A COASTLINE

IS AN

IMMEASURABLE

THING

A COASTLINE IS AN IMMEASURABLE THING

A MEMOIR ACROSS THREE CONTINENTS

MARY-ALICE DANIEL

An Imprint of HarperCollins*Publishers*

HarperCollins books may be purchased for educational, business, or sales promotional use. For information, please email the Special Markets Department at SPsales@harpercollins.com.

Ecco® and HarperCollins® are trademarks of HarperCollins Publishers.

A hardcover edition of this book was published in 2022 by Ecco, an imprint of HarperCollins Publishers.

FIRST ECCO PAPERBACK EDITION PUBLISHED 2023

Designed by Paula Russell Szafranski
Frontispiece © robin_ph/stock.adobe.com
Maps © Mike Hall

Library of Congress Cataloging-in-Publication Data has been applied for.

ISBN 978-0-06-296005-4 (pbk.)

23 24 25 26 27 LBC 5 4 3 2 1

HB 09.11.2023 0652

CONTENTS

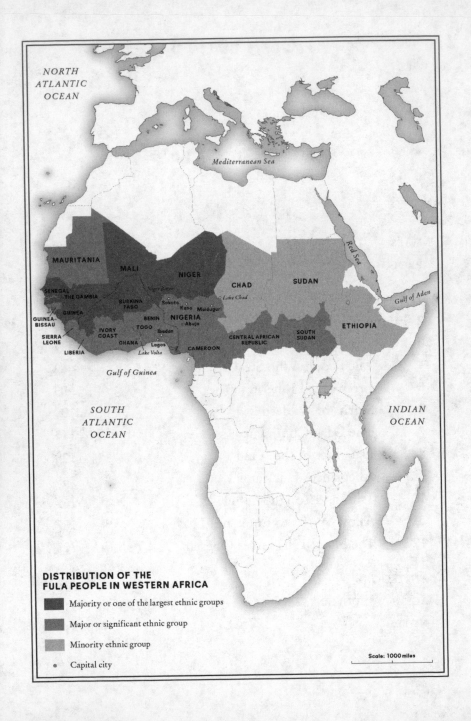

NORTH
ATLANTIC
OCEAN

Mediterranean Sea

Red Sea

Gulf of Aden

MAURITANIA

MALI

NIGER

CHAD

SUDAN

SENEGAL

THE GAMBIA

Niger River

Lake Chad

BURKINA
FASO

Sokoto

Kano

Maiduguri

GUINEA-
BISSAU

GUINEA

BENIN

NIGERIA

Abuja

ETHIOPIA

IVORY
COAST

TOGO

Ibadan

SIERRA
LEONE

GHANA

Lagos

CENTRAL AFRICAN
REPUBLIC

SOUTH
SUDAN

LIBERIA

Lake Volta

CAMEROON

Gulf of Guinea

SOUTH
ATLANTIC
OCEAN

INDIAN
OCEAN

**DISTRIBUTION OF THE
FULA PEOPLE IN WESTERN AFRICA**

Majority or one of the largest ethnic groups

Major or significant ethnic group

Minority ethnic group

⊙ Capital city

Scale: 1000 miles

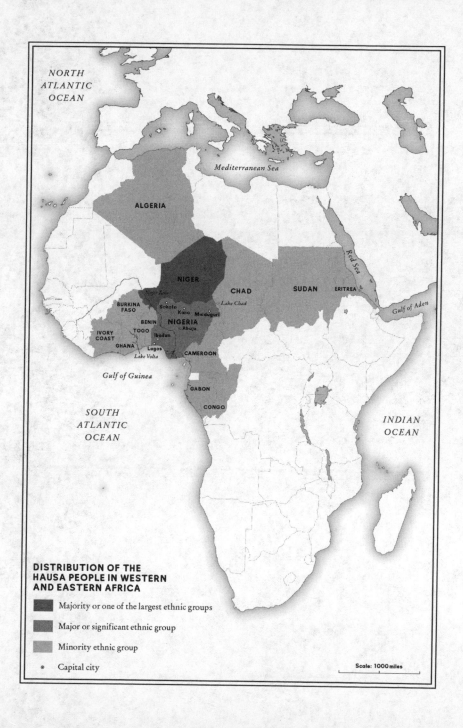

NORTH
ATLANTIC
OCEAN

Mediterranean Sea

ALGERIA

Red Sea

NIGER

CHAD

SUDAN

ERITREA

Niger River

BURKINA
FASO

Sokoto

Lake Chad

Gulf of Aden

Kano   Maiduguri

BENIN

NIGERIA   Abuja

IVORY
COAST

TOGO

Ibadan

GHANA

Lagos

CAMEROON

Lake Volta

Gulf of Guinea

GABON

CONGO

SOUTH
ATLANTIC
OCEAN

INDIAN
OCEAN

**DISTRIBUTION OF THE
HAUSA PEOPLE IN WESTERN
AND EASTERN AFRICA**

Majority or one of the largest ethnic groups

Major or significant ethnic group

Minority ethnic group

⊚   Capital city

Scale: 1000 miles

A COASTLINE

IS AN

IMMEASURABLE

THING

PROLOGUE

My cousin Galaxy's baby fell out of a two-story window and survived. They called the baby a miracle child like they called my brother a miracle child when he was thrown from a motorcycle only to live.

Some Fulani clans insist the universe was created from a single drop of milk, out of which came blindness, sleep, pride, worry, and death: all the natural nemeses of men.

Gizo, a trickster spider, employs clever deceptions in pursuit of prey or easy profit. If you hear a noise late one night like a baby crying outside—no matter how pathetic the wail—you must ignore it.

There is one uncle no one in my family visits because his house sits at the end of a road full of frogs, and there you hear only the sound of bodies popping beneath car wheels.

And what if the wind is powered by manipulative spirits of the Sahel, who whisper of wealth but seek to vex and devour?

Such are the stories I would hear about my family and

native Nigeria during the decades we spent adrift—unreal, sometimes lurid, always labyrinthine accounts that drew and repelled me.

I was born in Maiduguri, Nigeria—birthplace of Boko Haram, the terrorist militia that specializes in kidnapping the girl child. A concoction of three religions, four languages, and thirty-two addresses across three continents made me who I am. For the first decade of my life, I was raised in England until my immediate family moved to the USA, our final adopted home. Too many to count—the phone numbers; postal codes; zip codes; area codes; ways of thinking and being in Africa, Europe, and America.

Answering the question "Where are you from?" has never been easy. My history straddles dueling cultural systems: I am a dual citizen of Nigeria and the United States. I've been told by paternalistic Nigerians that I am not "really Nigerian"; xenophobic Americans imply I'm not a "real American."

Restlessness, rootlessness. In this country, I've lived in Nashville and New Haven; Mystic and Maryland and Manhattan; Koreatown, Los Angeles; Detroit on the riverfront with clear Canada views; the Brooklyn before the Brooklyn now; Chicago. My parents and both siblings eventually put down roots twenty years ago within the large West African community surrounding the American capital.

But I remain shiftless. I meander and move for work, school, love. I inherited a spirit of such extreme *exophoria*—that uncontrollable tendency of eyes to gaze outward. My ancestors were traders and herdsmen who roamed the Sahara in search of water. My immediate family and I are transcontinental nomads, relentless in our own pursuit of something less material. Only five of us migrated to this part of the world.

We seek a real and imagined country.

Still, the closest thing to "home" I have found are the dreamlands called California. Five hundred years ago, a famous Spanish fairy tale drove early modern men—in all their madness—to pursue a prophesied utopia. European explorers scouting the American West sought a legendary California: an enclave almost Eden, where the only metal found was gold. When they came upon the place they decided must be their promised land, they named it "California"—manifesting an object of exquisite desire into reality. California is *thought-form*: conquistadors wanted something so badly that they made it concrete. They created their own golden state, their golden beginning.

I might remake it into some form of a happy ending.

Myths; maps; etymologies; genes—all the ways I have tried to tell the story in me. I am a product of the past and peregrination. I have had to confront many things about my family or about myself I once considered consecrated truth. I work with poetic license; deal in false information; traffic oblique or outright lies.

When I write, I write the same sentence over and over in a process of revisionism, inching closer to truth. Consider this claim: "I was raised a Christian because my grandfather was the only successful convert of missionaries who visited his village, buried within the Islamic stronghold of Northern Nigeria. His apostasy in 1955 was not well received. He hid in a tree after converting; relatives tried to poison him for treachery."

I first wrote that down half a lifetime ago. In each retelling of our familial "facts," the story changes slightly or significantly—maybe someone misremembered the day or century. My grandfather was one of few converts, but he was not the *only* one. And it was not only him who had to hide in that tree, but him and my grandmother both. They were married; she was thirteen or fourteen, so much younger than I thought.

"Nigeria" is a fraudulent simulation of the British Empire. Its legacy is incongruity; it is arbitrary. If "Nigeria" as a country doesn't make any sense, then it is never enough for one to simply know, or to simply say, that one is Nigerian without further explanation. Understanding where we are from—who we are—is a task of nuance and nuisance. The many influences that inform my ethnicity reflect a millennium of cultural melee. When I began this project, I could not authenticate my mother's birth date.

If this all sounds confusing, it is—even to us Nigerians. We come from a nation better perceived in dreamscapes: Nigeria was made in myth. A storytelling tradition forms the foundation for any sense of Nigerian identity. Our nationality is unnatural—*so narratives must make this nation.*

Nigerian stories are architected over time, tellers taking elements of truth and shaping them into fables—tales with a moral lesson animated by animals and objects, gods and ghosts. In West African fables, humans meet helpful halfmen, busybody demons, meddling ancestors. In fantastic settings, creatures contend with each other as allies or saboteurs.

In my father's tribe, official storytellers were local celebrities, famed by festivals where they showcased songs and stories in rhythm, in dance. Orators were usually the oldest people, but merit played a part in their selection, as stories were performance art as well as edification. These elders recognized tribe members who had done something noteworthy and incorporated their experiences into tales. When my grandfather suffered a stroke and forgot how to speak three of the four languages he knew, storytellers spoke of the blessing in a quieted mind.

These chroniclers—tasked with sharing information about war, wrestling contests, and the hunt—were the record keepers of the tribe. Storytellers collaborated with village chiefs to establish, then perhaps embellish, the important "facts" of the stories they told. Their stories were performed in both the tribal dialect and the lingua franca of the area, so even outsiders might understand. Children learned and repeated lyrics, committing them to common memory. A song was composed to insult or challenge another clan. Another song was written to counter an insult perceived; this back-and-forth went on for generations.

Late in the year, after the crops had been stored, came the appropriate time for telling. Under the moon following harvest, these storytelling sessions were one of the few times everyone left their farms unattended to gather together. Moving from one village to the next while listening to neighboring clans' stories, one could perceive subtle differences in their ideals and ethics.

This communal tradition began dying out soon after the arrival of missionaries and modernity and is seen no longer in my father's region. Nigeria's indigenous mythology remains under threat across both its north and south—condemned by Islamic and Christian authorities alike in favor of their respective gospels. Wherever the Bible became the gospel truth, our mythos was marked *untruth*.

I turn my hand to a new narrative of my own making.

This is the great undertaking of Pan-African literatures. *Africa is not a country*: so goes a long-running joke amongst its natives. Of course, it is a continent of fifty-four nations—but one so often undifferentiated or presented as a monolith. Africa is routinely flattened in representations that cater to a Westernized world audience. Homogenization ignores Africa's contours to churn out those easy tropes and stereotypes.

Those fly-studded children begging for charity; distended bellies in famine; and all time is wartime; and everywhere apocalypse. Framed within such false devices, a story becomes untold.

I am charting the far-flung corners of the Black Diaspora that I inherit and inhabit. I present you variants of truth—possible, probable, and implausible versions of history. Origin stories extracted from everything that I've been told, that I have chased down. Many stories ensconced within the North of Nigeria have only been passed down orally until now, the time of this writing. My directive is *unearthing*—the root of a thing, a name or a narrative. In my engagement with the past, I pivot away from nostalgia. I want to pull something useful—elemental—out of this maelstrom: into the afterlight.

What follows is
feeling my way to bare, buried fact.

1

FORTUNE FAR AWAY

In my childhood, in a self-created canon, I was a princess.
I am confessing to the way I lied to my primary
schoolmates by telling them I was Nigerian royalty. My
English peers believed me because my native culture was
completely foreign to them; they knew *nothing* about it.

In every end-of-term school portrait, I appear as the only
Black child in the class. I was motivated by the remote possibility of becoming less strange. And by the possibility of
being valuable—something other than the clueless, shabby,
charity-shop African.

I never attempted authenticity when I disclosed the assets
of my dynasty:

"My father is king of three cities plus a river; at his corona-
tion, he was crowned the wrestling champion. My family has
sorghum and sugarcane fields, one room of terra-cotta masks
made in our likeness. My bride price could be the highest
in history, paid in gold. I sleep as I want under stars. I keep

horses. And flamingoes. My subjects name their firstborns after me and address me, with a deep bow, *Princess Nana.*"

I had no idea that with these lies, I was tying myself to an inglorious national stereotype. To the tune of billions of defrauded dollars, the character of the "Nigerian prince" is one Westerners are apt to believe out of ignorance. The 419 scam, named for the section of the Nigerian criminal code it violates, paints a lavish image of Nigeria as a golden goose. A hustler posing as a prince bamboozles his victims via wire fraud by promising them millions. So effective is this scheme that the FBI warns Americans:

Be skeptical of *all* individuals presenting themselves as Nigerian.

The scammers continue playing the long con; the long game; the nonsense game.

An email might begin: *I am Prince Mohammed Abacha, the son of the late Nigerian Head of State who died on the 8th of June. If you are conversant with world news, you understand better.* One might wonder why their emails are rife with grammatical errors, but this apparent design flaw is intentional. Every message is deliberately illiterate and implausible to attract only the most gullible. Relying on artificial intimacy with victims instead of viruses or spyware, 419 reflects a relationship to the West that is utterly rotted—tainted with the same cynicism as my lies to wide-eyed age-mates.

Maybe—I might begin to supplant my history of hyperbole and half-finished truth.

I do have one claim to nobility: my paternal grandmother was a kingmaker, part of the tiny committee of women who chose and crowned the next chief of their tribe upon the death of the living one.

In Nigeria, each tribe has its own definition of "death." For one tribe, death officially occurs only when intestines have been exposed to the air. In my father's tribe—Longuda—their chief is considered dead when his head separates from his body. When a chief physically dies—the first, fake death—his body is placed on a gurney that is raised up to the open roof of a special hut. Only the select in the kingmaking committee may enter. Every day, they attend to the corpse, burning incense around it. The decomposing chief's head is left hanging over the end of the elevated gurney. When his head finally falls off (whether it does so naturally or whether it is provoked in some manner is known only to the committee), head and body are buried together. Each day incense smoke is seen rising from the hut, the chief is considered still "alive." The extended period of death preparation allows for mourning: maybe it's also a clever maneuver of the committee, a way to gain time to groom the next king.

Through the stories of this paternal line, I was told that I was blessed before birth.

The Longuda tribe posits that there is a cave atop a distant mountain with a hidden chamber full of precious gemstones. Simply looking upon this cavern bestows fortune. Only a few can reach it; the journey is plagued with pitfalls and requires a large personal measure of perseverance and faith. The few who make it there and back become worthy of a special position within the tribe. All Longuda parents pretend they have seen the cave. This is their way of promising their children a glad and golden future. Personally, I never had need for Santa Claus; everything I wanted was surely coming to me because my father did reach that cave as a young man. Oh, yes—it took him one year, but he survived by eating grass. From the foot of the mountain, he climbed stone stairs he chiseled himself.

This mythology yoked destiny to distance and placed fortune far away. Maybe such myths made my parents look beyond Nigeria and leave, believing we were next in some lucky line: our logistics laid out in legend, our path preordained. Maybe they reckoned themselves the equals of our intrepid ancestors, nomads who harnessed the hostile estate of the Sahara—those pioneers in whose fantastic footsteps they proposed to follow.

England never figured into my father's dreams.

Both my parents knew so much about their mother empire because in school, their geography, history, and literature classes focused on the United Kingdom—even after Independence. They could tell you about wildflowers around Windsor but not about those fifteen rivers of the aptly named Rivers State. Unlike my mother, my father didn't like what he learned. He didn't consider the possibility of leaving Nigeria until our situation became dire.

Though my parents at one time had decent prospects in Nigeria, we couldn't remain there long past my infancy. Before I was born, they were both hired to teach at the University of Maiduguri, their position somewhat stable during the 1970s. In 1979, the Nigerian currency was as strong as the British pound and stronger than the dollar—1 naira equaled 1 pound or 2 dollars. Now, the exchange rate is 0.002 naira to 1 pound; 1 pound sterling gives you 500 naira; a dollar gives you 400. The kobo, a coin worth 1/100 of a naira, is so worthless beggars will throw it back at you.

Soon after my birth, the university stopped paying its faculty during one of the characteristic collapses of a postcolonial bureaucracy. My parents made immediate plans to escape the failing state—traveling separately on hazardous roads back to their home villages to locate original records, then filling out mountains of forms by kerosene lamplight through increasingly frequent power outages.

Receiving hard-fought student visas to England, they enrolled in doctoral programs—my mother in zoology, my father in pharmacology. My mother's research focused on crop protection and pesticide safety. They continued to study the subjects they were first drawn to as young intellectuals hoping to one day improve their country's disintegrating environment and public health. They were unaware they would become part of Nigeria's devastating "brain drain," when the educated left to seek opportunities abroad. Everybody who *could* go *did* go; soon, the positions necessary in any functional society were left empty.

When they moved the three of us children to the Thames Valley of Southern England, my parents imagined our time in the West would be temporary—they would learn practical skills, after which we would return to a healing home country. England would be a safe harbor to wait out the perfect storm of our unluck. Our journey hinged upon haphazard hope in the wilds of the widest unknowns.

As is the Fulani way—the way of her tribe—my mother was fearless in the face of our relocation. Before we left for England, she gave away most of our family's things: items she thought we would outgrow before we returned. Throngs of people from all over the city came to say goodbye and take my baby clothes.

My parents packed hardly any possessions—no books because England *must* have better books. Electronics would be incompatible. Our clothes would have little utility in the English climate. My father borrowed a winter coat from an acquaintance who had recently visited London and brought back this uncommon apparel as evidence he'd really been to England. For my father, the dearest things he left behind were his record player and record collection, sentimental markers of his youth. He still tries to reconstruct his curation by scouring eBay for rare editions, once behaving out of character by splurging on a $200 record he could only find in China. When we left Nigeria, he had the full expectation of returning to his music one day.

He could not know an uncle would pawn his precious record collection. He could not know how many relatives he would never see again. As we huddled on that soggy island, our telephone never stopped ringing with news of death. Grief traveled to touch my father continuously during the racking decline of his last living brother, who battled barely treated HIV then AIDS.

We were the lucky ones to leave. We would be together, alone.

The date we left Nigeria—*September 12, 1988*—was the day after a solar eclipse, like a sun setting on the British Empire. That September, experts warned that England's economic forecast predicted recession. My family was midair over international waters as Prime Minister Margaret Thatcher made her famous "Bruges Speech," laying out her vision of England's place in the world. She narrates "the story of how Europeans explored and colonised—*and yes, without apology*—civilised much of the world." In her rhetoric, colonization is a "tale of talent, skill and courage." "Disposing of some myths" about her country, she declares that "Britain does not dream of some cosy, isolated existence." Leaving its former colony, my parents knew all about Britain's dreams of empire, not isolation. Crossing into English airspace, we arrived still with myths. My mother hoped Britannia would provide for us, as in atonement to abused children.

"I approach the age my mother and father were when we

arrived in England"—I first formed this sentence within my mind so long ago that it is no longer true. I am thirty-four at the time of this writing; my mother was thirty-one then, and my father, thirty-six. I am retroactively aware of how my young parents must have suffered. I pity my parents in past tense. They did not know what wreckage we would wade through as lonely immigrants in lonely lands.

England looked blanched, like all color had been boiled out of it. It lacked that characteristic angry red Nigerian dust that gets into *everything*. We were impressed by well-maintained roads and manicured lawns, features contrasting with Nigeria's chaotic cityscapes and the wildness in the bush. My father liked that English rice didn't have little stones in it, a thing that always bothered him. He had read about, but never seen, apples.

Soon after our arrival in Reading, my mother enrolled me and my older brother in day care. He was five at the time; I was three. I came home in tears every day because I was utterly confused and couldn't communicate. My eight-year-old sister had already begun schooling in Nigeria, so her language skills were strong enough for her to continue without crisis. English was taught in Nigerian schools, but it wasn't spoken in our household. My mother withdrew me from day care out of pity, though I would have learned the language much faster had she ignored my tears.

I knew little English at three and four while ensconced in our exclusively Hausa-speaking home. I absorbed like a sponge in my fifth year through constant television and my family's efforts. My sister taught me English at playtime; my parents started to speak it more to prepare me for school. As we all began to talk in a hybrid of English and Hausa, the proportion of English words increased each year, and the balance shifted. By six and the start of Year 1 at primary school, I was an intermediate speaker. Fluency came quickly after that. I write, speak, dream in English now—I write poetry in it—so it feels strange to think back to a time it was not native to me.

For those years I was isolated from the outside due to the language barrier, my brother and sister were the world and my means of communicating with it. The three of us struggled most with finding translations for Hausa words that have no clear correlate in English. Take the word "*ba*," usually spoken with an upward inflection, as a question. A sentence spoken in our house might be: "We're having sausages, *ba*?" We brainstormed substitutes and finally came up with the slangy Briticism "innit?" which sounded brutally unnatural.

In trying to translate a word like "cupboard," little sense can be made of it when broken into its individual components, "cup" and "board." It was specifically this ordinary little word that prompted me to begin thinking in a linguistic system where "a cupboard is a cupboard" and *not* a word with a parallel I might find within the stores of the language I knew better. I forced myself to stop translating words from English back to Hausa and instead to try thinking only in English. I recall the night I first dreamed in English. Dreams then were nightmares about going downstairs alone with the light in the hallway dead or dying; they were sprees of chocolate coins and candy bars that looked like honeycomb.

My father developed a penchant for high diction and would teach us posh British vernacular: those words he was fascinated by while improving his own English and that he'd be proud for his children to incorporate into their vocabulary. Asking us to do our chores, he'd request we get to it "with immediate effect and alacrity." At six, I knew that "perambulate" meant to walk around, through, about, over. *That we had walked; that we were walking still.*

When the first Gulf War ended, I was five years old. I thought its end meant there would be no more news. It seemed the war was the only thing on the nightly reports, so once it was over, I thought it took the field of broadcast journalism with it. I was happy, as I hated watching the news my father always kept on—not because it was boring or frightening, but because too many English words still confused me. I also thought there'd never be another war. Once the bombs stopped falling, it didn't occur to me that another should come along.

I lived in the shade of incomprehension in our first house in Reading, and my earliest memories are muted in grays. Deadened in the ashen backdrop of English damp; dismal lace curtains; the playground pavement. As we settled into our second house—the one we'd live in for our remaining five years in England—my English was much improved. The memories that formed as I was beginning to intimately understand the language are punctuated with color. I see the particular paisley of a duvet cover, vivid and minute.

I remember 106 Addington Road in detail. Our house had a redbrick exterior that always looked mottled, like drying blood, because of the frequent English rains. A black wrought-iron gate in front of the house swung into green grass. In the back, a high wooden fence caged a half-paved garden. It was a semidetached house, so we shared a wall with neighbors on one side. They'd bang on the wall in protest whenever we were too loud, rattling the porcelain in the parlor's wooden cabinet. One day my whole family, including my parents, started banging right back.

We had one tiny bathroom. Every Saturday, my mother washed all our clothes by hand in the bathtub while we children scrubbed underwear in the sink. Together, we'd hang the laundry in the backyard on a slipshod network of clotheslines slung low enough for me to reach—so low that the garden became a hazard, an obstacle course of colorful plastic tripwire, where tall guests bowed their heads. The muggy weather was uncooperative; it would take days for laundry to dry, the process requiring mad dashes during a downpour to bring clothes back inside. Then to wait for clearer weather and rehang them. When I learned to ride a bike, it was between messy rows of bedsheets that hampered my path and broke my falls.

On the first floor of the house, there was a kitchen; a huge spare room our landlady sometimes divided and rented out to tenants; and a parlor whose double doors opened to the back garden. Behind that plot, there was a detached garage on whose roof we climbed to pick the bitty sour apples that fell from the tree bursting up through it. The rear exit of the garage led to an alley and the lot of a metalworking factory, which my siblings and I would sneak into after hours. It was a favorite play area—we climbed on giant industrial machinery and used unsecured tools for sword fighting—until a foreman caught us and scared us into never going back.

On the second floor, there were three bedrooms. I wasn't allowed in my sister's. And I wasn't allowed in my parents' bedroom except when I claimed to be sick, and then I was tucked into their bed to watch *Sesame Street* and *Reading Rainbow* all day. I slept in the second-biggest bedroom with my older brother; only two years apart, we were the closest in age and coconspirators.

My brother prized his position as the only boy—a position that got him out of many domestic duties and afforded him more freedom and a wider latitude of acceptable behavior. He was the first to make friends with neighborhood kids, finding the beloved Nigerian pastime of football just as alluring when played on the concrete of its country of origin as on the grassland we'd left behind—the main difference being that he had to wear shoes instead of playing barefoot. We played football everywhere, outside and inside, all the time. The ball was the universal language of boys, and we kid sisters were the hangers-on, taking risks to prove our adequacy.

While pulling one of these stunts inside our house, running down the hallway with the ball, I tripped over a wrinkle in the carpet and fell face-first through the double-glazed glass door. A shard tore a jagged path an inch below my hairline, bleeding profusely, as head wounds do, through entire rolls of toilet paper. My mother rushed us to the hospital, all of us soaked in my blood. The Fall was my first emergency. When the wound healed, it formed a raised keloid scar in the shape of a crescent moon, which made my siblings nickname me "Gorbachev." My scar is a defining feature of my face; my evangelistic mother would have preferred a cross to a crescent.

My description of our house in Reading might make it seem charming, even quaint. In reality, it was so dilapidated that when I returned to England as a teenager, my friend Ashley confessed that her parents didn't like her coming over because of the extent of the mold and dust. One good thing about being a child is not minding certain conditions intolerable to adults. *You could draw patterns in that dust.*

The house belonged to a Jamaican woman my mother didn't get along with, and the furniture was all hers. She had too much of it, but we weren't allowed to move anything. All her knickknacks accumulated so much dust—especially in the parlor, where she kept a white cabinet filled with ceramic teacups, silver teapots, and clay ballerinas and mermaids. She didn't want us handling her cheap figurines, even to clean, and the layers of dust were her way of knowing if we'd touched anything. In the springtime, we'd wake up to find thin silver trails by the doors that opened to the outside— slimy, iridescent trails made by the snails rampant in our garden. We never worked out how they got in, so we could never stop them. When my siblings and I held overnight stakeouts to determine their point of entry, the snails never came.

Rent was 250 pounds per month, a below-market sum, but we were responsible for the old house's maintenance costs, which we couldn't manage. The area we lived in wasn't too close to the council estates—the "rough" part of town. In our neighborhood, you could tell the class difference house by house: those who could afford renovations and repairs and those whose homes fell into disorder. You could pass a gorgeous cottage, and the very next dwelling would be coming apart, with boarded windows and holes in the roof. The garden of one house on our street was so overgrown that greenery obscured the windows on the first floor. A main childhood goal was to cross the grass and peek inside: to settle the question of whether the residents kept dead bodies inside.

Our house faced a chemist shop, a dress shop, and a halal butcher's owned by a multigenerational Pakistani family with a daughter my age. I was often dropped off there when there was no one to look after me, and they gave me packaged pastel nougat for free. I still search for anything like it. For the longest time, I believed I lived near Roald Dahl, my favorite author in childhood—who had died just before I knew of him, when I was four. Even now, I don't know how this delusion got so firmly fixed into my reckoning of reality. I repeated the sincere fiction to my friends in America, until the day I finally thought to look it up: a day I became more ordinary.

Reading: pronounced like "redding," not "reading." I always make the distinction that I grew up in Reading. Not a suburb of London. Not "near London." Not "around London." Located by the River Thames—also called the Isis—Reading developed as a major port along the river route leading east all the way to London. When I was a child, our sporadic trips to London seemed to take forever, as we ate my mother's cold fried chicken out of tinfoil in passage to Madame Tussauds or the British Museum, on those rare occasions we could afford to visit. As an adult, I was startled to find out that London is easily accessible by rail in under an hour. When I was growing up, Reading was not a bedroom community of London, as it is now becoming; people who lived in Reading worked in Reading.

Reading is not a city, but a large town—a county town, the seat of municipal government. It often avoids getting stuck in that seeming state of perma-recession much of the UK struggles to pull out of. Its population is three hundred thousand, and it is known for its football club and for the Reading Festival, one of the largest public events in England. Berkshire County is famous for picturesque rural walks, well traveled by Wordsworth and other Romantic poets.

The streets of Reading are arranged in grids: it is difficult for anyone, even a child, to get lost, so I was allowed to venture on my own early. By five, I was going across the road to buy household items for my mother. By six, off I went farther down the road to buy one-pence candy. Roaming the streets nearby—names like Blenheim Gardens, Foxhill Road, and Donnington Road—I got to know every house, recognizing its inhabitants by face or quirk. I knew who had a sociable cat and who didn't appreciate me picking flowers from their garden.

We lived a twenty-minute walk from the town center. Even though we went there every weekend, the pedestrian center of town remained unimaginably exciting to me. It was the domain of adult activities—commerce and business— and I loved going with my mother on all her errands. To the travel agency to inquire about flight prices to Nigeria, then to Barclays bank—where I filled out deposit forms with fake information while she was busy at the counter, and where I opened a savings account with exactly one pound. We came home stinking of fish from "Smelly Alley," the street of fishmongers.

The town center developed around the traditional heart of an English settlement: an abbey, which used to be a required structure for a town charter. Built in the twelfth century, Reading's abbey was one of England's wealthiest. It stands preserved in the middle of the modern shopping district, its gravestones centuries old. Its cemetery was the spot for teenagers to drink together amongst gnarled tree roots growing around the graves, obscuring the names of their ancestors.

My family started attending Wycliffe Baptist Church so early that in my mind, this church always existed. Having been pulled out of day care, I didn't have outside company my own age: my "social life" revolved around my siblings, my parents' brand-new friends, and church, always church. We belonged to Wycliffe during our entire tenure in England, joining it simply because it was the closest Protestant place of worship. Church took up most of our Sundays—not because the service went on for interminable hours, as they do in Nigeria, but because afterward, we loitered in the car park.

My mother hoped to import the custom of reserving the entirety of a Sunday for gossiping. My siblings and I ran around the parking area long after all other children had left, then we leisurely walked home as a family, extending a trip that should've taken ten minutes by stopping to greet any person we had even the most tenuous connection to. My parents discovered that the Nigerian habit of dropping by houses unannounced was tolerated much better by the private, more formal English on Sundays.

Invited to introduce our family during our very first church service, my father launched into a speech peppered with random, archaic British words—an *"expergefactor" was an alarm clock; a "compeer" was a friend*—sparking the crowd's curiosity. After the service, he was approached by a man I perceived as a cuddly, funny-looking giant and his pretty wife. Uncle Simon and Auntie Polly became godparents to all three of us children. Married young like my parents, they were childless, and they delighted in us.

My godparents were religious—"Born again"—but they were the sort of modern, liberal Christians I am now surprised my parents embraced. Uncle Simon was a visual artist, and I credit his influence for my parents' acceptance of my choice to become a writer. Despite the renowned literature of Nigeria, there remains some stigma around writing as a profession. For my mother's tribe, poets have an unsavory association with the street musicians seen as little more than beggars. The full-time pursuit of creative writing is discouraged as impractical, and many immigrants push their children toward stable professions: careers in law (my sister is an attorney) or in health (my brother is a pharmacist). And me, I was supposed to be a doctor, like my father.

Uncle Simon would paint portraits of me with shaggy braids, my head framed in a halo of cool reds. In photos of England, you see us picking apples in their backyard and opening their gifts on Boxing Day. We loved going to our godparents' house because it was the opposite of the rented house we made do in—it was theirs and it was intentional, ornamental—dressed in the signature of Uncle Simon's playful painting. It was a home, and we were happy there, except during get-togethers with their relatives. At those times, in a house full of white English people, my siblings and I were a little too loud, too unruly.

Our godparents took us places we never would have seen otherwise, like Windsor Castle, a royal residence in use since the eleventh century. My parents lacked time, money, and all interest for the old-world charms of our new country. I walked Wordsworth's walking paths because of this couple, who made it their business to acquaint us with their England.

They were our introduction to the obscure, intimate aspects of English culture—that staid, restrained old character. Whatever bits of etiquette we didn't pick up through general observation, we learned through them. My brother was informed that culottes are not really unisex. My mother learned that "You gained weight!" is never an appropriate greeting, no matter how tenderly she meant it. I learned enough shame to stop cracking open chicken bones to suck out the marrow.

In exchange, my family shared our own ways. As a people, we Nigerians are gregarious, having a reputation for being louder than Americans. One of our verbal tics is repeating phrases for emphasis: we love the sound of the human voice, none beyond our own. Political debates rage through the night, which outsiders predict will break out into physical fighting at any moment, misunderstanding our excitability as aggression.

Our national temper is overmuch. The way I put these norms into context for people who know me is to explain that amongst other Nigerians, I am considered shy. As someone who talks too much, who talks to strangers too much, who has some difficulty modulating the volume of my voice, I use this personal comparison to prepare uninitiated guests for the unmediated melodrama of a typical Nigerian gathering.

Nigerians are notoriously hospitable. I say "notoriously," because if you ever refuse a second helping in a Nigerian home or attempt to pay the check after drinks out with a Nigerian buddy, you're in real trouble. We stop by any neighbor's house anytime, unannounced; we in turn hold our homes open. Nigerians invite themselves to every event taking place in the community (where I'm from, having a "closed" wedding is still a recent and rare concept). At weddings, a boisterous man might appoint himself MC by commandeering the microphone and launching into a succession of increasingly desultory and drunken toasts, speaking at length on any topic crossing his mind. This self-appointed master of ceremonies might not be close to—or even known—the couple.

Uncle Simon and Auntie Polly got to witness that side of us only other Nigerians see. Once, we asked them over for lunch, and they arrived on time only to discover that we were all still asleep. In Nigeria, no one expects guests to show up at the appointed hour—in fact, it's considered rude, because one should assume the hosts will not have everything ready. At our house, we sometimes dressed up Auntie Polly in Nigerian clothing. Here was something totally new: a Western woman in our clothes. My mother expertly constructed her head wrap to a towering height that gave the petite, pallid lady authority. My godparents were the only white British people we became so close to; we remained reserved around others. Not shy—*Nigerians are never shy*—but ill at ease.

Reading has become far more diverse in recent decades, especially due to its proximity to London. It now boasts 150 spoken languages within its population. According to a recent census, 75 percent of the town population is White; 14 percent is Asian; 7 percent is Black; 5 percent is counted Mixed or "Other." During our time there, immigrants in Reading were mostly Pakistani and Indian. These incomers, also leaving former colonies taken apart piecemeal by the British, tried to salvage something from their traumatic ordeal with the Empire.

Around town, my family was a sight to see.

Only two decades ago, I saw more Black people in American movies than around me. Apart from our Jamaican landlady and the daughter she sent to collect our rent, we saw no other Black faces in the surrounding streets. A year before we left England, one other African immigrant family moved into the neighborhood. Within weeks of the Ghanaian family's arrival, the young son George acquired the nickname "Smelly George." It stuck to him for typical, made-up, xenophobic reasons—that his mother's cooking smelled bad and lingered on his skin. I remember him for the new anxiety he provoked—the fear of being given my own insulting name.

Somehow, we found the Bellos, another Nigerian family of a rare breed: Christians from the north. Within Reading, the Bellos were our only link to Nigeria, and it was unlikely and lucky that they happened to be from the north, whose population is not well represented in the West. There were three children close to our own ages—two boys and one girl. We arranged ourselves into inseparable squads of three girls and three boys. They never attended our same schools because their house was in a different catchment zone, but they joined us at Wycliffe Baptist Church every week. We would plead to be excused from Sunday school to sit with the adults, then we'd scheme ways to pilfer the silver thimbles of wine diluted with Ribena blackcurrant concentrate.

When we and the Bellos referred to ourselves as "cousins," we did not mean by blood, and we had to clarify this repeatedly to the English. But we also did not mean we were "cousins" in the way Nigerians refer to unrelated acquaintances of flexible degrees of closeness as "cousins." We were tighter than that—chosen family. After we moved to the US, they migrated here soon after. We made a tiny unit of Nigerians who seemed to stalk each other around the world.

A coincidence confirmed our belief that we had found each other by Providence. Years after my family met the Bellos in England, we came across a photo taken at my first birthday party held back in Nigeria. In it, I am sitting in front of a colossal pink cake; dozens of salivating children crowd behind me. In this blur of faces, we spotted the two eldest Bello children. They must have been in our city for some reason, and having heard about my party, simply showed up uninvited, as West Africans do. We had no idea that we had once encountered one another.

There was no Nigerian or West African community in Reading to speak of then. For the decade we lived in England, the Bellos were the only Nigerians we faithfully communed with inside the country. Both our families started putting up Christmas trees, a tradition not followed by anyone we know in Nigeria, where the holiday is less secular. Our mothers would perform experiments on packages of Tesco frozen chicken, trying to make the flesh taste like home: wild chickens freshly killed then fried are an entirely different animal. Our fathers brainstormed commodities for an import-export business. And we children provided one another brief reprieve from being alien.

Maybe I was six when I found a book in our spare room, probably donated by the church. The book was an interactive treasure hunt involving an actual fortune buried somewhere in England, which would be awarded to the first person who could decipher the clues hidden within a series of elaborate drawings. Though their setting was England, the enchanting images felt like the spaces inside an African fable. A rabbit in one scene appears in the next, somehow changed. The rabbit beside a cryptic symbol; the symbol again, inverted. The rabbit in the woods, multiplying.

The rabbit was my guide, a thing natural and normal. Every day, I studied the pages by the millimeter, determined to be the first to solve the clues traversing alien territory. The clues across a temperate landscape: broad-leaf and spring-flowering forest. *Foreign, ephemeral forest.* I spent much of my young life looking for touchstones in this imagery. This mystery, I thought, connected me to thousands of other seekers who pored over the same English terrain as I pored over every pale hint and shadow on the page.

Many years later, after we left England, I would remember my obsession with that treasure hunt and look it up on the internet. I learned that the clues had been solved and the treasure had been found *years* before the obsolete cultural artifact made its way into my hands via the book donation bin.

It had always, ever, already been too late.

2

IRREGULAR UNIVERSE

My siblings and I shared a childhood best characterized as a competition for very limited resources. Being the youngest, I usually lost. Nightly, I entered the tub last to reuse their dingy bathwater because hot water was expensive. We were left to our own devices in an irregular universe. Within it, we managed scarcity. Fending for ourselves, we were cutthroat, sometimes cooperative. We never solved the mystery of *who* always removed and hoarded the batteries from our remote controls, and for what. A favorite team activity was making sweets with the items found in the only cupboards we could reach. Our special recipe was a concoction of condensed milk powder and strawberry jam rolled into messy balls, which we tried to sell to perplexed passersby on the street in front of our house.

In Nigeria, there exist levels to poverty, such that even the middle class can afford full-time childcare. Even while scraping by as lecturers with consistently delinquent salaries, my parents were able to employ a nanny. My mother relied on our nanny and never fully developed a sense of what kind of parent she would have to be when shouldering her role alone. She was strict and authoritarian in some ways and unusually lax in others. Any amount of violence in movies was overlooked; using swear words was *never*. We set our own schedules of unstructured time to run wild. We were never, ever allowed to spend the night at a friend's house, but we had no bedtime and slept till whenever. We skipped school more than recommended and enjoyed unlimited television time. Once one of us kids had physical custody of the remote control (the rule we came up with to avoid fistfights), we would watch whatever we wanted as long as we liked. Church on Sunday was the only nonnegotiable.

Our relative privileges in Africa had no bearing on our new impoverished reality. The furniture in our house and the clothes on our backs came from other people first, often from car boot sales. On weekend afternoons, vendors would line up their cars on local fairgrounds, offering used wares from the trunk—the "boot." Even children my age noticed class markers like our secondhand clothes; our ceilings sagging with water damage; clouds of stuffing bursting through the seats of our bronze Beetle.

In that junky Volkswagen, we collected old clothes for the semiannual sales held to raise money for our school. Each class had a different fundraising activity, but my mother quickly signed up to collect donations for the clothing drive, whether or not she was supposed to. I called these missions our "Rubbish Nights." Our family would be assigned several streets to drive around, looking for garbage bags marked as donations and left on the pavement in front of houses. We piled them into the boot and the back seat where I sat, so many of them that I disappeared. My mother always volunteered for this duty so my siblings and I could sort through the worn clothing and select what fit us. It was the only way we could afford necessities for our wardrobes. Our immigrant antics were resourceful but never subtle. Our classmates often recognized some item of clothing they had donated the week before it made its debut on us, the never-proud new owners.

My parents will always be Mommy and Daddy. To me, those are just their names. When I started Year 1 of primary school at six years old, my English was good enough, but the names I used for my parents outed me on day one. In general, Nigerians call our parents Mommy and Daddy long into adulthood, not associating these terms with immaturity. We don't discard them in youth in favor of Mom and Dad. The rest of my classmates proved they were grown-up by shortening their parents' titles when they said goodbye. I seemed childish in comparison.

My family hadn't figured out what to do about names.

Out of respect, instead of saying their names, I was supposed to call both my brother and sister Yaya—meaning "elder" in Hausa. I never did. My mother tried to make me and failed.

One of our tribal traditions that did not follow us was the practice of giving parents special titles. According to this custom, we address parents by referencing their firstborn. After the birth of my sister, Uwani, my mother and father became Maman Uwani and Baban Uwani. One of my uncles—just to please me—subverted this convention, calling my mother only Maman Nana. In Nigeria, I never heard my parents called by their first names. In England, I heard them become Harold and Sarah.

In Northern Nigeria, as everywhere, it is an honor to name a child after someone. But one cultural norm mandates a nickname for any female child named after an older relative. This rule helps to avoid the taboo of yelling the shared name in anger when the girl child misbehaves, especially within earshot of the elder. The tradition doesn't apply to young boys, who are called by their given names even when their behavior provokes loud reproach. Out of respect for my maternal grandmother, Mairi, it was obligatory that I be given a nickname to distinguish us.

At school, I was called what I was called at home—Nana. Though, to my ear, the English pronounced it incorrectly, stressing the first syllable. My father spelled my name out loud and called me "En ay en ay." His silly pronunciation confused people we'd meet, who thought I had this unusually repetitive name.

My brother, Ishaya, was named after no living person; his name is the Hausa version of Isaiah, the man called "The Prophet" in the Old Testament.

My sister's name is Lydia, which is also my paternal grandmother's middle name. Likewise, she was given the nickname Uwani so that no one could be heard impatiently calling for "Lydia" all over the house. My sister, thinking the name Uwani sounded ugly, always went by Lydia in England. She had to explain to her friends why her family called her something different at home. I wouldn't meet this problem until later.

My center of the world was Redlands Primary School, which I attended for Years 1, 2, and 3. Year 1, I copied a girl named Fiona, curving my arm the way she did when she raised her hand, because a certain Jack liked her, and I liked Jack. Year 2, my class grew cress in a small plot to make buttery tea sandwiches. Year 3, we walked to the community pool to begin swimming lessons that were abruptly interrupted by my family's move to America—to this day, I can do a flawless doggy paddle and no other strokes.

Before the morning bell, students swarmed the playground, a concrete mass informally sectioned off into the little kids' area and the big kids' area, where it was understood that Year 3s and younger were not welcome. In our section, we little kids played tag around the periphery of the older children's football matches, wanting to be close to them while awaiting the day we might join. First thing each day, the entire student body attended an assembly. In the auditorium, also used for lunch and indoor sports, our septuagenarian principal taught us songs. To her, I owe my eclectic recollection of folksy English, Welsh, Irish, and Scottish songs; Andrew Lloyd Webber's "Copenhagen"; the South African national anthem; so many sea shanties.

One autumn evening every year, Redlands hosted an arts showcase. My fondest memories of England: seeing the school nearing nighttime as an entirely new building; my sister playing calypso music in her steel drum band; me finally being allowed to hold our camcorder to record her. A less fond memory is watching from the sidelines as four classmates performed my original choreography to my father's record, the Temptations song "My Girl." I'd introduced them to this music and taught them my dance before they kicked me out of the group for being "bossy."

My parents arrived in England as tea drinkers: a British custom eagerly adopted in Nigeria. Our daily breakfast was tea and Horlicks, a malted wheat powder, mixed with hot milk. Apart from this, the meals my mother prepared were mostly Nigerian, especially for my father, who refused to eat pork and potatoes every day.

We ate so much rice that as an adult, I have never once bought rice to cook—I'm the rare African who got sick of it. Almost every night, my mother would boil a pot of long-grain basmati rice, which we hauled from the Indian-run bulk food store two streets away. This rice she made into *tuwo*, mashed rice molded in the hollow of a dried squash shell—each firm sphere makes a portion. On weekends, she'd prepare and freeze stews to accompany the rice. Her special stew was made from tomato paste, ground onions, garlic, red peppers, and red palm oil, which gave the already-red stew an even brighter hue and left permanent orange stains on the clothes of careless children. She made *egusi* stew with ground pumpkin seeds simmered with beef and spinach; or a stew with a groundnut base; or *miyan kuka*, made from powdered baobab leaves.

My mother cooked the traditional cuisine of her rural girlhood, attempting to adhere to the recipes her mother had taught her. *Moin moin* is a savory pudding she made with corned beef, black-eyed peas, and beans. We children helped with the painstaking process of making *moin moin*. After pureeing all the ingredients, we stuffed the mash into tin cans. We placed the cans in a big pot with a shallow pool of water, leaving them to cook under a tinfoil tent to trap the spiced steam.

With my parents' harried schedules, the communal meal-times observed in Nigeria disappeared. We ate few meals together as a family, and we kids enjoyed free run of the kitchen. We always wanted English junk food, our tastes quickly turning against the healthier Nigerian fare. Of my mother's meals, I ate the chicken skins and the crispy layer of burnt rice peeled off the bottom of the pot. My older sister was responsible for feeding my brother and me and served us English pork sausages and fried potatoes ("bangers and chips") daily. We loved all English snacks and sweets; we still gift each other imported custard cream biscuits and browse the international food aisle hoping for Cadbury's candy. We have never recovered from our great disappointment in American chocolate.

Whenever my friends came over, they recoiled at the unfamiliar dishes, the pungent smells and gooey textures of foods whose components they couldn't identify. West African food does not prioritize presentation, and many ingredients were totally new to their palates. My best friend, Ashley, cried one afternoon eating supper at my house because my mother's homemade yogurt had lumps in it. She went home early, and my family laughed.

On special occasions, my mother would make ludicrous amounts of food. Some recipes we adapted out of necessity, lacking certain ingredients we couldn't easily find in Reading. Certain dishes called for modifications to make them more palatable to English guests. Maybe we'd use fewer spices, maybe we'd serve them with Heinz tomato ketchup. On those days, my mother did take great care in her food's presentation. She would serve stews in the one set of serving dishes we owned—white china bought on sale at Marks & Spencer—covered prettily with layers of sliced onions.

For these affairs, she restocked in London, maintaining our supply of *yaji*, a fiery red pepper powder; dried tamarind pods used to make rice porridge sour; and seasoning for *suya* beef skewers, a common street food sold along roadsides all over Nigeria. It was my father who always made the *suya*, spending hours slicing beef flank into the thinnest possible strips using the sharpest knife in the kitchen. Children were never allowed to help with this precise and dangerous task, and my mother was known to cut the strips too thick. My usual kitchen duties were chopping a barrelful of fresh okra; unwrapping the foil shells of Maggi seasoning cubes; and picking out floating debris from soaked beans.

Reflecting the Nigerian tradition of spontaneity in sociability, most of our parties had no purpose or reason. We held them at random a few times a year, usually on Sundays after church. Our usual guests were the Bellos; our godparents, Simon and Polly; and a handful of immigrant neighbors and colleagues, mostly Indian or Pakistani. A few African families (Tanzanian, Cameroonian, Kenyan) rounded out the list, coming from London or places farther away. We saw these families too infrequently to form tight bonds, but when we were together, we reverted to West African prototype, becoming lovers of life and full-throated.

In the Nigeria I know, a child's birthday party is held just as much for adults as for the child, usually being open to the entire local community. My English classmates found my birthday parties confusing. All my parents' friends would be in attendance, shooing us out of the way. My father would play his favorite music: West African Highlife; Western music like George Michael, Michael Jackson, and ABBA; secular Nigerian music like Fela; and gospel pop. There'd be no clown, potato crisps, goody bags, or kids' music. My mother served her typical heavy buffet of rice and meat; cake and candles were an afterthought. Children were expected to amuse ourselves somewhere out of sight. My playmates' parents were unsure whether to stay or leave.

My siblings and I tried to make our parents change their customs for our birthdays. We pressured them to commit to conventions like strict start and end times, instead of hosting nebulous, all-day affairs with guests floating in and out. We decorated the house with balloons, bought candy, and made goody bags to give away. We petitioned for snacks and drinks our mates would enjoy. By the time we left Reading, we'd successfully relegated the adults to the parlor (their serious meals laid out alongside) while we children took over the backyard—with our own music and bottomless sugar supplies in a decorated space that could have almost belonged to our English friends.

Uncomfortable moments were routine for me—usually related to language issues—but I was rarely outright ashamed of my native culture at this early age in primary school. Our apparent poverty was my problem. One pound was enough to buy all the sweets I could want, but I started to think beyond candy and want things like new, normal clothing.

As the second daughter, I wore clothes that had first gone through a long period of secondhand ownership by my sister before being handed down to me barely holding together. At seven, I reached the Age of Salvation—the age I was taught that a child is of sound enough mind to accept Christ and stand before His seat of judgment. I couldn't even dress myself neatly.

My father considered himself dapper and wore reasonably current English fashions. He followed trends in Nigeria during the '70s: bell-bottoms and platform shoes. My mother was much more modest and conservative; she wore what English women wore—those who were thirty years older. For festive functions, we all still wore African clothing. On these occasions, we were Nigerian men and women: *seriously dressed*. To Nigerians, clothing is a competitive sport where people vie to outdo each other at every party or wedding. For fancy events, families buy bolts of matching fabric and engineer individualized styles that flatter each member. Our coordinated outfits make spectacular photos.

In Nigeria, traditional clothes are not bought off the rack.

You first spend a long day at a textile market to browse and bargain. Maybe you leave a stall to show the vendor you're serious about what you're willing to pay; you return a few hours later. Your fabric is cut as its price is haggled still, then you take it to a tailor, one in a long row of sewing shops that ring the outside of every city's central bazaar. You choose a design from hundreds of timeless and modern fashions compiled in catalogues and photo albums, or you draw or describe your own original style. Tailors are affordable, so this custom couture adorns the entire population. Anyone can start a local trend by designing an eye-catching outfit envied and copied by their neighbors.

Northern Nigerian clothing is grandiose: the billowing structure called a *babban riga* translates literally to "big dress." Attire for men, including the big dress, is as expressive and flamboyant as anything made for women. His formal outfit features loose trousers under the *babban riga*, which is a wide robe whose history we trace back eight hundred years to the kingdoms built by the prosperity of desert trade. The robe is protective in this climate, and is a status symbol, a voluminous form with ornate detailing cascading to the ankles. In it, the figure of a man imposes. A *hula* or *alasho*—a hat or a turban—tops his look.

Women wear a "wrapper" called a *zani*, a large rectangle of material that encircles the lower part of our bodies like a wrap skirt. My mother carried me on her back in babyhood, folding me tightly in her *zani*. We pair it with a matching loose or fitted blouse. The décolletage and the sleeves of the top can be limitlessly customized for taste, modesty, and formality—add buttons, beads, ribbons, pearls, sheer layers, waves, ruffles, and fabric flowers. My look in girlhood was a blouse with short puffy sleeves and intricate stitching on the front to camouflage food stains. In later years in Northern

Nigeria, I had to cover my arms and raise the neckline, and the skirt swept the floor. In the US, I keep the hemline of the skirt this low because I love the long column of color.

The material used for our outfits can be cotton, linen, heavy lace, satin, synthetic. Girls are taught how to evaluate the quality of textiles. You must test the elasticity and shun papery textures. Counterfeits look stunning on one side but fade when you turn them over. On high-quality fabric, a repeating pattern should be precise. "Wax" refers to a print dyed in a process that produces saturated hues. Tens of thousands of uniquely named wax-print designs communicate information and ideas, like region and religion, pop music and politics. A radio once meant "modernity." Mathematical equations signal "education." Busts of Queen Elizabeth II for colonial nostalgia. Padlocks say, *Lover, don't leave.*

In the final step of getting ready, women fuss over each other's *geles*, head wraps made of a stiff, crinkly fabric that is stacked high on the head in a statuesque composition, like a tulip, a cone, or a crown. The precarious structure must be secured using a technique that immediately makes clear which women are out of practice. I always needed help tying my own tulip, and it was a feat getting it to stay put. Even today, a *gele* turns me into a fumbling child.

To have our clothes made, my mother relied on the Nigerian community in London, and she took me with her to seek the seamstresses on Liverpool Street. Having neither the time nor money for frequent trips, we couldn't always return for a final fitting and alterations. I began to prefer seeing our traditional clothes on my mother rather than on myself. I was chubby, growing awkwardly on the English diet; her slim figure remained the same. Once a year, my school hosted Multicultural Night, when students and their families were invited to wear their native dress. On these evenings, the school, with its sizeable South Asian immigrant minority, became a sea of saris vibrating against the monotone palette of little England. My mother brought a pot of her tomato stew and wore her best wrapper—looking, or so I thought, more beautiful than any other in the hall.

I still wear wrappers casually around the house; I fold one around my waist and carelessly tuck one end of the fabric at my side. When my parents have Nigerian visitors, the way I tie mine is always mentioned as a compliment or a criticism.

Sometimes, when my father came to pick me up from school, he came barefoot.

I do not remember if I was embarrassed by this.

Social awareness came slowly.

My sister was far more self-conscious; she jettisoned our cultural idiosyncrasies. For her, shame was a near-constant presence as she navigated an elite Catholic girls' school. St. Joseph's Convent School for Girls was exclusive, expensive, and run by strict nuns. She gained admittance by taking the entrance exam, and after she did well, the school gave her one of two full scholarships covering tuition. The other recipient was an Indian immigrant; they were the only students of color out of sixty-six new admits.

St. Jo's served the upper class from all over Berkshire County: the kind of place where rumors of royalty abound. At the convent school, my sister and her classmates observed the Catholic Church's traditions, including twice-daily Mass, and learned its catechism, just as my father had in his own youth. At St. Jo's, my sister played six mandatory sports—tennis, horse riding, field hockey, gymnastics and dance, swimming, and track and field—two per term. The curriculum required Latin plus two more foreign languages; she chose German and Spanish.

Five years my senior, my sister was at that age when clothing mattered the most. St. Joseph's girls wore uniforms of a dark brown skirt, cardigan, and blazer; a mustard button-down shirt; knee-length brown socks with mustard stripes; a brown bowler hat; and black saddle oxford shoes. Most students hiked up the calf-length skirt during encounters with boys from their brother school, Reading School. My sister received a clothing voucher for the shop in Reading's town center that had outfitted wealthy students for hundreds of years. She got to pick out two of everything—brand-new—and for the first time in our new life, her clothes were as good as everyone else's. Outside school, she still lived in a higgledy-piggledy wardrobe; because it took her so long to amass her babysitting wages, by the time she could finally afford a pair of Doc Marten boots or tie-dyed leggings, the trend was long over, and she once again became the odd girl out.

Her friends went shopping in the town center, went skating, had sleepovers, flirted more at Reading Boys'. Saddled with younger siblings, her role as caretaker hindered her social inclusion from the moment the final bell rang, when she walked across the road to pick us up from Redlands and see us home. Sometimes, her friends would join us, and we'd take the very long way home to first drop them off in nicer parts of town. My brother and I were little help to her. I still feel guilty about the time I purposely washed the dishes so badly I was never trusted to try again. Free most Saturdays, she'd walk to a music school to learn the steel drums—an activity chosen because it wouldn't interfere with babysitting and it was free (she really wanted to play the clarinet, but her school charged a small fee for rentals).

She writes plays now, setting them in that ruinous grave-yard in the town center and borrowing faintly remembered dialogue from those long walks home. A Protestant in a Cath-olic school; a poor scholarship student; the only Black stu-dent in her year: my sister experienced an insecurity I came to know well—the way you looked or spoke or behaved was never right. We felt an overwhelming instinct to find people who looked, spoke, and acted like we did. Then a barren grief upon the realization that few such people would be found.

She regrets leaving England, thinking she needed a little more time. She has the motto for St. Jo's—"*Optima Deo*," meaning "My Best for God"—tattooed in Romanesque script across her back.

Many Nigerian families like ours were torn—first from our homeland, then from one another. We arrived at a time when the counties around London were "full of Nigerian babies," according to one social worker. For three decades starting in the 1950s, thousands of children in West African immi-grant families were fostered by the white British working class in a system known as "farming out." Typically, they were the children of African students who paid privately for their care, meaning there was little oversight. The children placed in these arrangements experienced even stronger feel-ings of disconnect and disorientation. Farming out continued through the 1980s, so I consider myself lucky. Even though my parents fit the profile of poor, overworked students with no support system, we children were able to remain at home.

For much of my childhood, one or both of my parents went missing from my life. For long stretches of time, my fa-ther was absent, studying in his drafty room near the Univer-sity of London, where he earned his doctorate. He rented the dodgy flat in London to avoid a daily commute from Reading and came home on weekends sporadically, once or twice a month. When he was home, he liked to buy fresh red grapes in bulk, and we all helped him make jam, which he took back in jars to make cheap white-bread sandwiches. He worked at the university hospital, babysitting test patients in drug trials, even accompanying them to the bathroom because they had to be under constant supervision. I would be shocked in adulthood to realize how close we were to the chimerical city that kept my father away, its distance from us seeming oceanic. Less than an hour away. We barely saw him.

Because of my father's extended absences, my mother ran our household as though she were single. She worked afternoons at the fast-food chain Wimpy. She made burgers and mopped while my brother and I ruined coloring books at our table in the corner. She tutored a pair of Indian siblings, Bobby and Pretty, whose time with her I resented. On Saturdays, I would go with her by train to the depressing industrial town of Slough, where she taught students who were falling behind. She took a fourth job, a night shift, scrubbing toilets at the University of Reading, where she was getting her PhD in zoology.

My mother's doctoral program paid a modest stipend, and when she graduated, we were left without a source of income; the Nigerian university sponsoring my father's education had abruptly terminated his funding with no explanation or recourse. After that, we received slim government assistance in the form of rent subsidies.

Then one year, it was my mother's turn to leave—for Oxford, where she went to complete a postdoctoral certificate in education. As our permanent parent, my mother made us whole. Her year away was devastating, living in my mind as the most distressing event during our time in England. All five of us traveled to Oxford to move her into a graduate student hall—into a crummy room with one communal bathroom for the floor. We spent the day getting her settled in the new home where we would not be. We children couldn't understand how she could leave us, stalling until night and the very last train back to Reading. That ride home passed in a shroud, the cheerless capsule hurtling away from my mother, my mooring in a remote land.

"Just the five of us" became "just the four of us" whenever my tiny family unit was broken apart and scattered. My sister becoming *mother*: my father, *memory*. We five shared feelings of envy toward those friends and family we had left behind in Nigeria—envying their cocoon of familiarity, of abundance in constant community—as well as guilt that we might fail them. We tried to think we must be building toward something.

No matter what, my parents sent money back to Nigeria to support our extended family. They paved the path for relatives to join us in a place that offered better. As the immigration process can take years, our family now living in England arrived only after we left. My mother was the first girl to attend school in her village, and she championed her younger sisters' educations and prepared their egress to England. Following in our footsteps, my aunts and cousins held a road map—they quickly found success and stability.

Our own progress was never linear.

My father describes his professional field as a hierarchy in which he couldn't move higher as a person outside the system—as all recent immigrants are—no matter how hard he tried. An administrative assistant once called him a "bloody foreigner." He began seeing how there was no opportunity for advancement in his department unless he learned unwritten rules, and he came to invest all available energy in understanding the culture, molding his subtle personality to the roles he might adopt—the indispensable assistant; the listener; the uncomplaining colleague who shouldered more than his share of responsibilities.

Always at my parents' backs slithered that flavor of fear: *of failure*. Failure spelled worse things than not making rent. Failure made you a liar—for all those promises you made yourself and your children about your purpose, their potential.

In my childhood, on official documents, I was a "resident alien."

More diplomatically, I was a "third culture kid," a term referring to "children who accompany their parents into another society" during those integral developmental years when one's sense of individual and collective identity is formed. We "kids" are immersed in the cultures of both our place of origin and our place of immigration. Our third culture reflects what we bridge, how we build. Our first two break down, so we make another way. Being shuffled around the world can induce advanced intercultural literacy. It can also induce a floundering cultural identity, a feeling of not having a home—or of having one and being lost to it. Third culture kids share a cultural station with others of similar experience, yet we never seamlessly fit anywhere.

What does it mean to be from a place? Is it an accident of birth? Are you from the first home you remember? The place you lived the longest? Is it something earned, like citizenship? Something learned, like language?

During the entirety of our English decade, nothing even *began* to become our own. My family unit was isolated on that island in the North Sea. If we had moved somewhere near Nigerian community—perhaps if we were able to travel to London more often—I might not feel so acutely wounded by the separation from my culture. The four other people in my immediate family were for so long my only reference point to our native culture. To this day, I'll come across some custom and not know if it is widespread throughout West Africa, local to our region and particular to our tribes, or just a family quirk. When an English friend asked me why my father eats his rice and stew with a whole banana on the side, I did not know.

Learning how to tie my own head wrap, I used to study photographs of my cousins, but I never felt as though I knew what I was doing. For a long time, my parents believed that we would soon be returning to Nigeria for good, so concerns about a deteriorating relationship to our culture were never as pressing as the more practical concerns of our marginal lives. We would reconnect when we returned.

My England was a maze: my formative years spent on the outside looking in while waiting to be swept somewhere else—*perhaps back and back.*

3

LAND LIKE A FIREARM

IF YOU HOLD AFRICA LIKE A GUN,
NIGERIA IS THE TRIGGER.

You're pointing the gun down at Antarctica.
In the topography of this exercise,
Nigeria is positioned right at the crux:
both the trigger and the part called the "action."
The territories of my tribes—in the column
of the Sahel—are contained in the magazine.

A live weapon makes a decent metaphor
for terrain I intend to take you through,
calibrate for you. A gun makes a map;
a diagram of diaspora; a counterbalance
to the mechanism of memory, an object
that leaves such satisfying weight in one's hand.

Land like a firearm—moving parts of nomads,
animated by the kinetic energy of war and industry.
Imagine Saharan sand as gunpowder,
my kindred as kindling. Our oil is oil.
And if this fantastic schematic begins
to collapse like ill-made machinery:

Remember the unfulfilled promise of open fire . . .

By one measure, I was born in the least lucky place. The dead-last location on this Earth to face a glad future and fare well. *The Economist* magazine's Where-to-Be-Born Index ranks the lucky ones in the lottery of life. My Nigeria came in eightieth place—out of eighty countries.

I was born near the border Nigeria shares with Niger, the same nation the World Economic Forum designated the worst place in the world to be born a girl.

A third omen: my birthplace of Borno State is labeled "extreme"—for both its coordinates in the extreme northeast of Nigeria and for the extremist religious violence that has plagued it since the 1960s. In the view of the United Nations Commission on Human Rights, this is critical killing ground. Atrocity and I share a place of origin in territory given the official title: "The Home of Peace."

Borno State's capital city, Maiduguri, was established in 1907 as the center and the military headquarters of the British Empire's new Northern Nigeria Protectorate. Neither side of my family has any roots in Maiduguri. I came into the world in this precise place only because my parents were lecturing at the University of Maiduguri. I was born in its teaching hospital, which was targeted for destruction ten years ago;

two terrorists were caught planting incendiary devices near the maternity ward.

In the seat of terror of the Sahel, I was the toddler with the worryingly skinny neck who refused to eat unless I was taken outside and distracted with the lethargic movements of lizards. In all my baby pictures, I am wearing a thick line of kohl to protect my eyes from desert dryness and evil. I am scowling from the heat of my uncle's Peugeot 505, where they perched us for poses.

Islamic insurgents see Maiduguri as their new caliphate—an empire of religion, a sacred state. Boko Haram is a terrorist organization that "recruits" child soldiers and child brides by simply taking them, infamously kidnapping 276 schoolgirls in Chibok in 2014. The Global Terrorism Index—weighing incidents, injuries, and fatalities—ranked them the number 1 terrorist organization in 2015. Boko Haram pledges allegiance to ISIS, the so-called Islamic State of Iraq and Syria, giving Nigeria the dubious distinction of being the only country outside the Middle East with territory controlled by ISIS.

The name "Boko Haram" translates to "Western education is forbidden" and embodies the rebel goal of removing all traces of Western influence from Nigeria. They have been hugely successful, murdering hundreds of teachers in attacks in schools across our mutual home state in the north, resulting in their ruin and closure. Most never reopened. The jihadis oppose anything apart from their own interpretation of Islam, essentializing their mission as so many radicals love to—*making the female body their battleground*: forbidding girls basic education; impregnating stolen child brides; deploying girls in their best blue burqas as dissembling suicide bombers.

They call themselves "The People Committed to the Propagation of the Prophet's Teachings and Jihad." Upon their dawning in 2002, their new mosque and madrasa drew impoverished Muslim adolescents from all over Africa with something like a promise: to "purify the land."

Maiduguri is really two cities become one: the old city and its sprawl. Beyond that, the bush. In Nigeria, "the bush" refers to the uninhabited, rural areas outside villages and towns. Or *almost* uninhabited, but for bushmen who make a way scavenging in this wild. Wild animals like monkeys, hyenas, rats: bushmeat. Sometimes, the inhospitable bush becomes the only place of refuge—the place desperate people go to hide during a "crisis."

This is the status quo: there are quarters within Maiduguri where Boko Haram cannot be routed—which remain under permanent curfew—and a state of emergency persists across several northern regions. So, in my family, we use the word "crisis" to mean a period of *particularly* intense butchery in the north. Crisis there means suicide vests at police headquarters or bombs detonated on market days. A dozen gunmen unleashed around a city. A bus set alight, women and children locked inside.

After we left for England in 1988, my family returned to Nigeria in various configurations over the years depending on what my parents could afford—for Christmas, for a slate of spring weddings or a burial. Sometimes, my siblings and I traveled with only one parent: a precaution to ensure one surviving parent if the other encountered a fatal crisis.

But we never returned to Maiduguri, having no permanent ties to the city that is seasonally watered by a river, seasonally ripped apart by explosives. City of one or three million: there can be no accurate population count because of the chaotic spate of refugees fleeing. My family joins at least one million people who left and must be subtracted from that number. I remember nothing of my birthplace.

I was born a nomad amongst the settled. The area's dominant Kanuri tribe is traditionally sedentary in the expanding desert, their fortune in the form of the Ngadda River.

In the local Kanuri language, *"mai"* means "king." And *"duwu,"* the Kanuri word for "thousand," is synonymous with infinity. Thus, Maiduguri names the place of one thousand—or of innumerable—kings. The city bears this name because of an ancient custom amongst its denizens to wear ceremonial gowns not only for festivities but also as everyday attire. To newcomers, the city appeared full of kings, and it seemed a place of endless enterprise. It remains a center of commerce: the terminal point of a colonial-era railroad extending to the coast, and a vector of perpetual traffic and diesel exhaust, where armed ambushes target cargo trucks on their way elsewhere.

And markets made it. Markets in the old city called a constant tide of strangers. They brought animals in every stage of their consumption: as livestock, as hides, as skins, as craft leather goods and dried snacks. Traders brought our staples: rice, millet, maize. They brought pinkish gum arabic, the stiffening sap of the acacia tree, sold by weight in unrefined form like great mounds of confectionery. Men brought trade and their tongues. I was born in the birthplace of a trading dialect called Nigerian Arabic. Most geographic features in this area have two, three, or four commonly used names in various languages.

I was born in the land of black cotton swamps. The blessed, promised place. The lucky land near the seasonal river where, despite everything, the state motto remains: "The Home of Peace."

In a sinister superlative, Nigeria is ranked the twelfth most likely to fail in the index of the characteristics of fragile and "failed states." My frail nation was conceived in pursuit of profit and palm oil. Europeans divided Africa arbitrarily, apportioning it according to what they craved. Our borders appear in a geometry of greed, divining our natural resources into dividends. In the incursive fifteenth century, the Portuguese were the first to attempt to commandeer the coasts of West Africa. In those early days, exports of natural resources by sea and overland via desert routes courted the interest of competing foreign states. Europeans built coastal fortresses to protect monopolies amidst import-export wars.

Gold and ivory. Petroleum and people.

For four hundred years, the West African seaboard served as the site of chattel slavery, the kidnapping of over twelve million humans. Nigeria is a central birthing place of the Black Diaspora. It was largely from there, from slave castles lining slave coasts, that the violence of our separation was set into motion. The Euro-American slave trade ended in the nineteenth century; then began decades of indirect rule imposed through military might, economic exploitation, and proselytization.

Nigeria was a Frankenstein colony—cobbled and coming together bizarrely. Partly engineered as a prospect of the Royal Niger Company, Nigeria was first privately "owned." The Royal Niger Company, established in 1886, existed under various names and finally as a subsidiary of the Unilever corporation until 1987, the year after I was born. British imperial strategy lay in helping such companies dominate trade markets; bit by bit, corporations began to exert ruling powers.

England in the early Machine Age had a high demand for palm oil, used as a mechanical lubricant, so it annexed the delta where crude oil bides within the flesh of the palm tree's fruit. Sometimes, the colonizers deceived tribal chiefs into signing away their territorial rights with contracts in convoluted English. If met with resistance, they razed whole villages. They desecrated the corpse of our precolonial Nigeria. Nowhere within the vast networks and institutions they built did they make room to preserve what had come before.

During the "Scramble for Africa" from 1870 to 1914, Europeans increased their control of the continent from 10 percent to 90 percent. A series of military conquests handed Britain a decisive victory in 1914. The territories pieced together by the British in league with other European nations were officially named "Nigeria" that year.

They had their colony. Their continent.

An in-law recently bragged that the Bible is the only book she's ever read—will *ever* read—in her life. There is a famous quote about the impact of the religion that Europeans brought, an observation of the Kenyan leader Jomo Kenyatta: "When the missionaries arrived, Africans had the land, and the missionaries had the Bible. They taught us to pray with our eyes closed. When we opened our eyes, they had the land, and we had the Bible."

. . . Yes, after all of this, we had the Bible.

And we had the Holy Quran.

The first exploratory Christian Europeans established strongholds that came at once into violent ideological conflict with the territories already claimed for Allah. Christianity arrived on the coasts alongside early European opportunists and penetrated inland wherever missionaries built all the cornerstones of civic life—schools, churches, and administrative offices. Christian communities huddle close to rivers because many missionaries traveled by boat when mooring their settlements.

Conversely, Islam descended from desert—from northern warlords and eastern scholars who came traipsing down the Sahara one thousand years ago. In the north, *malamai* (Quranic teachers) preside over a network of madrasas, Islamic schools that often take the place of liberal education. Southward, in an opposing tradition, missionary schools train students in the Christian faith. About half of Nigeria is now Christian. Islam claims almost all the other half. Constantly clashing, these organized religions cooperate only to marginalize traditional spiritualities.

One Nigerian state might have a 99 percent Muslim population while its inverse has 1 percent. A political map of Nigeria presents a country bisected: Christians in the south segregated from a Muslim north—territories bound by belief, separated by a real, invisible line. The point where our two Abrahamic faiths meet marks the capital, Abuja, which rests in uneasy compromise in the center of the country.

Nigeria's divergences hounded the British as they tried to manage their multiethnic dominion. When they decided Nigeria's borders, their mindless construct dissected clans and bisected tribes. This touched my family personally; two grandparents spoke French, not English, because most of their tribal congregation extended into areas colonized by France.

A 1907 telegram to the Colonial Office reveals the official British agenda. Item 1 reads: "Pacify the country." In the northern region I come from, the British encouraged divisive tribalism. They appointed minority tribes to rule bitter majorities, disregarding traditional systems of governance—simply empowering favored subjects instead, having unfit local chiefs and emirs report to them. Their catalogue of mistakes still plagues us.

England tried to tame its Crown colony, but it defied easy management. In 1960, after forty years of formal colonial rule, a series of compromises between indigenous ethnic groups established a new constitution for self-governing regions of Nigeria: *a republic.* Finally, independence. Queen Elizabeth II remained the honorary head of state until 1963. During the long period of resistance to her colonial regime, Nigerians collaborated toward that common cause. But the inevitable problems of newly created nations began to fester immediately after Independence; within a decade, the country erupted into grisly civil war. Fortunately, the billion-dollar Biafran war ended in 1970 with reconciliation rather than reprisal.

The past presents a problem for the idea of "Nigeria." We feel specters of the people and powers who carved this unlikely land without logic.

Structurally, our states do not mirror any kingdoms that preceded them. The thirty-six current states of Nigeria originated from three administrative regions: northern, western, and eastern. There was no popular input or outpouring from its people during the genesis of such strange states; postcolonial military regimes unilaterally dictated their conformation, often by illegally changing the Constitution. The present architecture of Nigeria is more stable—a nominal democracy slightly less volatile than during its days of dictatorship. The country's morphology was settled by the 1970s, but sectarian strife is built into the bones of its careless conception. Having previously belonged to various unaffiliated kingdoms, the people never clamored for Nigeria's creation, never cried out for nationhood.

Statecraft such as this was only very recently embraced.

Nigeria is daunting to get to know. Traveling from one region to another, different areas of the country seem to have nothing in common. The mangrove forest overgrowing; half-hearted forests; some swampland; gorgeous grasses; the brushwood where nothing good grows, not even ubiquitous date palms and oil palms; medial mountains; weird rock formations that disturb the subtropical scene and make mirages improbable. It took years of civil war for the population to agree to live as one body politic.

Understand Nigeria through another ongoing war—a war between water and dust. Dust versus Water: vicious drought during the dry season meets violent flooding in the rainy season. Dry lakes stand where water bodies were. Even the language to describe the landscape reflects this conflict: the two possible roots of *Sahel* mean either "sea coast, shore" or their opposite, "grassy plains." The Sahel region forms an arid flank straddling the southern boundary of the Sahara and the savanna grassland underneath. A horizontal strip running along the African continent, one end to the other. The Sahel's lower edge underlines the borderlands I come from. *Think of the Sahel as desert coastline.*

Our central capital, Abuja, is Africa's first planned city. In rural villages, mud and thatch provide building materials. A nearby world away are skyscrapers, suburbs, and shantytowns. The city lights of Lagos might best be imagined like the life cycles of supermassive stars. My Lagosian friend Jide warned it would eat me alive, eat me whole. Still growing on the southern coast at a rate of 20 percent each year, this megacity is prophesied to become the first habitation of one hundred million: the most populous place on Earth. It is also sinking.

The excess of Nollywood, the third-largest film industry in the world, glosses over gratuitous poverty in some of the world's largest slums. One slum in Lagos occupies an entire floating island; Nigeria is a place of plenty where there is never enough. With two hundred million people, it is the largest nation of Black people in the world. Due to a high birth rate, some statisticians project that by the end of this century, its population will surpass China's. Of its people, Nigeria gives the world wealth at an irreparable cost. A "brain drain" sees the departure of much of its educated citizenry and the depletion of its intellectual resources.

Where it does well is *innovation*—our people are known for our entrepreneurial spirit and virtuosity in the creative arts, especially music. The same country where "bush tea" medicine causes fatal liver damage is the center of the brilliantly emerging African tech industry. Nigeria contradicts, and in some stubborn ways, it orients itself in a rear-facing stance that stalls progress. It can feel stuck in the overbearing religiosity of a conservative social order; twenty years ago, moral outrage over a beauty pageant led to street battles where two hundred died. Nigeria developed prematurely, thrust midcentury onto the world stage. Full of early industrial promise, it was once expected to pattern South Korea and China in terms of exponential and explosive economic growth (in the 1970s). For many Nigerians, that future indeed followed, but it never came for the fortuneless north.

A resource curse is a phenomenon in which, counterintuitively, an abundant resource exacerbates a country's economic problems. Despite its oil and mineral reserves, Nigeria routinely appears at the bad end of international indexes ranking issues related to quality of life. *Maternal mortality rate. People living with HIV/AIDS. People dying of HIV/AIDS.* Concerning poverty, poor health, and human rights abuses, I've often thought cynically or sadly, "*Of course* Nigeria is on this list."

I am also not surprised that one Gallup global survey places Nigerians as some of the most optimistic people in the world. And this optimism is tied to optimism about our country—one rated high in "Corruption" but always rising in "Connectivity" and "Competitiveness." We peg our personal fate to its fortune.

"Which tribe?" is the first question one Nigerian asks another.

Nigeria is a nation of nearly 400 tribes, speaking 502 languages. Each tribe has its own language or dialect, and they differ widely in religious practices and cultural norms. Evolving over centuries, ethnolinguistic groups combined, conquered, collapsed. Tribes absorbed others by bloodshed or through language diffusion, intermarriage, and alliance. Some splintered upon encountering the Sahara, kept apart by the arduous desert crossing; drought-resistant tribes adapted to desertification. By the early nineteenth century, the ethnic affiliations we call "tribes" coalesced—in terms of tradition, religion, and language—into roughly the configurations they form today.

For hundreds of years, facial scars marked pride in one's tribe: the popular way to inform strangers and kin alike of where you belong. The visible rites are cut into faces by skilled people owning the sharpest knives, after which plant dyes and charcoal paste stain and heal the wounds. Tribal marks convey the famous qualities of a tribe; some carry luck itself within their grooves. They are relics, charms, even résumés. Some are meant to reveal how well the bearer withstood the agony of its making. One pattern means your tribesmen are swordsmiths, another that your people make music or come from kings.

In my immediate family, none of us five bear tribal marks. We are anomalies in Nigeria: a fully baptized family in the overwhelmingly Islamic north. We are also oddity in the West, where most Nigerian immigrants arrive from the central or southern parts of our country. Not once have I met another African in the West who claims the Fulani or Longuda tribes that we do. Similarly, meeting immigrants who speak our native Hausa is rare. If we do come across another from Hausaland, they're invariably Muslim. That I was raised a Christian is a testament to the tenacity of a few missionaries who strayed into my mother's nameless hamlet.

In the short-term period after Nigerian Independence in 1960, a few of the largest tribes dominated politics. Smaller tribes—attempting to increase their political capital—began demanding shares of power and enjoyed some success. When the central Nigerian state consolidated its own authority, the significations of tribe started a downward slide. Now, "tribe" is more a cultural, communal system than a formal, political property. Tribal affiliation isn't decided by strict regulations, blood quantum rules, or official enrollment. *You are claimed.*

Or you are not. My family has spent countless mealtimes hashing out our thorny tribal identities. Keeping in mind the permutable nature of "tribe," there are four possible answers I could give someone asking for my tribe—each with varying degrees of accuracy:

Fulani, Hausa, Hausa-Fulani, and Longuda.

"Doors of No Return" refer to the gateways from which slaves were stolen during the Atlantic slave trade, positioned at the mouths of the castles and forts standing at various slave ports. Once the enslaved crossed this threshold, it was the last they saw of home. My immigrant family passed through no such portal, but we look back to our land and wonder at what has been torn and taken from us.

After some time away, Nigeria acquired the obscure title "Back Home." A place of consuming heat and an unmanageable ensemble of relatives. It was the place my parents would threaten to send us children back to whenever we misbehaved. The menace of exile molded our behavior, a deterrent more effective than the prospect of corporal or divine punishment. When I stole my brother's giant chocolate egg, which he won in a bank raffle, I was told I was going to be sent *Back Home*; a phone call was even feigned to make arrangements for my impending departure. I was left to sit with this deception, paralyzed with the inevitability of my banishment.

Now I find myself in an opposite exile. I have not gone Back Home in ten years due to homegrown violence, the accelerating terrorism perpetrated by Boko Haram in and around the city of my birth. Nigeria looms before me like a ridgeline barely discernible through mist over darkened water.

Boko Haram enjoyed a resurgence beginning in 2010 after a new strategy of mass prison breaks freed hundreds of prisoners; this group has caused 350,000 deaths in 20 years. The US State Department has issued a "Do Not Travel" advisory for my birth state. The government web page is emblazoned in bright orange banners that emphasize the severity of the risk. *Be extra vigilant when visiting banks or ATMs; Do not physically resist any robbery attempt; Keep a low profile; Stay alert in locations frequented by Westerners; Establish a "proof of life" protocol with your loved ones.*

In 2019, the president of Nigeria declared Boko Haram "technically defeated." That same year, the governor of the state wherein they rampage ran out of patience with unsuccessful federal intervention. In response, he attempted to secretly recruit a force of ten thousand "hunters with voodoo powers" who would be protected against bullets by magical amulets. Hundreds of vigilantes—skilled hunters but untrained soldiers—were seen melting into the bush. They would be armed beyond the machetes they arrived with, trained for three weeks, and prayed for. The governor solicited the daily prayers of thirty ulamas (religious scholars) located in Islam's holiest city, Mecca. He hoped to undermine the faith of "pious" insurgents. *I wonder what ulamas think of amulets.*

Despite these military and mystical efforts, my family started canceling trips home, and our caution set us in a ceaseless drift ever further from our relatives. My last visit home was in 2011, when I was twenty-four. That makes a decade of distance from that red West African dirt: too long a time since I set foot on the real, raw earth that gave me up.

There is one national football team for Nigeria; there are no tribes on the pitch. This unity partly explains why football is so culturally significant to a country otherwise divided along many kinds of lines. As I grew up, my father watched any international match Nigeria played in—they were the soundtrack to my childhood. During World Cup qualifiers, anytime the Nigerian team came close to scoring, he'd jump to his feet and start yelling, "A chance for Nigeria!!! A chance for Nigeria!!!"

The rest of us would join him in his chant. My family often synchronized like this—like some kind of chain reaction to uncertain identity in uncertain existence. We all wearied of feeling like curiosities, so we compulsively echoed one another. Each of us was one little, leftover, or lost piece in some puzzle to be deciphered. A mystery, *unmuddled.*

We make more sense mythologized.

4

THE PEOPLE WHO
STEAL THATCH

In one possible origin story, my paternal ancestor was captured as a slave and then released. The family legend goes that my father's great-grandfather, born in 1890, was kidnapped at the age of nine along with other children as they played outside one ordinary day at the turn of the last century.

In his village, there was no system of defense against raiders and slavers. His supposed captors were Arab men on horses who came riding from the north through a narrow gap in two large hills. They sold stolen children into slavery across the Sahara, as far as present-day Libya. At that time, a caravan route from Nigeria to Libya was traversed by merchants and traders of all kinds, including those in this lesser-known trans-Saharan slave trade.

According to this story, my great-great-grandfather was taken to a watering hole, an unidentified oasis and grand bazaar somewhere in the sun-blinding mass of desert beyond Lake Chad. And there he was sold. I want to know how long that journey takes—by foot, beside camel, on horseback. *Do I want to know his price?*

Before beginning the second leg of the voyage to Libya, his new masters performed a thorough inspection of their "merchandise" and discovered that he had sores on his skin. They mistook him for a leper. His skin condition still runs in my family on my father's side, but only resembles leprosy to the paranoid. It is a hereditary fungal infection with the scientific name *Tinea versicolor* (my family invented for it the silly term "frou frou"). Lightly raised, brownish spots of a quarter inch spread across one's back; a type of yeast that naturally occurs on skin and thrives in hot climates grows out of control. It was the sun of the long march that afflicted the boy.

Nowadays, it is easily cured by taking antifungal pills, washing with Selsun Blue anti-dandruff shampoo, staying out of the sun. It is neither painful nor contagious. Then, my great-great-grandfather would not have known whether he would live or die. He was released because of presumed leprosy—thus, perversely, my family considers this skin condition *lucky*. I am disfavored for never having had it.

My forefather began working as an assistant to a merchant who guided him as he traveled home. All the merchants spoke a Berber language, and he was able to learn some of their words and communicate. He found his way down to his village in Nigeria by going back via the same route he had come. To get home, he walked through a gauntlet of ranging geography. *Sahel. Sudan. Sahara. Sub-Sahara. Savanna. Steppe.* He would have seen shrubland, scrubland, grassland—no woodland.

He knew his people by their tribal marks (three vertical scars on their cheeks, then three radiating out from the corners of their mouths like whiskers). Identifying the distinctive markings, he reunited with his family an unknown length of time after he was taken. We do know that he lived a long life in freedom and had many children. Because of his spots, we, his descendants, joke that he was more "leopard" than "leper."

Though my father never laid eyes on it, he claims that somewhere there exists a leather patch with Arabic writing. It indicates our ancestor died a free man.

There is so little recorded about my father's tribe, the Longuda of Northern Nigeria. An oral tradition means that most histories were never written down, and the rare paper texts were not preserved. The few, shabby attempts at tribal histories were written by biased British anthropologists and routinely included absurdly offensive inaccuracies. At times, it is obvious to me that the local people were pulling their legs—so preposterous are the reports. *No*, villagers did not believe they became birds, a flock that could fly away when annoyed; they only wished so.

There is also that colonial tendency toward historical revisionism and outright cultural destruction. Europeans did keep records according to their colonial interests, motivated by profit or proselytization. But even given the British knack for bureaucracy during colonialism, there was no reliable system for maintaining genealogical records in either of my parents' areas. The oldest such records were church rolls, and the earliest of these date back to the early twentieth century, a mere one hundred years ago. Church documents from the Danish Lutheran congregation most Longuda belong to were rarely translated, never archived. The entire north suffers chronic neglect, lagging in literacy rates and lacking a basic literary infrastructure: the publishing houses, libraries, and well-maintained archives enabling the survival of print.

I have found only one book detailing the Longuda: about their innovations in ox-plowing. The tribe's origins are not well documented. As the Longuda have always been sun worshippers—the name of their primary god translates to "the sun above"—some of their origin stories point to roots in Egypt and its powerful sun god, Ra. In one tradition, they came from Yemen; in the Longuda language, the word "Yemen" still means, "We have left." Sometime in the distant past, a great migration out of Yemen or Egypt or elsewhere involved some Longuda who left to follow the setting sun westward. In the middle of the Sahara desert, they had a dispute and divided themselves into two groups. One group stopped following the sun, and instead headed east, ending up in Uganda. Where the west-seeking Longuda settled was the place they loved enough to stop chasing after the sun. They fell in love with a river.

I do not always believe my father's stories. I do believe in his story*telling*.

My father's method for determining the veracity of any story places a high value on consistency: if you hear the same story within your own family and then again around your own village and the next, it's more likely to contain elements of truth. For him, the stories that hold the most emotional weight—regardless of accuracy—are those that explain certain mysteries, like the earliest conflict precipitating a long-standing tribal rivalry. (That all-important original insult.) In one famous incident, a fabler from my father's tribe called the chief of a nearby village a *servant*—doubly humiliating both the tribal leader and his settlement, which was larger and should therefore have been acknowledged as superior. In swift retaliation, a composer from the injured party accused the rival chief of being a thief—firing back that servants are nobler than thieves.

The tribe's name, Longuda, was bestowed by the British, who could not pronounce "Nungura," the name the tribe itself used for their land. The tribe eventually adopted the Anglicized name, and history was scribbled over and subsumed into the Queen's English. The tribe first called itself Nungura Ba—the People of the Land of Nungura. "*Nungura ya*" means "one person" and refers to an idea of oneness that united the clans sharing that land. The various clans performed different functions within the larger tribe. My grandmother's people were known as healers, and my grandfather's were rainmakers.

In my mind, the Longuda tribe seems always to recede and diminish; I am not close to my father's small side of the family. I don't speak or understand the Longuda language very well, an endangered language spoken by one hundred thousand tribesmen. Limited to two states in the northeastern part of the country, their numbers make up less than 1 percent of the Hausa or Fulani tribes of my mother's side. That the Longuda remain, even this small, is a main point of pride. Small tribes were absorbed by other tribes after a military defeat, so we know that the Longuda were undefeated because they were never subsumed under a victorious tribe's rulership.

The Longuda tribe is exceptional in that it is the only matriarchal ethnic group in Nigeria. The chief was a man, but he was always chosen by women. Women owned most property; if they inherited land, they continued to own it solely in their name after marriage. If marriage produced a child, the husband forfeited all his own land to his wife. Now, though, their matriarchy has eroded and is more romanticized than observed. The Longuda still trace their family line through mothers, using the rationale that when a woman gives birth, everyone knows she is the child's mother, while the father's identity is less certain. The logic is that a child can only *fully* belong to her mother.

My father says that most Longuda would not consider me Longuda because he married outside the tribe; thus, his offspring don't count. With the Longuda, children are still encouraged to claim their mother's tribe as their own. And so, ironically, my rejection of being Longuda and my affinity for my maternal tribal line is my most Longuda trait. However, Nigeria as a whole is patrilineal. Some government forms have a line to specify your tribal affiliation, and you're expected to pick your father's. As a result, on official Nigerian records and in the opinion of the state, I'm Longuda.

I *never* say I am.

My father makes sure to note that he was born on a Tuesday evening, though this holds no particular significance. He was born in the village of Guyuk, in the northeastern Adamawa State, on July 22, 1952. His parents and all four grandparents were born and spent their lives only a few miles away from the room where he was delivered in the dark of night by goat-fat candlelight, brought into this world by an elderly neighbor and seamstress who doubled as the only local midwife.

In his native language of Longuda, his nickname, Khimka, means "Cherish what you are given."

My father's full formal name is now Harold Ishaku Daniel. His father chose the aggressively British-sounding first name in homage to Harold Macmillan, the aristocratic former prime minister who supported African decolonization. Ishaku is Isaac. He wasn't born with all his names; he has no birth certificate. In the church registry, his full name was simply Harold Ishaku. It wasn't until he entered the university, when the registrar's office started asking for a middle name, that he gained one more name. He decided to list Ishaku as his middle name and use the last name Daniel, his grandfather's name, which his extended family had recently settled on after a squabble. His grandfather, the earliest convert of his clan, took the name Daniel upon baptism at the age of eleven. Like Cher and Madonna, he was just Daniel. The missionaries who encouraged renaming didn't mind him adopting a mononym; he must not have needed a longer name to stand out nor a surname for administrative purposes. Before his name change, he was Tapwarakan Butereni.

There was controversy amongst my paternal relatives while deciding their family name because they had options—the practice of automatically taking the name of one's father was only one generation old. Previously, names were chosen for places or occupations; where you came from was more important than who your father was. Once the family argument was resolved, "Daniel" replaced "of Banjiram," referencing a nearby town. The name Daniel is concentrated as a common last name only within my father's particular area; this extreme localization leads us to believe that the story of Daniel was a favorite of missionaries there. The few Nigerians named Daniel likely trace their name to an ancestor with an affinity for the eponymous hero of the Biblical book. Perhaps those converting to a minority faith were heartened by his miraculous survival in the lion's den.

Guyuk was traditionally the place where the chief of the Longuda chose to reside. It is still the "capital" and the cultural center of Longuda tribal life. The name "Guyu" meant "people who steal thatch." Because their land didn't grow the high grass used for roofing huts, neighboring tribes accused them of stealing it—though in truth, they bought or bartered for it. The British added a *k* to "Guyu" to make it "Guyuk" for unknown reasons.

My father's family was influential in his birth village, one of twenty-five Longuda villages in a cluster. His grandmother made and sold clay pots good for storing food, a skill she passed down to all the women in his family, which soon earned them a reputation as the makers of the biggest pots around. One entire room of his childhood home was taken up by what was verified to be the largest pot in the region.

His family's poverty was relative. They weren't in that very top class of society occupied by a handful of wealthy people, but they lived on the rung just below that, in the class of skilled workers who had some formal education and held jobs requiring training. His mother was an adult education teacher and medical assistant who liked to call herself a nurse, though this title should be understood in a colloquial sense. His father was honored in the village as the champion wrestler, going by the stage name "So-So," a slang term for a bath sponge—he always bounced back. He taught a subject called "rural science" and later worked in customs in the airport so far away in Lagos, an airport routinely found on lists of the world's worst. It was better then.

In Nigeria—positioned just out of reach of the ever-expanding desert—*water is life*. Our waterways are so fundamental that many tribes revere them as deities.

The village where my father grew up is the place where two rivers meet. The Benue, which begins in Cameroon, passes through Nigeria before emptying into the Atlantic Ocean. The Gongola River starts in the highlands of the Jos Plateau and joins the Benue in a confluence. During the rainy season, you can stand at the top of the gorge surrounding the rivers and see two distinct waters. One yellow river is smaller and flows swiftly, while the larger of the pair goes slow, a darker brown hue without hurry. Having different currents, they form rapids where they meet, so you cannot swim in his people's dangerous portion of river. They go there to irrigate farms, wash clothes, and pluck fish from the brackish, breaking conflux.

This confluence is the life-giving *essentia* that sustains his clan: the staging ground for my father's boyhood. Situated near these rivers, the village then was mostly farmers and fishermen and a few markets where they sold the fruits of their labor. Communal activity revolved around the harvest, which took place in December after farmers finished storing their staple crop, sorghum. Christmas coincided with harvest celebrations, resulting in syncretic practices—traditions jumbled together, mirroring the eclectic and hybrid origins of Christmas itself.

At specific times of the season, hippos would emerge, and the entire village turned out to watch them. As one cannot hear well across large bodies of water, there would always be a scout, usually a child, standing on the riverbanks and signaling to oblivious fishermen if a hippo was getting too close. Most people left the hippos alone—they capsize your boat if you harass them—but the bravest people hunted them. These hunters were heroes because of the danger in hippo hunts and because they distributed the meat to bystanders. Killing only the males to avoid decimating the population, hunters provided communal meals for generations; hippos taste just like beef. The hunts were more dangerous in the distant past, when hunters used spears and harpoons, as they had to get quite close to the animals. When came guns, the hunt became easier but less heroic. Hippos went extinct there, no longer surfacing in the river. The last few were captured and carried off to game reserves.

There was only one car in Guyuk, a Land Rover belonging to the chief that had to be physically wound up to start the engine while someone inside the car pressed the accelerator. The house my father grew up in didn't have matches because his family could not afford them. Matches had been new magic to my father's grandfather, who was the firemaker of their village. In the savanna belt, high winds are typical, so people do not leave low fires going in their open-air kitchens. After the night meal, they are doused; the next morning, they again need to be lit. My firemaking forefather owned specialized equipment and flint shaped like a bow, and he was efficient and fast. After he made one fire, my father and other children helped carry the flame from house to house.

They had no electricity or plumbing. As the eldest, my father performed many tasks in service of the gargantuan feat of procuring water and food in a remote society. Daily, he fetched water for his household from the river—until the village built a single communal pipe; the pump was opened a few times per week, and a half-mile-long line of people with buckets would come to take away as much as they could balance upon their heads.

Before the arrival of Christianity, it was to the sun the Longuda gave thanks for their lives and livelihood. In addition to the central sun deity, every family revered a host of minor gods, making idols to represent them, assembled in a home shrine that was the focal point of their spiritual practice.

The Longuda retained beliefs that frustrated missionaries. Death was generous only if you died "properly," after which you wouldn't come back. If you died *improperly*, you would return as a spirit invisible to all humans except a special few, the seers. An "improper death" was defined as any for which the exact cause of death couldn't be determined. These unlucky spirits were chased off with a spear at the beginning of a hunt.

Christians, Muslims, and "pagans" used to get along in my father's region because there was "nothing to fight over," according to him. The Longuda tribe even formed councils to serve as intermediaries and calm tensions between actively warring Christian and Muslim settlements in the north—their tiny ward an oasis. Though traditional beliefs remain prominent, the Longuda tribe is now nominally Christian.

My father's grandfather was the first in the entire Longuda tribe to have a Christian baptism. He renounced the "sun above" to look east toward Judea. After his conversion, five out of six of his children were female, and others in their matrilineal tribe took this as a lucky omen since males marked the ending of a family line. Thereafter, his neighbors sought his blessing and said they accepted his savior as their own.

By the time of my father's childhood two generations later, everybody in his Longuda clan claimed to be Lutheran, reflecting the missionaries who settled in the area. The quibbles of new converts revealed unique cultural concerns. In the fledgling patriarchy of the Longuda, one recurring argument was over seating arrangements in their cramped chapel. If, according to the Apostle Paul, women must never speak in church and should only speak through their husbands, how could they do so while seated in a segregated section, separated from their men by an aisle?

When he was in primary school, my father met the very first missionary who had ever come to Guyuk. Dr. Bronam returned from Denmark when he was ninety to see the place he won for Christ, wanting to witness its transformation and die happy. The whole community came out to see him; all day, there was dancing and pageantry. The children sang a song they were taught in the village's only school ("Today is our day of joy!") before dedicating the unfinished second school that was being named after their white knight.

The new nation of Nigeria: its creation when my father was eight years old marks the main event of his childhood. He remembers emotion more than detail—that everyone was happy, though he did not understand why. He hoarded the little green cups and green-white-green-striped flags that were handed out to children and kept them safe for decades. The atmosphere of optimism expired within years. Soon, civil war. In 1967, when he was in secondary school, he began seeing war planes flying overhead on their way to suppress the secessionist Biafran State. Uncles joined the military and never came back.

My father's first school was a Roman Catholic primary school in a neighboring town. Children were allowed to enroll there if they could pay the yearly fees and were big enough to touch one ear with the hand of the opposite arm when reaching over their head. The school was a walk of many miles from his home. He was taught Catholic catechism and attended daily Catholic Mass. For secondary school, he transferred to a boarding school in an actual city much farther away—in Yola, the capital of the state.

My father speaks four languages. Longuda was his first language, spoken at home. Bachama, the language of a larger tribe straddling Longuda territory, was spoken in schools and amongst his Bachama relatives. Hausa was spoken in marketplaces and on buses; it is my first language, and it is the lingua franca of Northern Nigeria and much of West Africa. English was not spoken in his home but was taught in school.

As he grew up and became more aware of the world around him beyond his tribe, he was limited by a crippling lack of access to information. Some schoolteachers had radios, and some stores in town centers did also; otherwise, besides what was shared secondhand by missionaries and visitors, there was virtually no news from the outside filtering in. He and his schoolmates could not afford newspapers, so mostly, if they did not learn about something in school, they did not learn it at all.

Several months after the giant leap for mankind, my father saw the footage of the first spacewalk when some Americans arrived at his school with videos and a television. When *Apollo 11* landed on the moon in 1969, the United States Information Agency dispatched representatives from the American embassy, located at that time very far to the south in the then–capital city of Lagos. The cultural ambassadors were sent to schools all over Nigeria, even to the distant north, to tell schoolchildren about the moon landing: a mission of soft power spreading the message of American exceptionalism in the vacuum left by one receding empire.

In general, the Longuda didn't get along with the British because the tribe wasn't compliant, particularly due to British interference in their process of selecting chiefs. Many Longuda committed acts of sabotage. A driver transporting a British bureaucrat would inconveniently run out of gas in the middle of nowhere. If asked for a count of barrels of groundnut oil, workers in a processing plant would report wildly different numbers each time. Each miscount and recount cost time and reduced the efficiency with which the

British exported the raw materials extracted from Longuda lands. For such acts, one of my father's uncles was hanged in his village's market square on a charge of "rebellion."

In both church and at school, my father was taught that Black people descended from evil and should be grateful that white people came to spread the good news and grant them the opportunity to rejoin the holy tribe—to be grafted into the unsullied lineage of Israel and Abraham. For a very long time, he never independently considered what it meant to be Black, African, or Nigerian. His major identity was his tribe. Tribalism was so entrenched—so masterfully exploited by the British—that one did not look further than that. Almost everyone looked the same, so Blackness was the default. At the same time, Blackness was regarded as inferior—this belief a byproduct of colonial conditioning.

The white man—also called the "red man" by the Longuda people—was something special. He had machines like bicycles, guns, and cars—machines that were like magic. My father's grandfather told him about white people powers, which he witnessed firsthand when organizing their hunts. When they spotted their prey—or simply when they were annoyed with something—they could point their metal stick at it. The stick would make an awful, loud sound, and the offending thing would die.

And they told you stories about the origins of the world, stories that pointed to a knowledge of all matters—access to the esoteric and underlying truth of all things.

As children, my father and his local friends saw white people as such alien and ascendant creatures that they once believed the cruel joke of an older child—that the feces of white people were made of chocolate. Though they failed in their search for evidence to disprove this fiction, the fact that they didn't dismiss it out of hand reveals the extremes of colonial propaganda. In school, they learned nothing about the trans-Atlantic slave trade—even about the people taken from Nigeria—so he remained ignorant of those centuries of struggle. When he heard about "Black Power," he didn't think much of it. But he did sing the lyrics "Say it loud; I'm Black and I'm proud!" because he liked the rhythm of soul.

My father was punished by missionaries for speaking his native Longuda; they wanted students to speak only English. His English improved, but this new proficiency made him vulnerable to an affliction known as Brain Fag (short for "fatigue") Syndrome. Symptoms resemble an anxiety attack and include rapid heartbeat, nausea, muscle spasms, and blurred vision. The feeling of something crawling beneath your skin. It was first observed in Nigeria in the 1960s: a localized syndrome that only impacts West African students in former colonies. One theory is that a student's brain begins to protest against the culture clash of the colonial educational system.

Curiously, the more fluent a student is in English, the higher his risk of experiencing this mental collapse. Self-imposed pressure to succeed may be a major risk factor. My father decided he wanted to be a surgeon after a doctor saved his brother from a knife injury. That doctor advised him to stay at the top of his class. One night, as my father sat down to study, his hand began to shake and scramble his writing. He couldn't comprehend what he had written. When he opened his mouth to ask the empty room what was happening to him, the words that came out were nonsense. He remained in this speechless state of fog—almost in a fugue—for hours.

The most palpable connection I have with my father's tribe is through his stories.

My paternal relatives all live in Adamawa State. I remember only two visits to my father's side. Because my mother's family is much bigger and far more close-knit, it always made more sense to spend most of our time with her people. Given the difficulty in traveling by road in Nigeria, we usually skipped visiting his side altogether. My mother was the one who made the effort to stay in touch with relations. My father rarely did. I had the feeling he feared calling home because he received so much bad news about his favorite people dying one after another. I never spoke to his family outside brief phone calls at Christmas. Interpersonal interactions with them confounded me. Nothing normal ever came out of my mouth.

On one trip, I remember waking up mid-evening and hearing my mother crying in another room. The black curtain that divided the rooms was so heavy it muffled her voice, making her sound unfamiliar. I must have slept through an argument between her and my paternal grandmother. I don't know where everyone else had gone; it was just the three of us. When I asked my mother what happened, she wouldn't tell me. She still won't. In my house, there was never much parental propriety regarding what we children should be exposed to—all adversity, arguments, and emergencies played out in front of our eyes. The exception was the turmoil in my father's family, which was always cloaked in secrecy.

Informed mostly through eavesdropping, I suppose my grandmother thought my mother wasn't good enough for my father. Maybe my grandmother, a former kingmaker, had political reasons for objecting to my father's choice. During her time, Longuda men maneuvered to find powerful wives. One could win a good marriage by displaying attractive qualities like grit and sobriety. Marriages were voluntary, rarely arranged: even the Longuda tradition of bride-stealing was performed only with the bride's consent. Marriage was encouraged to be kept within the Longuda tribe but prohibited within smaller clans. My father finding a bride outside his tribe was not out of bounds, but maybe his mother wanted for him a prominent Longuda woman.

It could be my parents are not well matched in their intertribal union. They clash over the reasons or explanations for any divergence in their tribal ways, arguing around the obvious possibility that tribes do things differently. The generation before theirs was the last to widely bear tribal marks; my parents disagree about why their own became the first to set aside this almost compulsory practice. My mother claims marking was phased out due to Christianity's prohibition of bodily mutilation. The scarification process is not always sanitary, so my father counters that it lost popularity as people became more educated about infection. The truth is a mixture: not really a mystery.

In 1994, when I was seven years old, we returned to Nigeria for a few weeks, for the only trip in which we spent as much time visiting my father's side as my mother's. One of my father's uncles was getting married—they weren't close, but you can never run out of relatives to visit—so my parents arranged a long stay. The wedding week was supposed to be spectacular.

By this trip, I was fully fluent in English. My sole task was to pack my own clothes. On every trip to Nigeria, we were laden with gifts and supplies for our relatives; I was allowed only a backpack and told I'd have some clothes made when we got there. I reserved my meager space for an ensemble I'd found in Marks & Spencer specifically for that trip, a rare new outfit bought without consideration of versatility or practicality. Able to choose anything I wanted, I selected an ankle-length, grass-green skirt with fabric pleated like an accordion and a cream silk blouse with ruffles around the neck and wrists. Some monstrous midnineties version of something an eighteenth-century dandy might have worn in a baroque salon. Over these two pieces, I fastened the gold buttons of a velvet vest with swirling watercolor in burnt orange and heavy maroon. The final look became a long-running family joke.

As with all trips, we flew economy class with British Airways, which maintains regular service to its former colonies around the world; out of familiarity, it's the only airline my mother trusts. On our flight, a Nigerian man was being deported. In handcuffs, he sat between the two marshals escorting him, becoming increasingly agitated as the seven-hour flight went on. In a sudden outburst in the sky, he began screaming that he would *never, never, never* return to Nigeria, that God would bring down the plane. The Nigerian passengers, both Christian and Muslim, grew alarmed, and for the remainder of the flight, the cabin was charged with an atmosphere of panic and prayer.

When we touched down and disembarked onto the tarmac outside the terminal, we felt relief, even as were assaulted with the atmospheric onslaught that welcomes you to Nigeria. Heat, the burden of humidity, and the oddly sweet smell of petrol and burning rubber. Stepping out of the conditioned capsule of an airplane is a very specific sensory experience of Nigeria—unsettling, unnaturally sweet.

Then, the famously chaotic airports. A state of anarchy is fueled by the tendency of traveling Nigerians to overpack, not only overburdening each suitcase far beyond its capacity and weight limit but also carrying too many per person. The pandemonium is stoked by another Nigerian tendency to argue, finagle, and negotiate—in this situation, in a nervy effort to avoid paying excess baggage fees. Upon landing, the problem becomes getting through immigration, which may be sped along with a "donation" that puts you at the front of the line or into a private room for processing. One tactic involves loudly announcing your tribe, hoping an official will be biased in your favor and call you forward.

Clearing customs, we were picked up by an older cousin. Nigeria was on the cusp of a five-year stretch of a brutal regime ruling from 1993 to 1998. The previous year, military dictator Sani Abacha seized the presidency after a coup; he had absolute power until death as the de facto president. He was popular in the North of Nigeria, and as we drove through the streets, we saw him in the meticulous uniform of a full general on posters adorning vehicles, walls, and storefronts.

My cousin pointed out the new government buildings and the old—what was useful to the new regime and what was only part of the past. We drove on a raised highway across a river and stopped at its side for *kileshi*, large sheets of roasted and dried beef dusted with powdered groundnuts and pepper. My mother loves *kileshi* so much she was later caught at the customs inspection trying to smuggle some back to England.

We met a roadblock and were stopped by the military police. If that was the first time I had an AK-47 pointed in my face on such a trip, it did not make much of an impression. Police and soldiers were commonplace, never a welcome sight. My cousin got out of the car with a prepared bribe. *Talatin?* Is thirty enough? One naira was worth an American nickel, and thirty naira would buy one can of condensed milk. The soldier laughed. Hearing our British accents, he assumed we were rich. *Kara!* More! *Dari Tara.* That's all my cousin had, nine hundred naira—at least, that's all he lied and said he had, and that's all they found when they searched him, us, and the car. There are ways of hiding money in old Mercedes.

We split our time between village and city, Banjiram and Yola. I still associate my father's part of the country with relative tolerance and freedom. I remember being allowed to ride on the backs of many motorcycles and romping around acres, free to pick and eat a farm's wild sugarcane. I'd sit in the sun and warily watch stray dogs stalk some slow-moving rodent. I explored the immense lot of earth in various states of fertility, setting the far fence as my ultimate destination and finding the land prone to surprise. Beaked snakes. Other snakes. The unidentifiable.

My great-uncle was married in a private park outside the city. For the wedding, some relative composed a one-lined theme song with the repeating lyrics, "On your wedding day, Bifam, we are wishing you a happy day . . ." All morning, it was blared by the band through faulty but powerful speakers. The bridal party took up the catchy tune as we all followed the bride and showered her with naira notes. She made her way dancing from the rented cabins serving as dressing rooms to the main event hall, winding through grounds dotted with white tents set up for the banquet. The tents would shield guests in case the rainy season came early—a sign of good luck, which was fervently prayed against by the bride.

That night, my mother and father danced on the stage in the spotlight—to music they knew and everyone else knew but I did not know. I coveted the feeling of belonging you find in knowing the songs of a place. I became anomaly. And I felt that same hot, itchy twinge of hypersensitivity as when my father and I are trapped in a moment, together, too long. The air too close. I was trespassing inside the storybook where I once did not exist.

5

FROM HER I INHERIT

If I say I am Fulani, this is to say I go without fears.

The creation myth of my maternal tribe assures that death was long ago defeated.

Essentially, we need not worry.

The Fulani origin story traces the universe to its first matter: a molecule of cow milk. The Fulani are cattlemen. They herd most of Nigeria's cattle, who they name individually based on coat color and distinctive features. Christen her Fossossereeye if she is mottled like snakeskin. Name him with one horn Toll. Black hair encircles the eyes of Finii, as if he wears kohl. Our prayers protect cows from infection and make them fat. More than other tribes, we mistrusted the white man because he could not call to cattle.

The first Fulani man came out of a river. After him trotted out a sole calf, which was followed by another and another until our primogenitor had his full drove. Condemned by a river god to become a vagrant, he lived by the grace of animals. Since that first miraculous herd, cows have sustained us. We measure wealth in heads of cattle. They are wedding gifts, the cement in new family unions. Fulani herdsmen cannot bear to eat dairy cattle, who are like family. Their intimate bond with beasts became scandal—the slander that Fulani men marry cows still circulates within other tribes. Some accuse us of valuing cattle "more than human lives."

I feel the closest emotional lineage to the Fulani tribe—I am my mother's daughter.

She in turn is *her* mother's daughter.

My mother still ferments yogurt and clarifies butter, reprising totemic practices she learned from my grandmother. My grandmother claimed to be a "perfect" Fulani and saw her tribe as distinct from all others they settled amongst. My proud grandmother had Fulani tribal marks and tattoos that weathered with age and finally almost disappeared. Triangle scars with one-inch sides began at the corners of her mouth and ended just past her dimples. Lines scratched inside were scored like wire bristles; the pattern of striation gave her skin jagged texture. For markings, the Fulani prefer thin over wide. Businesslike, straight lines down Fulani foreheads indicate expertise in breeding cattle. Grandmother had a lizard tattoo on one cheek, of ink made from cashew shells. The lizard grew slimmer until it looked like a trampled snake.

This is how sedentary farmers characterize the Fulani: "They are like birds."

We fly away.

Fulaniland: former English territory lies a few miles from former French territory.

A coarse copper monopolizes every memory I retrieve from barren borderlands: that particular rusted hue of the dust that invaded our homes, eyes, our shoes. Nightfall was only that dust forcing its way even into skylight. The sun bleaches the sclerae of eyes; they appear orange like blood moons—this jaundiced effect is particular to Africans and protective, an adaptation against ultraviolet light. Everywhere outside, you see Red Fulani, one breed of cattle raised by Fulani pastoralists. The breed is a hybrid between indigenous African cattle and zebus imported from India since the Middle Ages. Of course, Reds appear as russet, and their long horns curve into elegant or gnarled half-moons. They are beloved of the Fulani for their tolerance of the desert heat and defiance against thirst.

Strands of the history of my warlike Fulani tribe—which arrived in Nigeria via Islamic incursions from the east—were noted by our own scribes. We piece together much of the rest through our oral tradition. My grandfather diagramed our knotty family tree, and my mother considers his timelines accurate. I trust but verify. According to my grandfather's genealogy, his first cousin was the then-sitting president of Niger, Mahamadou Issoufou, nicknamed "Jan Jan" for the redness in his skin tone. I was skeptical—until the president called our house to offer condolences upon my grandfather's death.

My family's Fulani clan crosses into Niger. Because the Niger-Nigeria border was established by the British in their usual thoughtless manner, sections of the Nigerian north have more in common with Niger above than with the rest of Nigeria to the south. When my grandfather was alive, I'd practice my schoolhouse French, wanting to communicate with him and the many relatives we visited in Niger after passing through checkpoints that created an unnatural separation in our tribal turf.

I remember one lonely truck: BORDER PATROL inked across its back in green lettering. The lower edge of the Sahara almost makes a neat, natural border alongside the artificial, political border that divides Niger and Nigeria. The desert was originally a treacherous forest, which cut off people on either side from each other ten thousand years ago. Now, Sahara's dust bears life—its winds spread mineral nutrients to regions around the world, feeding the far Amazon.

Since the 1980s, scientists and their satellites have been tracking the expansion of the Sahara desert. It has grown 10 percent in the past century due to decreased rainfall. Deserts naturally expand and contract seasonally, but the Sahara continues to creep downward—the term "sub-Saharan" will soon be a misnomer for the Fulani tribe, who will be entirely consumed. The desert also wants to wander.

The Fulani are untethered. In fact, the Fulani are the last remaining migratory tribe in West Africa. A third of the Fulani raise livestock, making the Fulani the most populous pastoral group in the world. For this reason, we may know more than any other people the contours within West Africa's expanse, and the intricacies of its interior. My wayfaring tribe reaches as far east as the Red Sea. Due to dispersal, the uncertainty in demarcating the Fulani is too great for the exact tribal population to be known: estimates range from ten to fifty million. The Fulani form a minority of 8 percent in Nigeria.

Finding little grazing land and less water in the expanding desert, more Fulani find themselves forced to stay still. My grandmother's people have settled for six generations, an uncommonly long time. My grandmother inherited cattle from dairy-farming, cheesemaking relatives whose living bound them to land. Their bequeathment of livestock tied her, too, to ground fit for pasturing. She later sold her animals to pay my mother's school fees, making them the means of my mother's migration.

My grandfather was a traveling trader before becoming a

farmer before becoming a pastor. He raised camels, goats, and fowl, and he grew guinea corn, beans, and millet. He was the first in his family line to settle in place. Now, the Fulani who settle—called "Town Fulani"—come into regular conflict with their transitory tribesmen, those "Cattle Fulani" who move with herds seasonally. Intertribal violence between the two subsets of Fulani is no longer contained within the tribe. Fulani itinerants wage war against anyone who threatens to turn their grazing lands into farmland.

The Fulani live in combat wherever they go. Water wars follow season after season of drought. In the last decade, thousands have died in these clashes. The Global Terrorism Index that ranked Boko Haram the number one terrorist organization ranked Fulani herdsmen number four. Wars over resources inevitably turn into battles with a religious bent; almost all Fulani are Muslim, while many "enemy" farmers belong to the Christian minority. Some Nigerians see Fulani nomads as an invasive species who violate "laws as readily as they do borders."

The Fulani planted the Holy Quran in the sand.

It was this tribe, through two centuries of military campaigns called the Fulani Jihads, that Islamized much of West Africa. "Jihad" has three shades of meaning and is a word often misused or misunderstood. The first refers to a "holy war waged on behalf of Islam as a religious duty." The second means "a personal struggle in devotion to Islam especially involving spiritual discipline." The final connotation is any "crusade for a principle or belief."

All three definitions apply to the Fulani Jihads of the eighteenth and nineteenth centuries. They began in 1727 in present-day Senegal, the Gambia, and the Guinean Forests, when Fulani Muslims organized against all odds to challenge the chieftaincies resisting Allah. Collaborating with Muslims from other tribes, Fulani-led militias took down powerful empires and established religious states wherever they won. 1804 brought the decisive Fulani offensive that destabilized any rival kingdoms still standing. The victors, led by the scholar and warrior Usman dan Fodio, "The Commander of the Faithful," established the largest West African state at the time, the Sokoto Caliphate. Driven by a desire to reform his empire of twenty million into one religious accord, he promised *revolutionary* jihad—a "Movement of Restoration."

The Fulani were unsuccessful in their ultimate expansionist aim. They wanted to extend the reach of Islam beyond the sand to the water of the West African coast—all the way to Southern Nigeria, where the continent bends. In claiming the Fulani tribe as my own, I must reckon with destruction waged in the name of God. I am alienated from the Fulani over their fierce Islamic identity.

I and all my Christian relatives stand apart from the broader congregation of Black African Muslims. Until my maternal grandmother and grandfather accepted Christ, the entirety of that family line had followed Islam (with diverse degrees of pagan practice). These two converts made up part of the 1 percent of Fulani who follow another religion. "Fulani" and "Christian" are practically antonyms.

My grandmother's people had steadfastly adhered to Fulani tradition, guided by a moral code called Pulaaku, "the Fulani pathway." Pulaaku regulates relationships between relatives and strangers; men and women; foes and friends; apprentices and elders; animals and their keepers. It asks of us integrity. To be Fulani is to abide by principles of grace, moderation, humility, hospitality, impeccable caretaking of cattle, and courage. To stay on this path, adopt a brutal work ethic. One Fulani proverb assures that "no matter how deep a body of water, there is fine sand at its bottom." *There is a way through everything, every abyss.* Each generation passes Pulaaku on to the next, a marker of Fulani identity. Not so for my mother, whose moral instruction came from the Bible—my grandfather broke that covenant.

Before converting to Christianity, my grandfather won a male camel at a local festival—the top prize in the category of "wayward dancing." He competitively danced and played the drums at such festivals. From what I can gather, "wayward" referred to things that were haram—forbidden in Islam. He danced at feasts, birthdays, and weddings, and was paid in goats. He performed the dances from distant tribes that he learned during his wanderings and charged a premium for those exotic displays. Once in Niger, wealthy newlyweds gave him a female camel to join the male—to mate and make milk.

At one festival, my grandfather was accosted by a boy from a local madrasa who had been sent out to solicit charity and was afflicted by leprosy. They got into a scuffle—reasons unclear—and my grandfather was infected. Unlike the misdiagnosis that freed my enslaved great-great-grandfather in family lore, his leprosy was real. Just like that parallel narrative, my grandfather's disease marked a turning point in his fate—giving him a new faith. He recuperated in a Christian hospital, where missionaries ministered to him during his convalescence. What he liked about Christianity was the tree of life in Heaven whose leaves cure all maladies.

His conversion shook his entire village. He hid in a tree after his relatives found out and wanted to poison him for this treachery. His parents forced him to a pagan priest, who recommended a drastic ritual: they would lock him in an outhouse and leave him there overnight. The conspirators believed that offended spirits would enter the makeshift prison to avenge my grandfather's rejection of their power. He should die by morning.

His mother made medicines for women in labor. She was an herbalist and an occult dancer. Before Christianity and Islam outlawed their dancing, women like her wielded influence as priestesses and defended the survival of our old mysticism. When the outhouse was opened the next morning and my grandfather was found alive, she brewed him a "tonic" that would either cleanse or kill him. The drink did neither, and his mother never spoke to him again.

After his dangerous conversion, my grandfather *resubmitted* to Islam and took a new wife—then went back to Christianity to christen the recent marriage's new child. Born again, again. Despite this lapse, he became a pastor, and my mother's religious life was one of strict observation. Their large family of ten children was very poor on his pastor's salary drawn from donations. They made up the bulk of the attendance at his church, which drew a sparse but zealous crowd from surrounding areas. Of these ten preacher's children, one-third have been recalled to Islam.

After the Fulani Jihads, the ascendant warlord Usman dan Fodio urged an end to all syncretism between Islam and traditional spiritualities. He was not entirely successful; tribal taboos and superstitions persist to this day. I come from a line of women instructed to avoid speaking too much to their firstborn children, a Fulani taboo that protected the child from those—living or dead—envying the blessing of a wished-for child.

My grandmother took this superstition further, refusing to even speak my mother's name. Her precaution meant my mother never heard her own name escape her mother's mouth. Beyond superstition, there was a motive behind this practice; my grandmother followed it out of respect for her firstborn. Refraining from uttering her name granted the baby special status. In a Fulani family, if a father dies, the firstborn becomes the head of the household and assumes responsibility for his or her late father's wives, animals, and businesses. A mother's position in the family is lower than that of the firstborn—even a one-day-old—so she must not presume to use their name.

My mother was urged to call her mother by her first name to demonstrate her rank. And she did call my grandmother "Mairi" until she went away to boarding school. Hearing children from other tribes calling their mothers "Mama," she started to as well. Her affectionate gesture was never reciprocated. Instead of using her name or a nickname, my grandmother called my mother *ke*, meaning "you," which was intended as a polite, formal address. To my ear, it stings. Even going through childhood being spoken to less than her siblings—even being called "you"—she knew her mother loved her. But she wondered.

My mother refused to pass down maternal alienation to her children. My mother has left me her head-thrown-back laugh and off-key singing; not her long hair; her mad obsession with names. She texts me to suggest I change my name to Dan Daniel, in Hebrew meaning "God is judge, God is *my* judge."

She has said to me—unprompted and apropos of nothing— "*Yes, I want to live, too.*"

She always asks me to write her life story.

And she always begins, "I was born in Illela village, the first of nine or ten children."

She offers nowhere neat to begin. She was born in a place

not big enough to have a name—they called it Amanawar So-koto, meaning "a leper colony outside the city of Sokoto." Until recently, I thought she'd been born in little Illela be-cause that's what she always says. I now know that she only names Illela because it's the closest village anyone else might have heard of. Her birth certificate erroneously states that she was born in 1956, one year too early. She discovered the error decades later, after comparing her birth date with that of a close friend she knew to be one year younger.

My mother's maiden name is Saratu Mamman, both Christian and Muslim. Saratu is the Biblical name Sarah in Hausa. Mamman is a version of Mohammed. She has no mid-dle name, because in her local tradition, two names suffice. One nickname, Dala, is a corruption of the word "dollar" and signifies a wish for wealth. Another nickname, Jummai, classifies a "daughter of Friday." Her third nickname and personal symbol, Giwa, means "elephant": that she might be great amongst women.

As the eldest of nine or ten children (depending on if you count the half sibling produced from her father's sec-ond marriage), she had great responsibilities from a tender age. She pounded grains to powder using a mortar and pestle half her size—a strenuous task taking a little girl all day in the sun. Friday was market day, and she hauled the food her family would need for the week. She avoided the irritable turkeys and took care of the goats. Every day, her family drank fresh dairy, a diet uncommon in Nigeria outside Fu-laniland, where its people retain the "Lactase Persistence Trait," which subsides as you move south. Goat's milk yo-gurt with sugar was the customary sweet drink of hospital-ity, the first thing she served to any guest. It took so much effort to supply the household with enough water that to clean her hair, she sometimes used a plant called West African sorrel—*karkashi* to her—which held a slimy, viscous fluid inside its waxy stalk.

Then and now, most settled Fulani there were farmers. People lived in mud clay houses with grass-straw roofs, surrounded by guinea cornstalks for privacy. The toilet was a hole. There was no electricity or plumbing in any house, and all still lack these utilities, though the houses themselves have been rebuilt with concrete walls and zinc roofs. Her village was not far from a serviceable road, so she got used to the sight of cars passing near her outlying homestead. During the civil war, caravans of Igbos fleeing persecution flooded her roadside playground.

By this road and a bicycle, my grandfather traveled to surrounding villages and towns whenever a pastor was required. Amidst their own neighbors, this pastor's family stood alone in precarious peace—everyone knew them, and everyone could say, "That house is where the Christians live." A minority of 0.5 percent within my maternal family's Sokoto State, Christians debate whether to proselytize or to protect themselves by continuing Muslim traditions—so they might stand apart a little less. When my grandfather famously reverted from Christianity back to Islam to take a second wife (before being "saved" once again), his audacity as a Christian with two wives was scandalous *and* safer.

Hausa Christians also know God as Allah. Though my mother's Christian family was an aberration in their area, still they came together with the two hundred neighbors in their village for celebrations. Everyone attended naming ceremonies for newborns, seven days after a child is born. Her family went to neighbors' houses for Eid and other Islamic festivals, which they called Sallahs, after the Arabic word referring to prayers and benedictions. In a tradition with pagan roots observed by Muslims as well as her Christian family, people would gather to make demands of the heavens. During a lunar eclipse, they would go outside to chant in unison: "Sun, release your servant, your slave, the moon."

From her village, in the distance one could always see a mountain, and my mother grew up worrying that the world ended behind this barrier. When she was sent to school beyond the mountain, excited to finally find out what lay past it, she was old enough to know that she was not in fact approaching her doom: that she would not dissipate the moment she crossed into the unseen. She was disappointed to see only more of the same.

In the Fulani initiation ritual called *sharo*, one male adolescent flogs another with a cane; the initiate must not show he feels pain. If he does, he risks humiliation in front of the girls who went to watch, and then he might face difficulty finding a bride. Some die. To be scarred for life is a mark of pride. *Welcome to adulthood.*

My grandfather broke with such traditions after his conversion. My mother was never taken deep into the bush for any initiations. Her father's decision to send her away to school changed the trajectory of her life. She became the first girl in her village to receive an education and remained the only schooled girl until her younger sisters came of age. For a very long time, theirs was the only family educating their girls, and a spartan schoolhouse wasn't built near their village until thirty years later. Before its completion, all local schoolchildren had to travel far away if their parents were inclined—and could afford—to send them. The rate at which they do so remains low. More than half of school-age girls in the North are not schooled; a third of those children sent to school receive only Quranic education, which emphasizes religion over "literacy and numeracy."

When my mother left home, she and her father boarded

a big lorry to Sokoto; from Sokoto, they went to her new boarding school, a full day's journey over 150 miles away. She was seven years old. She would remain in this boarding school for seven years, only returning to her family during two annual breaks at Christmas and summer. The school, run by Baptist missionaries, educated sixty boys and girls from villages near and far whose parents were Christians. As students spoke many languages, class was conducted in Hausa, the lingua franca of the north. She learned to speak, read, and write English here.

When she returned to her village on school holidays, she was regularly entreated by the sheik of Sokoto State, an important Islamic religious leader. He dispatched emissaries wielding Qurans to her home to teach her how to pray and bring her back to Islam. Being the eldest child, she was targeted in the hope that she would influence her younger siblings. Her father allowed these visits to avoid trouble, but also because the Fulani never turn guests away.

At fourteen, my mother was sent to another missionary-run boarding school near a bigger city, Kano. Living away from her family and tribal community, my mother was isolated from many experiences other adolescents from her background shared—her own kind of cultural exclusion made her feel remote, like mine would a generation later. She was *also* always "off" wherever she went. In her new all-girls school with three hundred students, she found herself in conflict with the other girls because she was a rule follower and the uncontested teachers' pet. Their missionary teachers were British, Canadian, and American. Teachers beat students over their laps with paddles after infractions; my mother maintains that Canadian teachers were the most gentle.

As the other girls became defiant to the rigid religious instruction and iron-handed correction, my mother bowed to the missionaries. They held the keys to all salvation. She began to question any belief that didn't align with either Biblical teachings or scientific methods—two forms of truth themselves at odds with each other but still dear to her. Realizing an early aptitude for the sciences, she faced a lifelong, futile struggle to reconcile faith and reason.

Given her hurtful treatment as the unmentionable firstborn, my mother knew well how demeaning superstitions could be, how diminishing. That she must avoid trampling termite hills or risk a long illness; that on certain days of the week, she must not travel. She tired of tracking which animal was unlucky to meet across her path while walking to the well for morning water. *Lucky—the gazelle. Unlucky—the donkey. The hyena can smell impending, accidental death.* Too many places meant death to enter, like a room with an open door under a rainbow.

As she studied under the missionaries' eyes, she began to see her village and what it offered as insular and incomplete. Even her father's sermons, which she had lived for, now disenchanted. It wasn't enough for her father to become one of the few people who had a radio, a German-made model whose Berec battery was larger than the appliance itself. In her village, most inhabitants had never seen a single white person, so they were fascinated by her descriptions of her teachers. Once, she brought a doll home from school, and all the local children gathered to look at it, some convinced it was alive because its eyes moved. That was the first time they had seen a plastic doll. Armed with her education and exposure to the outside—and particularly proud of her knowledge of the Bible and the atomic table—she grew disaffected with her seemingly shrinking corner of the world.

At home, her father sheltered her because she was beautiful, and he suspected beauty would betray her. She began fighting with his second wife, judging her "unholy" half family. She became desperate to leave her father's house. During her final year in secondary school, her school principal, a British woman who was departing to retire in England, secured a way for my mother to take advanced-level classes in the UK. Her principal made the mistake of sending my mother home one last time to say goodbye to her family; her father abruptly changed his mind and withdrew his permission, trapping her in the house and not allowing her to leave in fear she would become "wicked" in the Western world. She was seventeen years old, and in the fashion of adolescents, being told "no" only sealed her desire for what was withheld. England became forbidden fruit.

She remained in Northern Nigeria and entered a national university newly founded to complement Nigeria's sole existing university—the place she would meet my father. On campus, she had to be protected by volunteer bodyguards from the Christian Student Union whenever she walked to the library, because so many men approached her to ask her to marry them. My father was one of those helpful volunteers. At university, she dreamed of becoming a doctor until the first time she saw a dead body and ran away. She ran toward an unconventional path. In my childhood, I had no shame bragging that she was the first person to publish research confirming the existence of a hole in the egg of the cowpea weevil; the hole is named after her.

How her life would have been different if she'd never left her home. How my life would have been different were I not hers. From her, I inherit that instinct that heckles some people—to revisit all the places you have left behind and think of how survivable your childhood was. That first time she went beyond the little mountain framing her village and saw more of the same scenery, she knew she could not rest there. We are alike in this measure: *of dissatisfaction*.

The spirit of striving came to me by her. So came other specters. From her, I have inherited startling dreams. In dreams, I hear last words of pilots over the black box; I see my sloughed-off skin running back to me because it loves me so much. My mother dreams of junk mail shoved inside the cracks of the Wailing Wall; she is convinced of demonic intent. To her, dreams are efficient communication with God. She says she can foretell a pregnancy by their signs. Sometimes a death. If I tell her about a disturbing nightmare I've had, she makes me say a prayer to "reject" its evil. I have stopped telling her, keeping them to myself, pretending that nothing so temporal and tissue-like could hold any power over me.

Once, I woke up to find that she must have come into my room sometime during the night, dipped her finger into anointing oil, then traced it on my window. Who else would leave a tiny cross for me to see first thing in the morning light? And then I saw another on the next window. Another the next night.

6

SPIRITS OF WILDERNESS

If I say I am Hausa, I am not sure that I am.
(You may come to understand this later.)

To start with, Hausa is not really a tribe. It is the largest
indigenous ethnicity in all Africa—a broad ethnic confederation ranging over West and sub-Saharan Africa, number-
ing eighty million. Concentrated in Niger and Nigeria, the
Hausa make up one-quarter of Nigeria's population. This
group is substantial in fourteen other African countries—as
far north as Mali; west as Senegal; east as Eritrea; south as
Cameroon.

Trade is the mechanism by which the Hausa spread their
influence; over centuries, they developed lucrative networks
to sustain a population across vast, harsh expanses. At their
mercantile peak, the Hausa were famed for blacksmithing,
leathermaking, salt mining, and textile production as well as
for trading grain, gold, hides, and henna. Every big city in Africa now hosts Hausa neighborhoods called *zongos*, from the
Hausa word for caravan camps, the auxiliary desert outposts

that support nomadic commerce. Hausa pilgrims on progress to Mecca travel a path of welcome along their itinerary: a tessellation of Hausa-speaking settlements radiates eastward in the direction the faithful face during prayers.

The legendary founder of the Hausa people was a crown prince who came to us from Baghdad. We call him Bayajidda. The heir of Baghdad, he was exiled from Iraq and *odysseyed* with his entourage of loyal soldiers until reaching West Africa. When he arrived in the place now deemed the spiritual home of the Hausa, he felt thirsty. Told there was nothing to drink, he learned of a great snake causing trouble for people in pursuit of water. The snake called himself "king" as he menaced a nearby oasis, permitting villagers to draw water according to his whim. Bayajidda besieged the well and beheaded the serpent, liberating the people from its jealous power. He kept the head for a trophy.

The sitting queen offered half her domain to its hero, but no killer came forth. Imposters tried to pass off snake heads that plainly did not belong on the reptilian carcass. Bayajidda emerged with the real serpent's head, then petitioned the queen for marriage instead of power. To grant him this, she would have to defy a convention forbidding queens to marry. She found him worth the violation and accepted his proposal. At once, Bayajidda won a consort and kingship, and they governed jointly. Supplanting a tradition of virgin queens, their precedent marked the shift from matriarchal to patriarchal rule in Hausaland.

As king, Bayajidda had many sons with both his queen and his concubine. His descendants by his wife founded the "Hausa Seven," the large city-states that flourished beginning in the fourteenth century. Bayajidda's illegitimate offspring produced the line of rulers over the minor states known as the "Bastard Seven." Hausaland at its height connected these fourteen medieval city-states, each supporting a specialized industry. The Hausa states sometimes warred with each other, and their integrity as a collective fluctuated. Nevertheless, they developed into teeming marketplaces, caravan districts, and centers of scholarship, hosting visitors from all corners of the Muslim and merchant worlds. *Places equipping those embarking on cross-desert journeys; places welcoming those returning.*

"Hausa" is the tribe I've been telling people I belong to my whole life.

Hausa is my first language and, naturally, the Nigerian language I know best. The Fulani tribe, the tribe with which I most strongly identify, once conquered the Hausa. For efficiency's sake, my mother might grudgingly claim the Hausa tribe because she also speaks Hausa best, but if you ask her what she "really" is, she will always say, "Fulani." Like my mother, when I say that I am Hausa, this is shorthand—a way of letting people know what language I speak, because language bonds the most.

Hausa is the twenty-fifth most-spoken language in the world due to its use around the Hausa tribe's trade networks. Its fifty million speakers make it the most spoken indigenous African language. The official use of Hausa may cause controversy, as in 2017, when Nigerian president Muhammadu Buhari delivered a message on the lessons of Ramadan in Hausa rather than in English. Because Hausa is spoken mostly by Muslims, many Nigerians were outraged, believing his language choice encouraged sectarianism and signaled preference in a country where religious polarity dictates national identity and politics.

Our legendary founder, Bayajidda, could not understand

the Hausa language when he first arrived in Hausaland. The Hausa phrase "*Ba ya ji da*" means, "He could not hear or understand before." Though he would come to be recognized as the founder of the entire tribe, his initial lack of our language was so egregious, so alienating, that the people had to mark him as wholly uncomprehending.

I am marked myself. I speak Hausa, but not the way those who stayed home speak it. It is a highly idiomatic language. On visits Back Home, while I could usually piece together all literal meaning, sometimes I got tangled in the figurative expressions rife in daily use. When my mother said, "*Ga fili, ga doki*," I knew she meant, "Here is the horse and here is the field," but I did not know she really meant, "Stop bloviating; stop talking about doing something and just do it." Or if my father stated, "*Rammamme kada maikibba*," I knew he'd said, "The thin person defeats the fat person," but I didn't know he meant that "the unexpected happens"—a meaning dependent on a cultural assumption that a fat person is much stronger than a thin one.

I do have a native's pronunciation, correctly articulating implosive and ejective consonants, sounds that non-natives would pronounce as *d*, *b*, and *k*. Hausa is a tonal language that employs the "creaky voice," which is known in the West as a "vocal fry" and associated with the "California girl"— that high-pitched yet guttural up-speaking that rises at the end of every sentence, turning it into a question. Most non-native speakers cannot speak in the correct tones; they also confuse gendered nouns. I was always subtly proud of getting at least these things right.

Arabic challenged Hausa in the nineteenth century, when the viziers—the Muslim administrators—of Hausaland instituted Arabic as the state language, used by emissaries, emirs, armies, and imams. The Hausa have a history of adapting

Arabic into our language: into our names and in the verse forms of a shared literary history. When in Nigeria, I was often called *hajiya*, an Arabic appellation. The Hausa tribe developed along the Hajj route from West Africa to Mecca because many Hausa Muslims made that long journey. They return hailed *al-haji* or *hajiya*, honorifics for the men and women who have completed the Hajj. In Nigeria today, the title is used liberally—when flattering a boss, complimenting a colleague, or luring a customer.

The yearly Hajj takes place during the final month of the Islamic calendar. This desert-crossing engine of mass move-ment became another routine disruption in the rhythm of my kin. A family of working migrants moves east together— historically by camel, now overloading lorries. They inch along the route incrementally, as it takes years to finance their onward passage. For some, the Hajj is the last journey taken in a lifetime, for which one leaves having no expecta-tion of return.

My family, although going in reverse, going west—we, too, have always been as pilgrims on progress.

Most of my memories of Nigeria are pulled out of Hausaland:
Twilight is the only speck of blue, the only thing like a body of water we see for weeks. A man in head-to-toe gray looks like the wall of smog just beneath a storm cloud. His veil helps weather the pelting of wind-whipped sand, which can rip skin from a face. He is walking across a dry field in the pale, thin hours after the fourth prayer and before the fifth. A few men are praying early or late, asking Allah to provide one hundredfold. They face not Mecca but each other, feet burrowing into the sand like fennec foxes. One man's prayer mat is painted like a doorway to a moon.

A woman with one bulging eye—because I was young, I called her Witch.

A girl with both eyes bulging—her infection could be easily cured, but it will not be and will spread to her brain.

According to the tenth edition of the *Encyclopedia Britannica*, published in 1902, Hausaland is "beautiful country, but the climate is insalubrious, and in many parts fatal to Europeans." River blindness has not been prevalent here for years, but still we are wary of black flies and certain worms. We do what we can about pestilence, sealing our beds inside suffocating nets hanging as barricades against mosquitoes, even as we resign ourselves to their constant nuisance. We light incense in a pit excavated in the cement floor—cut right into the Islamic green carpet in the living room—hoping to draw insects toward its scent and away from us. My sister shows me her arm after sleeping with it resting against the mesh netting; it is a constellation of moonlit bites.

A frequent wind disturbs me. Babies are held tightly against sun and wind and flies. Hens regard the lizard; the horizon is obscured by clay; flies tenacious as bark confound themselves with the work of preparing food.

There is yet blue light crawling out from under a door across the courtyard.

Kano is the jewel of Hausaland and, to me, the most beautiful city in Nigeria. It is the historic seat of Islamic scholarship and an ancient market town notable for minarets of mixed architectural styles; its history is best seen reflected in the glimmer of Islam's Golden Age. Its skyline of low-built, red-mud-brick buildings features a chain of flat roofs broken by parapets. Kano is eternal. Sections of the imposing city walls first built in 1100 still stand. The Palace of the Emir, constructed in the fifteenth century, has remained in constant use by those in power—emirs, kings, and jihadists. Gardens behind its gates.

In Kano, we'd stay with a relative who welcomed us into his white mansion, guarded with guns and dogs in a secure compound behind high walls and razor wire. I called him my uncle, and for years, I thought he really was, but he is not. A side wall of his house was painted with words of warning—THIS HOUSE NOT FOR SALE!—in order to avoid a scam where houses are sold fraudulently while their owners are away. He had fat animals that paraded around in the front. He had a capable generator, and when the electricity went out every night, there'd be just a blink and a hum, and the lights and television would come back on. We were, for a short time, ensconced behind this protective shell of privilege and power—economic power and the power of the electric grid.

I loved to walk through the madhouse Kasuwar Kurmi, a market that has been vital to trans-Saharan trade for over five hundred years. The late Middle Ages saw Kano as the southernmost commercial hub of the desert. In this role, the city became cosmopolitan, hosting travelers from far reaches—traders from Morocco, Libya, and Egypt came down and converged upon Kano. A wealthy city for centuries before colonialism, it would become integral to trade across the Atlantic after the British built infrastructure linking it to that second global network. Kano's "European Reservation Areas" were the quarters annexed to segregate colonists in luxury. Kasuwar Kurmi today shows off the wares of Hausa artisans—leather sandals from a breed of red goats; drums that mimic human voices; cloth in tie-dye, a technique the Hausa pioneered hundreds of years ago.

Everywhere, the horse, an immemorial Hausa symbol. The Hausa have a tradition of equestrianism singular in the lands of camels and cattle. Precolonial societal systems of Hausaland lasted so long and were so entrenched that the Hausa way of life has resisted assimilation with a measure of success, preserving an influential culture. Western ways have taken hold in the north to a much lesser extent when compared to the Christianized South of Nigeria, which has adapted Western conventions on an exponentially broader scale. Some Hausa traditions survive unchanged, withstanding the usually inevitable cultural collapse of colonization. To commemorate the end of the annual Hajj, a day is set aside for prayer. On horseback, the emir leads crowds of worshippers to the mosque.

The Hausa once had a nickname: the "blue men." In Kano, you still see the blue-dyed textiles Hausa clothmakers are famous for producing since their medieval peak. Indigo is the common color for men in their robes; for five hundred years, dye made of *Indigofera* shrubs has been stored in giant communal pits in the old city, where it glows during the vespertine hours.

For centuries, Hausa orators have reenacted the Bayajidda story at annual festivals celebrating our legendary birthing. Yet the clues the story provides about any actual, accurate origins of the Hausa cannot reliably be followed. Are the nomadic Hausa in fact indigenous? If not, how long ago did the Hausa tribe settle in the region of present-day Hausaland, and from where did it first migrate? Which people groups did the Hausa come into contact and mix with, or splinter from?

It is likely we came from the north, driven down from the Sahara looking for lakes. The Hausa are desert-faring—it fits that our legendary founder is a protector of water. The well where Bayajidda killed the beast is now a tourist site preserved as the literal wellspring of the Hausa people. It is notable that Bayajidda came from Iraq as an Arab warrior— the myth traces the Arab influences that swept North Africa then spread south to shape Northern Nigeria, and it nods to ongoing encounters between West Africans and people of the Middle East.

The mysterious origins of the tribe are seen in the enigma of the Arewa knot, another symbol of Hausa people. The knotted insignia has been used since the 1950s to represent "unity in diversity" within Hausaland, but this marker of regional identity might be prehistoric, appearing in antiquity. Its shape may have been influenced by Christian, Jewish, Islamic, and Ancient Egyptian symbology. Depending how you look at its pattern, it contains crosses, crescents, the Seal of Solomon, or stars.

The Hausa were first written into history by an Arab geographer, who ventured to compose a complete account of the extent of Islamification in Africa in the ninth century. Earlier than the turn of the last millennium? We quickly lose track of the Hausa. Within a century before our debut appearance in that survey of the Muslim sphere, we fade abstracted into legendry and symbol.

Arab Muslim clerics began drafting collections of stories about the Hausa in the sixteenth century. Around the same time, Hausaland's own scholars began to record Hausa history. Of my tribes, the Hausa have the richest legacy in terms of a written record, which is enshrined in recently rediscovered calendars and constellation charts, and in texts that survived the centuries. The *Kano Chronicle* was completed around 1890 but references texts written a few hundred years earlier. Largely legend, parts of it are still valuable contributions to the historical record: it has corroborated "kinglists" of Kano City rulers going back to 999 AD.

The *Kano Chronicle* recounts the history of those we consider the original Hausa people. It describes aboriginal Hausa clans, categorizing their gods by strengths and weaknesses. It talks of kings—the king who first brought camels to Hausaland; the king whose reign lasted a day and a night; the king so strong he caught elephants with rope. Dedicated to the Prophet Muhammad, the *Kano Chronicle* relates a prophecy given to the earliest Hausa people: one that predicted the end of their way of life.

Their apocalypse would be signaled by the arrival of a foreigner who would destroy their sacred tree, named Shamuz, then build a mosque upon the holy ground it once grew on. This word of warning spoken to the "pagans" hinted at the coming ideological battle that would see Islam defeat animism. When the people asked what they could do to avoid the coming calamity, they were told: "There is no cure but resignation."

The hegemony of Islam in the Hausa tribe began cohering from the eleventh century, when it was first introduced. Incrementally, it replaced the polytheistic beliefs of the early Hausa. A millennium of Islam has made this religion the cornerstone of most of the Hausa tribe's known history as well as its modern culture. Like the Fulani, this tribe is now universally Muslim—99 percent of a Sunni majority.

In Hausaland, calls to prayer become insistent and cacophonous as mosques compete in blaring the Adhan from their minarets. No matter where I go in the world, if I hear the call to prayer, it does pull something singing out of me.

The entire North of Nigeria recognizes the set of sharia Islamic laws to some extent, following a successful campaign launched by a governor in 1999. In three states, sharia can be applied by Muslims solely for personal matters. In the remaining nine northern states, sharia is the "main body of civil and criminal law." In these nine sharia states, it supersedes secular law and sometimes even contradicts the Nigerian Constitution. Right after sharia was established, riots erupted in several areas with formidable non-Muslim populations. We had to avoid these frays on trips home; Kano was in crisis during my teen years, when scores were killed over sharia.

Sharia is a comprehensive legal system that regulates violent crime and civil disputes; commerce and taxation; marriage and divorce. It differs from secular judiciaries because its legislation promotes "Islamic virtue" and targets "un-Islamic behavior," including so-called social vices like "alcohol, gambling, prostitution, unedifying media, and the excessive mixing together of unrelated males and females." Typical penalties span a range of fines and prison time. Amputation and execution by hanging or stoning are allowable but almost unheard-of, with actual occurrences each year in the single digits.

Around Northern Nigeria, religious police enforce laws deterring vice, poorly regulated by state agencies called the Hisbah. Tens of thousands of officers and volunteers patrol the streets looking for activities that violate sharia in their view, like wedding music or girls wearing sunglasses. Like "stylish haircuts" or two women riding one motorcycle taxi. Christians in my family are technically exempt from Hisbah regulations, but they face coercion after noncompliance. Having no authority to make arrests, Hisbah squads are supposed to summon real police. Yet, they arrive armed with batons, sometimes knives, and behave as vigilantes. Last year, a Hisbah policy dictated that store mannequins skirt idolatry and are potentially provocative. Officials waver between requiring mannequins to be headless and modest, and banning them altogether from clothing shops.

In the north, female modesty is enforced by both the religious police and by social expectations. Every girl of a certain age begins to wear a concealing garment that covers her head and neck, then extends halfway down her body, draping her shoulders and torso. The Christian women in my family cover their hair in public, too. The practice points to common ground between Christians and Muslims. In the New Testament, Paul puts it to his congregation: "Judge for yourselves: Is it proper for a woman to pray to God with her head uncovered?" Even outside Nigeria, growing up in the West, my mother insisted that my sister and I follow this protocol whenever prayers were said.

When we traveled in the north through states under sharia, my sister and I were always made to cover ourselves. I remember my family driving somewhere unimportant and getting stalled in traffic. When I dressed that morning, I thought a denim skirt that fell just above my knees would be perfectly appropriate within the confines of a car in which I was shielded from view. But when we were stopped in the gridlock, a man walking alongside us in the street glanced inside, saw just the tops of my knees, and became visibly agitated. I didn't realize what the problem was until my aunt reached over to yank my skirt down to hide the sliver of visible skin. His reaction made me afraid to leave the house. I wore the same skirt days later to play within the walls of our compound. Though no one outside family could see me, my grandfather became as upset as that stranger, and I was made to go inside to change.

Maguzanci is the most significant set of pre-Islamic beliefs held by the Hausa. Maguzanci upholds a pantheon of spirits who are illusory and illimitable as the wind. Collectively, we call them Iska, the Hausa word for wind. Only a few hundred incarnate spirits have been identified—they reveal themselves selectively upon hearing a specific pattern of drumbeats. Like humans, their moral qualities vary. Like humans, they are easily annoyed.

Deities are not ever-present or everlasting. Gods die. They deceive. Some celestials are more reliably good—the helpmate in childbirth; the gift-bearer; and the messenger who heals through happy dreams. Together, benevolent ones protect Hausaland from Yan Birni, the more domesticated spirits of the farm, and Yan Daji, the hard-to-manage spirits of the wilderness and the bush. Illness and ill luck follow humans after negative interactions with this ecosystem.

The magic of Maguzanci still survives, mostly in rural areas, despite the prophecy that Islam would eradicate it. Religious historian Umar Danfulani describes its existence as "an island within the ocean of Islam." As Islam took hold, traditional and syncretic practices were repressed—ancestor and idol worship; sacrifices of black hyenas and he-goats; the Holy Quran revered as a supernatural fetish item. Under siege, devotees of Maguzanci continue the ordering of our world via spirit possession. A hierarchy of priestesses work under one woman in the highest office and another woman called Mother of the Dance.

Priestesses are pathfinders in a behemoth network of superstition. They are experts on the personal preferences of spirits, wearing red if that is one's favorite color or brewing beer for the shrine. Unstable spirits are both cause and cure of human infirmity. Of incompetence and alcoholism. Those called upon in ecstasy may bless and plague. Maguzanci rituals are the opposite of exorcism—through invocation and incantation, spirits are summoned. *Wind* passes over and through.

My family carved a peculiar brand of evangelism into our little plot of Hausaland, forming something like a shield of protection around us in hostile territory. To my family, demons are the same spirits of the old religions. I questioned that our belief system should consider them real. Hadn't the might of Jesus vanquished all demons and all their afflictions? I was taught that the power to heal is a spiritual gift anyone may claim: pronouncing healing will manifest it. I was discouraged from saying, "I feel sick." Instead, I must declare that I am well: *"My bones are fat because I receive the good report of the gospel."*

When I was sick, my mother anointed my head with frankincense-scented oil, supposedly sourced from ancient groves in the Holy Land bearing the same olive trees Jesus quarreled with. She'd recite the prayers inscribed on the greasy pamphlet that came with the bottle, and with her finger "cross out" my crescent scar by tracing the Christian cross. From a book of prayers that promised to rout demons, she would rebuke "any spirit causing diabetes, high blood pressure, low blood pressure, heart attack, stroke, kidney failure, leukemia, blood disease, arthritis, lupus, Alzheimer's, or insomnia."

One trip Back Home spent in rural areas, my baby cousins gave me plastic bags of local water. They drank it; I thought that meant I could, too. And that was the time I almost died from a foodborne illness. I writhed on my bed for a week, vomiting everything that entered my mouth—first food, then soft food, then liquids . . . water . . . saliva . . . Finally, I could only heave. No hospitals nearby—there was no panacea but prayer.

My mother said God's grace was the best drug. Through prayer, I would be covered with the Blood of Jesus, a wonder-working tonic. My body became a battlefield over which my family waged spiritual warfare. All laid their hands upon me in shifts; they held vigils around the clock. As I drifted in and out of delirium, the sound of my mother praying in tongues—seemingly conversing directly with the Holy Spirit—inflamed the ambiance and all awareness. Until she also fell ill of a similar ailment, and the house was shrouded in silence and sickness. What could have taken a turn for the worse did so for the better, and we both made full recoveries.

They called us miracles.

7

THE DARK CONTINENT

In one misguided tradition, some in my family pretend we originate outside Africa. They devise distance from the Dark Continent and imagine we might elude it somewhere in the murk of antiquity.

My mother's family holds that our Fulani tribe is originally *un-African*. Usually, they point east to say we were initially Arabs, that we still have significant Arab ancestry. In another theory, my family looks for our line to the west. My mother insists that seven generations ago—at the point in history when the family tree her father recorded becomes unreliable—some uncertain ancestor came all the way from Albania. The story goes that he was a swordsman hired to conquer Africa for Islam.

My mother swears she has seen firsthand a sword brought into her family by the Albanian—a silver sword in a silver sheath. The supposed designs carved into it reveal the exact clan of its origin and the family who commissioned its making, like a crest. I believe her in the same way that I believe my father saw his own ancestor's leather patch, his document of freedom after slavery. One imagines that our silver sword would be priceless, but it was reportedly sold off by an uncle who did not receive much money from the trade.

While my grandfather was dying, he repeated something in a weak voice cognizant of running out of time. It was a name . . . He kept whispering the name of a tribe linked to Turkish mercenaries recruited from the Ottoman Empire four hundred years ago to fight for Allah in Africa. My mother holds on to his ailing whispers as proof. But Albania is farther than Turkey. And a whisper is not a witness.

In the Bible, Noah had three sons who survived the Great Flood. Missionaries taught my parents that Noah's progeny birthed nations. White men came from one son, Middle Eastern and Asian people from another. Black people descended from Noah's second son, Ham. Beginning in the sixteenth century, Ham was represented as black-skinned based on mistaken etymology conflating his name with both the Hebrew word for "burnt" and the Egyptian word for "slave." This interpretation has been thoroughly discredited, and it is now universally accepted that there exist no Biblical references to the race or skin color of Noah's sons. However, for centuries, the construct of postdiluvian race was a prominent reading of the Biblical narrative, used to theorize the origins of all races.

Ham was engineered into the Black man from which an accursed race descended. In my mother's missionary school, Ham was presented as the evil one. He was cursed—in some explanations because he saw his father unclothed, an abomination; in others, that witnessing a naked Noah was a metaphor for Ham's unspeakable wickedness. Blackness came to be known throughout Christendom as the Curse of Ham. It was tied to subservience—to a generational curse that ensured the status of "servant of servants."

Blackness was tied to immorality, then to aptitude. By the time of the Nigerian colonial period, racial pseudoscience had been refined, superseding the faux-Biblical formula for race. Race scientists began to use the term "Hamitic" to refer instead to a North African "type." They placed this distinct "Hamitic" race above the darker, sub-Saharan "Negroid" race. Hamitic people were supposed to be the missing link between sub-Saharan Africa, which was considered *savage*, and the more "civilized" North Africa. Race scientists credited Hamites as the sole Africans responsible for the entirety of the continent's contributions and progress. When my mother was born, skulls were still being exhumed around the Nile Basin: eugenicists hoped to prove by the shapes of their crania that the accomplished Ancient Egyptians were Hamites, perhaps kin to white Europeans.

Popular racist conjecture gave the Fulani "Hamitic" roots. The actual history of the Fulani is unclear—a way of life nomadic and rural left a small cache of records. Some Fulani oral histories postulate we came from Jordan. The etymology of the Fulani language points to the valley of the Senegal River, though one story claims that Fula developed spontaneously in a game between children of Arabic speakers: one day, they began speaking their own complete language unrelated to any other. It could have been as early as the fifth century that the Fulani began to migrate south and west from present-day Morocco or Mauritania. We may originate near the Red Sea, perhaps emerging alongside migratory early Egyptians. Modern Fulani are most likely an admixture of North Africans who abandoned Arab lands and the tribes they encountered while crossing the desert into West Africa.

Speculation about Fulani origins intensified during our colonization: stratifying heritage was an imperial obsession. A 1902 British report on Central Africa hypothesizes that the "dominant inhabitants" were the Fulani, who were "much more advanced in civilization than the other Negro tribes." One postcolonial ethnographer's observation echoes my family's allegations: the Fulani "like many North Africans— have a somewhat Arab appearance." Lord Lugard, a British governor of Colonial Nigeria, proposed that the Fulani had Hamitic or even Aryan blood. Lugard used his theories to implement a ranking system and install "superior" tribes as middle managers. His system was designed to discourage rebellion, supposing that subordinated tribes would be more willing to obey commands coming from people who resembled them.

The British were preoccupied with the theoretical ancestry of the Fulani because they wanted to endorse the tribe's "pristine" origin outside Black Africa. The elevation of the Fulani was predicated on such a pedigree—tribal promotion had a geographic prerequisite. England's Empire upheld the Fulani as elites across the North of Nigeria, even where they were a minority. My grandmother came from an insular Fulani family that settled instead of wandering; they could be sure they hadn't mixed with any Hausa outside their enclave. Preferred by the British for their "purity," her family suffered less discrimination due to their tribal status, despite their poverty. Many tribes still resent the Fulani.

Of the four tribes I might claim, I am probably most accurately Hausa-Fulani, a neo-tribe of blended origin. Where and how the Hausa and the Fulani combined—this points to a clearer picture of who I am.

Although I do not speak or understand the Fulani language, this does not disaffirm my identification with the tribe. The word "Fulani" itself is borrowed from the Hausa name for the tribe (in the Fulani's own language, we are the "Fulbe"). The Hausa language is by far the more influential of the two languages, spoken by four times as many people as Fula. Today, Hausa prevails amongst the Hausa-Fulani, and even people like my mother, who professes to be entirely Fulani, speak Hausa better than Fula.

The ethnogenesis—the development of one ethnic identity—of the Hausa-Fulani goes back six hundred years to the fourteenth century, when the Fulani people first arrived in Hausaland. The Fulani and the Hausa began as distinct peoples, but in a careening past, their histories mapped onto each other as they traded power. After centuries of suppression by the Hausa, the Fulani asserted their own control by waging holy war across most of the regions the two shared.

At the end of these wars: a new caliphate. The triumphant Fulani ruler Usman dan Fodio had seen his caliphate in mystical visions. He spun his dreams into an empire lasting ninety-nine years, one governed according to his belief of what Allah willed. After defeating his Hausa enemies and declaring their lands the property of God, he unleashed a host of "warrior-scholars" to put down insurgencies and promote learning in madrasas purpose-built to teach a broad public religion and science. In the caliphate that emerged from one man's fantasia, poetry revived: our century of expression—of ecstatic lyrics in Hausa and Arabic.

The "Governor of Believers" encouraged an incoming wave of Fulani to Hausaland, urging them to settle their occupied territory and enmesh themselves into Hausa society. "Fulanization" of Hausa culture proceeded under Fulani predominance. However, as the Fulani remained a minority population in most areas, a reverse process of their own "Hausaization" began in kind immediately. Fulani culture was absorbed by Hausa majorities in population centers across Hausaland.

The British exploited the rift and rivalry between the Hausa and the Fulani. Hausa soldiers were recruited by the British Empire to fight Fulani authority throughout nineteenth-century military campaigns. Their bellicose alliance was ultimately successful, and in 1903, the Sokoto Caliphate of the Fulani was dissolved and divided amongst the English, the French, and the Germans on terms settled amongst themselves. That spring in Sokoto, the British Army used cannons to breach the city gates and batter the city walls; the last of his line, the fallen caliph fled.

In a perverse maneuver, the British reappointed the Fulani to positions of prestige over the Hausa. The Fulani had made themselves a ruling class via jihad; once conquered by the British, they were installed again as the elect in a classic divide-and-conquer strategy. "Notes on the Origin of the Hausas" from a London journal in 1910 introduces the Hausa as secondary: "Next to the Fulani, the most important race in Northern Nigeria is the Hausa." With the Fulani once more placed over them despite their battle-tested loyalties, the Hausa believed themselves betrayed. Growing up, I heard Hausa horror stories about invading Fulani—how they burned the faces of those they enslaved to mark them. And some silly stories—how the Fulani couldn't eat corn, so full of dairy fat that made their stomachs curdle.

In the present day, an unflattering term for Fulani people is "caliphatarians." Intertribal tensions persist; the simple act of prayer may cause contention. When the Sokoto Caliphate was established, the Fulani were appointed as prayer leaders; they lead prayers in mosques to this day. But Islam binds the Hausa and the Fulani through a shared Muslim identity profound enough to fuse by faith. After centuries, they have integrated significantly; within Nigeria, they are classified in more and more contexts as one. Outside this country, they remain identifiable as separate groups, and their intimate affinity is not the norm. But Northern Nigeria behaves like a crucible for these two tribes, where they weld.

The historic battleground between my two tribes is the city of Sokoto. Here, the Hausa and the Fulani were thrown together physically in the close quarters of Old Sokoto, encircled and held together by ancient defensive walls.

The city's name is derived from the Arabic "souk," meaning "market," and Sokoto is still a market town. Walking around its bazaars, rarely will you see statues, their figures dangerously close to the old idols. You will certainly see two symbols in competition: horse and cattle. See them painted on the glazy calabash gourds we use for kitchenware or makeshift motorcycle helmets. As Fulani cattlemen reared the Red Fulani, the Hausa raised up the Hausa Horse from Arabian stallions and wild West African stock. These two animals—by their breeding, trade and transportation, meat and milk—generate Sokoto's wealth.

Sokoto was my family's home base whenever we visited Nigeria. It is the capital of the modern Sokoto State; it was the seat of the bygone Sokoto Caliphate, which now only exists in the person of the Sultan, who sits at the head of the Sultanate Council and leads the sweeping community of Muslims across Nigeria. Enshrining the tomb of its founding emperor, Sokoto has become a place of pilgrimage. Since the fall of its ninety-nine-year caliphate, religious extremists have tried to rebuild and replicate its triumphal peak. The insurgent Boko Haram recently declared the territories under its boot a contemporary "caliphate."

Some of the few Christians found for miles, in an atmosphere of religious tension roiling around them, my grandparents lived by a reservoir. Despite deadly attacks on churches during periods of religious crisis, when we visited, my family risked going to church every Sunday. The ECWA church we attended still stands in Sokoto; this denomination was first called the "Evangelical Church of West Africa," but leaders changed the name to the less specific, more optimistic "Evangelical Church Winning All."

The house in Sokoto where my maternal grandparents lived is almost the same age as I am, constructed in a typical communal style: The separate cooking hut is set far from bedrooms to keep them from filling with smoke. Living quarters surround a large outdoor courtyard, where clothes are washed and hung as more food is cooked and children play alongside errant chickens, turkeys, and goats. My siblings and I were taught how to kill the poultry animals we played with, chasing them out of rooms if they flew in through windows. At Christmas, we watched a cow butchered the halal way, its throat slit neatly and bleeding on the sand it sank into to die—more slowly than you'd expect.

I was kept inside the compound. For safety, sure. And for seclusion, and for space. Private domestic space traditionally cloisters the Hausa-Fulani female. A ditch at the end of the road was as far as I was allowed to walk alone to explore. There was no trash collection service, and piles of garbage accumulated in the near ditch—home to roving dogs, and the food supply for free-ranging city goats. The house had no internet, no TV. After I finished the few books I had room to pack, I could never find any more to strain my eyes in low-fuel lamplight. Once, I begged an uncle to take me to a storefront with an awning advertising a "bookstore" but found a stationer selling blank notebooks and accounting ledgers. We searched a large market with bookstalls; the only options in English were the Holy Bible or the Holy Quran.

Each time we returned to his familiar house, my grandfather insulted me upon first sight. He might say, "You look more like Ladi every time I see you." Ladi, the one-eyed crone with a hunchback. I am told that insults were how he got close to people. Removing the barriers of propriety, he supposed he might live a life in complete openness, hoping to one day reconcile his first wife to his second.

His two wives lived at opposite corners of the compound, on polite terms in their later years, though whenever I visited, my "junior grandmother" rarely came out of her suite of two adjoining rooms. She ate alone after the rest of us had disbanded. She had only one child with my grandfather, and their daughter grew up shouldering no resentment because of their ill-famed marriage. Still, the little girl stood apart from her giant half family. I knew my mother's half sister as the "or ten" in the number of siblings she has: "nine or ten." My grandmother treated her like one of her own, as one must according to Islam. According to some traditional beliefs, the child of the rival must be treated *better* than your own child. In Christianity, there are no guidelines for how to treat the child of technical infidelity.

After diabetes made walking painful, my grandfather would sit outside in the courtyard all day and night listening to BBC Hausa's global news dispatches on his radio. There is a well, shady trees, and mats rolled out for people who sleep under the stars when it gets too hot or after a heavy rain that clears the air and leaves its scent. We often went to Sokoto during the Harmattan—the season in West Africa of strong winds from the coast that yearly begins around Christmas.

The word "Harmattan" might come from the Arabic "haram," in the sense of an accursed thing. Within a desert bigger than one continent, dust storms can be bigger than countries. Once, on the day before we left Sokoto, there was a sandstorm. I remember my mother telling me to *come away from there, come away from the windows.* We ran around closing all the windows.

Imagine daylight turning to demi-night in seconds, crude sand being washed with tar and tossed into sky. Imagine that a still frame becomes disjointed and shaking, and then see only dark, and then hear heavy breathing. Imagine this continues for many, many moments. Straining to see outside through dust, the last thing I could make out was a goat being led by leashed throat, somewhere. Then dust settled, and a neighbor's daughter was missing. I asked my mother: *Is she dead, is she dead, is she dead?* I was assured the little girl lost would be found. I was told to sleep: after such a storm, we must have early prayers ahead of our return—for journey mercies.

My mother's family maintains that one forefather of the Fulani tribe was an Arab named 'Uqbah ibn Nāfiʿ. He was the general who led the Muslim conquest of the North African Maghreb region in the seventh century and was related to the Prophet Muhammad by clan. Through this man, some in my family claim descent from the Prophet himself. In one legend, ibn Nāfiʿ's armies found gold, luck, and water. Marching across the desert, they disturbed the sand underfoot and unearthed a magical golden cup from which flowed a spring. The source of this miraculous spring was a holy well located all the way in Mecca—the same well Allah created to save Ishmael from dying of thirst, whose waters washed the Prophet's heart after death.

The Fulani are in fact affiliated with Arab ethnic groups through close contact over their millennium of tandem migration—Fulani were early, key players in the Muslim world and in the advancement of its shared religion. Desert-faring Sahelian Nigerians intermixed with Arabs much more than did those West Africans farther south; one distinct ethnic group in Sokoto, known as Hausa-Fulani Arabs, is composed of the descendants of Hausa, Fulani, and Arab intermarriage. The millions of Fulani now in northern African countries have common heritage with the Arabs they live amongst. My Fulani family's claims of Arab consanguinity are not outlandish; it would not be inaccurate to call many of our ancestors Black Arabs.

But a link to Europe is pure fantasy. And I am troubled by questionable motives.

Growing up, I understood that my mother's family held lighter skin in higher regard. In the pre-Islamic and precolonial mythos of our region, fair spirits formed a cohort of lovely entities. Darker spirits were disagreeable—they were agents of ill-wishing. European supremacy reinforced this noxious preconception, which now projects insecurity and an inferiority complex epidemic in West Africa. Nigeria is the top consumer for corrosive lightening agents like skin bleach, used by 75 percent of its female population. For dark-skinned women like me, *better to burn off our skin.*

My family is in the habit of pinching babies' noses throughout infancy in a futile attempt to narrow them while the cartilage is malleable. They attribute certain familial and tribal traits to Arab or European lineage. These features include sharp noses; complexions with red undertones; long hair with a curl less kinky. In the view of race scientists, in addition to being "quicker witted than the dark agricultural Negroes," Hamites have a distinct physicality: "extremely linear in bodily build, extremely narrow-headed and narrow-faced, with a special narrowness of the jaw." A language of dehumanization was the through line in my family's indoctrination.

The Fulani are known to be proud; dignity is prized in the essential Fulani pathway. Perhaps my family seeks immunity from colonial taxonomies and malignant race science, like one British gradation of "the most pronounced types of the Negro race." Perhaps they want to distance themselves from the shame they see in subjugation.

They are wrong. Our link to the African continent is our only permanent bondage—we may not deny it; we cannot decamp.

I was thrilled when a DNA test reported that I am 99 percent African, with a decimal percentage of Arab ethnicity, and nothing at all to do with Europe. I never believed in my theoretical European progenitor, finding implausible the sequence of events that would have driven him from Albania to Nigeria. I felt vindicated when I reported my ancestry results, as if they were ammunition to totally reject our colonial programming. We could be pretty without being any part European—or anything other than Black Africans. If we look different than neighboring ethnic groups, it is only because there are multitudes in African phenotypes. Any attempt to distinguish ourselves by nostril flare or curl pattern is nonsensical.

Where my mother's generation internalized tribalism and racist colonial quackery, I reflexively recoil when my genealogy is denied. I suppose that my maternal family leans on our possible links to the Middle East and the *Monde arabe* because they associate that sphere of influence with eminence—with those merchants and holy men blessing our long-shared history of trade and prayer. *Surely, the best birthplace lies in the Holy Land*; through Allah's favor the Fulani divined their "right to rule." Maybe my family's insistence has more to do with prospect and fortune, less to do with beauty or skin color. Maybe it is more about fantasizing themselves part of splendid civilizations instead of the unhappy experiment in nationhood some stranger named Nigeria.

There must be pride in thinking of your ancestors so laden with gold that sinking camels struggled to stalk the Sahara.

8

DAUGHTER OF THE WIND

In Maguzanci—the occult Hausa cosmology that predates Islam—spirits live in family units exactly as humans do. Modeling the logistics of men, they sort themselves by "ethnicity and occupation." In this otherworld, spirits belonging to the same tribe live together in one house—*a residence built in some practical reverie.* The deities there are the divine representatives of living people in human tribes, and they mirror the qualities of mortal members. Of course, the tribal personalities of people and gods are presented from a Hausa perspective.

As above, so below.

Like its earthly incarnation, the House of Fulani is nomadic. The spirits of my tribe cannot endure peace. They abide in a state of possession, of pure impulse, of perpetual dissatisfaction with settled life. Calling upon our temperamental spirits invites malediction. Symptoms of the Fulani curse: the compulsion to wander, the inability to remain a body at rest. The Hausa—who found permanent settlements more frequently than the Fulani—cast the rival tribe as transients. Always, they see desert winds at our backs.

We Fulani are yoked to wind. We embody all intense and negative aspects of *iska*, the Hausa word for both "wind" and "spirit." Growing up, I knew that "*yar iska*" was the worst insult I could hear in Hausa. Its literal meaning translates to "daughter of the wind." Used to censure willful girls, it shames through a suggestion of promiscuity. The idea of *iskanci* refers to the behavior of a free spirit—as well as to craziness and vice.

My immediate family put no stock in Maguzanci myth. Still . . . what was that feeling at the edges of our lives? Something made us fitful. We wondered if the cause of such restlessness was rooted in our past like a generational curse—or if it hinted ahead, like an apocalyptic apparition. Over the coming years, as my family repeatedly moved from place to place to place, concerned relatives demanded to know:

What has possessed you?

In 1895, the controversial Irish poet and playwright Oscar Wilde was imprisoned in Reading, the town I grew up in, on charges of gross indecency. He would write of his years of hard labor in *The Ballad of Reading Gaol*. Upon release, he departed that same day for Paris, never again in his lifetime stepping foot on English soil. Exactly one hundred years later, in 1995, my parents gathered us three children to tell us we would also be leaving England, for Nashville, Tennessee, a place we had never heard of.

My first thought when my parents informed us of our impending move was the certainty that I would be shot.

Such morbid paranoia for an eight-year-old, but I knew no America beyond movie violence. As a kid, I loved to watch the Western *The Good, the Bad and the Ugly* with my father. In the opening scene, a duel between two gunmen leaves the loser with a smoking bullet hole in his brain. The killing was not overly graphic, but it always—*yes, stuck in my head*—because his wound punctures the exact place on his forehead where I have my crescent scar. My scar still feels sensitive at times, like whenever I think of this scene. I feel the tissue tingling in involuntary empathetic response. As we prepared to leave England, I constantly pictured myself walking down an American street and getting shot, imagining viscerally what it would feel like when a real bullet pierced my skull.

My father had gone ahead to Nashville in April, leaving us behind for four months. Both my parents' student visas were expiring, as they had completed their degrees, and we had no authorization to remain in the UK. We had no money, either, so my father spent his final few weeks in England scrambling to source some spending money. He borrowed from two colleagues: each gave him one hundred British pounds, which he confesses to never having paid back after losing contact with them.

He landed in the USA with a total of two hundred pounds ($250); he was that immigrant cliché of an empty-handed newcomer with a ludicrously inadequate sum of money. His new job teaching at Meharry Medical College paid $26,000 a year, and though for a family of five this salary hovered just above the poverty level, to us it seemed like a lot of money. When he left us, he couldn't afford the train that shuttled travelers from Reading to Gatwick, and instead took the Beeline Bus to his nine-hour direct flight to Nashville. When he disembarked, the colleague assigned to pick him up didn't know what he looked like—he'd told her to imagine Danny DeVito as a poor Black man.

After the Oklahoma City bombing on April 19, 1995,

only a few days after his arrival, we received a cascade of phone calls from worried family members in Nigeria and had to explain that he was nowhere near the attack; the USA was not as small as the UK. My father called us once a week to tell us first impressions of the US and stories of Tennessee. I loved that Nashville was "Music City," but my sister was dismayed after learning it was more specifically the home of country music, which she hated. She asked my mother, "Do they even *have* hip-hop in Nashville?" We built a caricature of a city around our nonexistent knowledge of the country genre.

While searching for an apartment, my father stayed at a La Quinta Inn, using vouchers issued by the medical school. Asking for tea in a restaurant, he was confused when presented with a beverage he had never seen before—iced sweet tea—instead of the hot black tea we drink in England and Nigeria. When he ordered meals and was brought an exaggerated portion, he had to ask the waitress, "Is this just for one person?" He was afraid he'd accidentally ordered too much and wouldn't be able to pay the check. When he told me about the concept of a restaurant where you pay one fee to eat as much as you want, I thought he was pulling my leg and didn't believe him. How could the restaurant make money if everyone could eat an unlimited amount, I challenged him— and why would anyone *want* to eat as much as they physically could?

The week before my mother, siblings, and I left Reading, we set out every evening to walk the town, going from house to house and store to store saying goodbye to everyone we knew—lingering with people we knew well, accepting well wishes from those we didn't. The pattern of motion in England is less mobile than in America; people relocate less, planting roots in stable generations, naming their houses. International emigrations weren't routine in Reading, and my mates thought my farewell a grand occasion. I wielded invitations to my goodbye party like a weapon. If any student displeased me, I revoked their invitation to an afternoon of living room dancing, sausages, and sweets.

I enjoyed the attention. There was a cachet in becoming American. It set me apart as interesting, compounding with my Blackness and Africanness: irregularities were finally working in my favor. My newfound "popularity" went to my head, and on the day of my party, I made almost every single classmate at the party cry—behaving in a bizarre, bossy way where I excluded this one or that at random, making pronouncements like, "Jordan can't have any cake!" or "Only my top three friends can choose which songs to play." I sidelined one boy from all activities and got angry when my brother started playing with him, saying that it was *my* party, so no one could talk to my guests but me. Some petty part of me, long pent up, wanted to punish my playmates for something that was not their fault—that I was never like them.

None of the furniture in our rented house was ours, so we packed no more than the regular luggage allowance for our flight. On the very last night before we left, we placed eight suitcases in the hallway, and these solid objects made the whole matter of moving real. After the packing was done, my thirteen-year-old sister begged my mother to let her go to a sleepover, something forbidden because my mom thought they were opportunities for trouble: meaning smoking, talking about kissing, or learning curse words.

On this unique occasion, however, my sister thought my mother would relent. Even my mother's friends, over at our house to say goodbye, urged her to reconsider her rule. But she would not. My sister stayed home with the loss of one last night with her friends. Her regret trickled down to me as well, and my memory of our final nightfall is nothing more than her anguish, unsettling as the insistent awareness of your own heartbeat. It clouded the house in resentment that hadn't lifted the next morning as we readied ourselves to go.

When I was small, I liked to be wherever I should not be—in my parents' wardrobe; behind the china cabinet; in the back lot of the metalworking factory behind our house, which was pockmarked with big pools of dirty water to play in. The day we were leaving, I went to the factory to hide. I was found and brought back to an angry mother who prefers to be at the airport many hours too early. Back at home, after the commotion of me going missing before our imminent departure, came the quietest moment: I am standing underneath the staircase, where we used to stack our phonebooks.

I think, "Can we really be leaving this house?" I would never see the flat expanse of garden under snow that was pure, white, and massive. Snow, blinding against bloodied brick. My mother's voice cuts my premature nostalgia: "Can you carry this box?" I pick up the box and complain, "Mommy, it's heavy." She says something in reply that I forget. Or was it that she said nothing at all? *I forget.*

It's curious which details of significant events stay in the mind long after the fact. *Which fade.* August 8, 1995, was one of the most important days of my life, and I don't remember if we flew out of Heathrow or Gatwick. This is the kind of detail I really should ask someone about. But I won't—because, like a child learning to ride a bike, who at some point begins to resent the stabilizing efforts of a nearby adult, I want to do it myself. I want recollections of that day to remain all mine—unadulterated, incomplete, but my own.

Preflight, the only thing I remember was the airport

bathroom. My mother, sister, and I went in together, leaving my brother in a lounge. As I washed my hands, my sister said, "We should go back." My mother mistook this to mean that she wanted to return to our house. To not get on our flight at all. So she asked her, "Really, do you mean that?" I remember the expression on my mother's face—the extent of her uncertainty. But my sister only meant that we should hurry back to my mischievous brother. The way my mother reacted filled me with a vague, nasty sense, and I was afraid of everything.

Then I wondered what it was we were stepping into.

When we landed and I saw my father, I ran into his arms and started bawling, surprising myself, as I had gotten used to his absences while he worked in London and didn't know I could miss him any more. I was overwhelmed even before the whirlwind: We were pulled out of the immigration line and taken beyond a bright, glittering sign heralding our arrival to Music City. Our bags were searched in a small room with an enormous American flag as a soldier in full uniform stood at attention, saluting. There was the first American gun I had ever seen—I asked my father if the soldier was going to shoot me.

My father arrived here on an H-1B Visa for skilled workers, but for the rest of us, my mother applied to the lottery for Diversity Visas. This lottery randomly selects hopefuls from countries underrepresented within the immigrant population of the USA; winners are welcomed as permanent residents on a path to citizenship. The lottery is free. It has an application process daunting to some but simple to a mother with long experience in both failing and functional bureaucracy.

It is unique amongst the nations of the world. A 2018 VICE documentary titled "The U.S. Green Card Lottery Is Basically Unwinnable" explains that fifty thousand out of fifteen million applicants are accepted each year with the goal of further diversifying our melting-pot republic. Natives of places well represented in the population—China, Mexico, South Korea—are disqualified. Today, citizens of every African country besides Nigeria may apply; Nigerians alone are ineligible, as our numbers have swelled. My family was lucky in our timing; my father found out about the lottery from an ad on the side of a bus.

Our odds of winning the Diversity Visa lottery were approximately the same odds as our lifetime chance of getting shot and killed in the United States: 0.3 percent (one-third of 1 percent). One out of every three hundred applicants wins the visa lottery, and one out of every three hundred Americans dies by firearm.

To be issued green cards granting us entry, we had to sit for a long interview. As the luckiest few, finally, we took the Oath of Allegiance: "I will support and defend the Constitution and laws of the United States of America against all enemies . . . I will bear true faith and allegiance . . . I will bear arms on behalf of the United States . . ." *So help me God.* As new resident aliens, we were released after a decade in chilly England into a Tennessean heat wave, promising to bear arms.

Thus began my American childhood.

Flying above, I'd marveled at blue oases in backyards; swimming pools were rare in English homes. American highways seemed impossible—*all this fits inside one city?* For us, it was unusual to see such motorways and no one walking—and the billboards! Each promising something decadent, like a gallon of free iced tea with the purchase of a bucket of chicken, or buffets offering an all-you-can-eat spread—*so my father hadn't lied.* America was a leviathan, a monster that dealt in gratuitousness in everything: highways, malls, the number of channels on television.

We arrived at our new home, Riverbend Apartments, which now has 2.5 stars in a single Yelp review: "Still have the same cabinets and drawers not working, but the place is looking better. The exterior is getting a fresh face which has a pleasant though dark palette. I still hear the squirrels sometimes and am anxious for the roof to be repaired which I am told will put an end to their egress."

The entrance to Riverbend sat on a straight stretch of road, the length of which still surfaces when I need to mentally calibrate a distance of one mile. The complex seemed colossal, its housing units divided by entryways and arranged along avenues. We lived on the first avenue. The cream-and-brown butter residences were separated by a hill from the cream and powdery blue of another block of apartments similar to Riverbend, only more expensive, better landscaped, and renovated. Winters covered the hill with snow, and my brother and I would sit in plastic buckets to sled down to the parking lot.

Our apartment had two stories—3 bedrooms, 2.5 bathrooms, a living room, a separate dining room, and a kitchen. When we first saw it, we were amazed. It was full of clean furniture not layered in dust; it had a balcony, another rare feature in England; I hadn't even *seen* a half bathroom before. I was gratified to find the fridge stocked with a new-to-me form of liquid sugar in juice drinks from Welch's. That things could be new; that a car or TV could be so large. Perhaps we had shaken off some of the trappings of poverty in only one day.

In my mother's trunk where she keeps stacks of our immigration documents, I recently found an old thank-you note trimmed in watercolor teddy bears and flowers. One side is titled "Mommy's Impression." She'd written: "A little uphill, there is a windy road branching from the main (not very major) road leading to a group of appartments. The appartments are in a semicircular arrangement. Ours is on the lefthand side. N12." Underneath this text, her drawn diagram of the apartment complex. I note her spelling, "appartment," halfway between English and French. Otherwise, her musings are accurate.

On the other side, still in her handwriting: "Nashville as I see it (Nana's)." I had written: "There's a very long road. Our house is somewhere at the end. It's quite big. There's grass and a few flowers here and there. There are lots of trees and plenty of cars. Our house has 2 stories and it is white. We have a white gate and purple fence. We have red, yellow, and white flowers and concrete pavements." This description is pure fantasy. Neither of us have any recollection of writing the note, and I wonder which house I was dreaming of; it wasn't any that I knew. There is a giant blue X through my own words.

Our first midnight in Nashville, my father took my brother and me in his Nissan Quest to the center of the city to see the replica of the Parthenon illuminated. Leaving downtown, we took the highway, now empty, and he showed us what it felt like to go one hundred miles per hour, making us promise not to tell Mommy. Even in the unfamiliar garments of a new city at night, I was not afraid of anything. When people talk about chasing American dreams, they are talking about a speeding white minivan on I-65: some sensible, secondhand model.

To the cheers of children, hurtling from one life into quite another.

That summer, Microsoft released Windows 95; there was a massacre at Srebrenica; superstar Selena was murdered. This was the summer we collectively did the Macarena; glued our eyes to the O. J. Simpson trial; thought Brad Pitt was the sexiest man alive. *Apollo 13* had just come out, and I was turning nine.

One end of the mile-long road that ran through Riverbend Apartments opened out to the grounds of the elementary school I'd be attending, as well as to a Waffle House, which we begged my parents to take us to every time we all headed out or headed home, so curious about what real American waffles might taste like—they never once did. The other end led out to a Walmart and Kmart facing each other in bared-teeth competition. In this mortifying shopping center, for years I'd make myself small to avoid being spotted by a classmate in the clothes section (having moved up from car boot sale clothing to bargain-basement bins tendering factory defects).

My father started teaching at Meharry Medical College, a historically Black school, while my mother looked tirelessly for work. We children were again alone. My brother and I developed an insane schedule that wild first summer in the States. We'd stay up all night in the living room watching MTV, whose music videos enthralled us with their three minutes of American aesthetics. In England, we flipped through only four channels. As soon as it was light, my brother and I went out, running on no sleep, drunk on the prospect of the new.

My sister receded from my life this summer, even though we shared a room and a bathroom. She couldn't get over leaving her friends the way my brother and I did, by tramping the neighborhood and making new ones. In her midteen gawkiness, she found safe haven in hard feelings and wanted nothing to do with kid siblings. She unfastened from us, conveying herself back to England in a routine that wore her down: extra chores to earn money for long-distance calls; longer and longer letters; days indoors crying.

My sister and I collided only once a day, in the mornings. We shared a bunk bed that had a queen frame on the bottom (hers), which narrowed to my twin bed on top. To get up to and back down from my bed, I was supposed to use the ladder, but I found it too tricky. Instead, I would jump over a small gap in the protective railing—directly onto my sister's mattress, landing right next to her resting head. Before I dismounted, I always made sure she was asleep and got ready to sprint to the bathroom as soon as this rude alarm jolted her upright and into hot pursuit. Years later, she told me that being woken up in such a way interrupted dreams where she was back in England, and that she hated me as she hated this summer for all its harsh awakenings.

My brother and I gravitated toward fellow immigrants; we relied on them to initiate us into the order of new Americans. I befriended a Laotian girl I always saw alone, whose parents never allowed anyone inside their residence. Only once, when I had to call home, was I admitted to enter the immaculate hush of a darkened apartment that exteriorized the girl's perpetual melancholy. I initiated one memorable discussion about electricity and plumbing with immigrants from Mexico and Vietnam—I thought *all* third-culture kids from third world countries knew mostly unworkable toilets and unlit houses. In fact, they knew different. From then, in conversations about our home countries, I avoided the issue of amenities. What we did have in common was a history of violence.

My brother's new best friend was the Vietnamese Phi, and I became inseparable with his younger sister, Kit. Phi and

Kit's parents were never home either, and we made lunches of boiled potatoes and butter. We smoked their father's discarded cigarette butts and felt sick and grown. Kit and I followed our big brothers around, so dogged in need for their company that we would debase ourselves by accepting any dare or challenge they put to us. Sometimes, they made us fight each other for candy bars.

Riverbend Apartments, true to its name, was right by the bend of the Cumberland River. All you had to do to get to it was cut through the woods and snake down a steep hill until you reached the edge of the riverbank. We never swam in the river, only tried to skip rocks across it or sunbathed on one large, flat boulder half-submerged in water. Every day, we tried to use the pool, but since swimming required parental supervision, more often than not we were caught by management and ejected when they made their lazy rounds after lunch. We spent hours scrounging for coins to buy junk food in the machines by the laundry rooms, even crawling around dirty roadside ditches to mine for nickels. We lived as maniacs every day until evening, only going home because of mosquitoes and for fresh plates of spaghetti and our mothers' love.

That classic summer of childhood—*you only get one*. Fireflies, always. For some, a first romance astonishes those humid months. This is the summer when Something Happens—finally *to* you instead of only *around* you. Just for you, the world starts moving, and you begin to move with it, staking some claim.

I bought assorted seed packets from Kmart, and in the wedge of unfit dirt between our patio and the parking lot, I tried to make myself a garden. I wanted to know about the kind of earth I stood on—its properties, the soil quality and composition. I missed the front gardens and back gardens of

England. Since I knew nothing about growing life, none of the cheap seeds ever sprouted or bloomed.

England can't be more different than Nigeria; Nashville can't be more different than England.

In America at first, my family felt ambushed. Once, I had exactly one dollar bill and tried to purchase a 99-cent candy bar. When the cashier rang me up, the total came to $1.06 with tax added. In England, tax is reflected in the sticker price, so what you see is what you pay. I had to put back the suddenly unaffordable chocolate. If my skin could blush, I would have blushed then.

My expectations of the USA were informed by my favorite movies, ones I'd watched in England on VHS over and over. My bloodthirsty impression of American cities was reinforced by *Lethal Weapon* (1987), a buddy cop movie with so much sex and violence it should never have been part of my catalogue. *The Karate Kid* (1984) explained lands to the west. Particularly instructive was *Coming to America* (1988), about an African prince who leaves home for Queens, New York, imagining that because of its name it would be the place to find a royal bride. Together, his character and I learned the gritty reality of 1980s New York in a crash course you might call "How to Not Get Shot."

I repeatedly watched *The Terminator* (1984), starring Arnold Schwarzenegger, an immigrant who'd made good. As a murderous cyborg that must learn to mimic humans, it is mostly his clipped Austrian accent that makes him seem a machine, an automaton. In a sequel, a teenager teaches him how to blend into society. *Back to the Future* (1985) was a gateway to the life of the American teenager, and the added feature of time travel exposed me to the trends of various eras. I was ignorant about how diverse the USA's landscape was, so each film did not represent a distinct, discrete locale. Instead, my mental image of the country stacked suburbia over an ocean of cornfields and asphalt; endless Californian coast annexed countryside and inner city.

Although these movies were a decade out of date by the time I put their lessons to use, it's lucky that so many blockbuster movies in the '80s dealt specifically with curious circumstances that find one freakish character trying to fit in despite some flagrant obstacle or abnormality. "American" was not human, I learned. It was metamorphosis. To become "American" was to play pretend until others bought it. To be an alien trying on the figments of a new life, trying out versions of a self.

When summer came to an end, the three of us were taken to new schools: my sister to high school, my brother to middle school, myself to Brookmeade Elementary beyond that Waffle House. Because of my reliance on unrealistic movies to instruct me regarding American life, I was profoundly confused by the school system. *Grease* was one of my regular movies, and the advanced age of the actors (playing teens while in their thirties) left me baffled by the concept of high school, which was "secondary school" in England. The actors in *Grease* looked older than my mother, so I thought high school was some kind of postdoctoral program.

My difficulty understanding how schools here worked started me off all wrong. Somehow, after my parents registered me, I was put into first grade instead of the fourth grade. I enjoyed finding school so easy and was unconcerned that all the "new" material my class was learning covered subjects I'd mastered a long while back. The mistake wasn't noticed until the third day—by my teacher, not by me. Who knows how long I would have remained smug and unaware?

In Nashville, we were the kind of poor that we knew might not be permanent. At school, I was on the reduced lunch program, where for thirty-five cents I received one entrée, one piece of fruit, and milk after handing over a bright orange ticket. *That alarming, obvious color.* We went to Long John Silver's on Tuesdays when kids ate free; I hated the cornmeal hush puppies that tasted like fried nothing. We went regularly to food banks, but unlike using the orange meal tickets, I enjoyed that; every week's package was different and full of the kinds of things my parents never bought—instant chocolate pudding, boxed macaroni and cheese, cans containing a surprise of noodles.

During our lean first year, my mother was a substitute teacher for all grade levels in schools around our district. Once, when she subbed for a kindergarten class, the kids lied to her, telling her it was naptime or playtime when it wasn't. Ignorant of the class's elaborate systems of fairness required to keep the peace, she told the "wrong" student to write the date on the board. Another student started crying that it was *her* turn. This set off a chain of escalating tantrums, until my mother called the principal and told him she couldn't do it anymore and needed to leave. She lasted two hours in kindergarten.

One day, she substituted for my fourth-grade class. I begged her not to do anything that might mortify me, but African parents have a very different idea of what their children are reasonably allowed to be humiliated by. During our class session, she walked around tense, tightly gripping her handbag and refusing to put it down. She was worried that

American children might steal from her after teachers at another school warned her to be careful. Noticing her wary behavior, a classmate asked her if she was "finna leave." It took a great deal of back-and-forth for him to explain that he was asking if she was "fixing to" leave—then, further, what *that* meant. Communication the entire class went like that.

I had asked her not to speak to me in Hausa because I grew shamefaced at the guttural edges of our language. I didn't want her speaking in English that much, either. She observed that Americans love to say "really good" when asked how they are. She asked us children about proper American English: if she could say, "God bless you really good."

All my wildest fears of humiliation were fully realized during the lunch break, when she pulled me into her lap in the middle of the cafeteria to spoon-feed me mashed plantain. I should probably have expected this infantilizing display to appall our preteen audience. At snack breaks throughout that year, many students had expressed real and feigned disgust at the sight or smell of Nigerian food in my Tupperware—so I'd stopped bringing any. My mother was trying to undermine their shaming; the spectacle of spoon-feeding in front of my classmates was her way of dismissing them.

Later in the schoolyear, my mother bought a liter of Coca-Cola and some snacks to bring to my class's upcoming open house. I was terrified of my class being reminded of her appearance as our substitute, so I stole the soda and snacks and tossed them outside in our unit's "dumpster" (also called a "Grundon" in Tennessee—both new words in my vocabulary). My mother searched for them all week before confronting me. I lied and told her I'd taken the whole liter of Coke to school to drink it alone. Perplexed by the logistics of this stunt, she questioned how. I said I'd hidden the soda in the bathroom and ducked in there during breaks to sip it throughout the day. We kneeled together and bowed our heads before God—I prayed aloud to beg forgiveness for my sins of theft and gluttony. I was really praying she would never again find cause to visit my class.

An unexpected theory: A certain modern American Southern accent—the accent of hill folk—is the closest one in existence to an eighteenth-century English accent. Voices of the early English settlers who planted themselves deep in the South are preserved in the time capsule of that drawl we recognize by its lagging and lilt. In England itself, the originating accent changed, becoming adulterated and unrecognizable after centuries. But isolated in out-of-the-way Appalachia, it can still be heard unevolved. That means Tennessee hillbillies sound just like the English who first colonized West Africa.

How strange I sounded when I found myself in Tennessee.

My elementary schoolmates pestered me—why this, why that. *Y'all wear clothes in Africa? Do y'all live in trees? Why you call it autumn? It's called fall!* Having no answers I wanted to voice, for a time, I became uncharacteristically quiet. My peers seemed years beyond me in maturity. These Americans were so eager to be grown. Discussions of the sex and drugs we saw on cable were commonplace, and I struggled to catch up. I made kids uncomfortable as they tried to figure out what I was, until they lost interest and left me alone.

It was the most awkward of all possible worlds.

I knew I was adjusting a little to the social environment when I began talking again.

At home, we continued to speak our hybrid of English and Hausa; the percentage of English steadily surged. We discovered Dolly Parton and belted "My Tennessee Mountain

Home" while deep cleaning together Saturday mornings, and we understood what country music was for. In public, we used Hausa to talk safely in the presence of outsiders. Unlike immigrants from Spanish- or French-speaking countries, who must remain guarded around Americans, we spoke a language we were sure no one else could understand. This encouraged my mother to talk about strangers right in front of them—or to talk about our own personal business. Often, she might've not even bothered speaking in Hausa; she used embarrassing English signifiers like "wig" or "food stamps" or "maxi pad" because the Hausa translation was Anglicized anyway or because there was no good translation at all.

I did try to train my erratic accent to match the Standard American accent heard in news programs. From movies, I mimicked Valley Girl uptalk. In a lucky coincidence, I found the Hollywood cadence familiar, because Hausa uses that same intonation. Despite attempts to sound like my mates, my Northern Nigerian–Berkshire English–Tennessean accent was a messy mumble that has never quite righted itself. Two decades later, my accent prompts the question: "No, but where are you *really* from?"

There were a few words I could not master; I could only say them a Nigerian way, a British way, or a Nigerian-British way. Even now, I have to force my mouth to make some words like an American. I must consciously combat stubborn instincts if I want to pronounce certain vowel sounds and avoid fielding questions about why I don't sound *standard*. "God," "water," "father," and "fall"—incidentally, key words of my childhood.

9

ALLEGIANCES UNCLEAR

An entity came creeping into our habitat: the novel chimera of American Racism.

We were the only Black family on our avenue, and it rattled us to encounter unwelcome. Finding some neighbors unfriendly, this was the place we started asking why. It's not that my family had never experienced racism before; I'd just been too young to perceive its full, unbridled dimensions. In Southern suburbia, I was learning. I became more conscious of my race as a feature that would ostracize me. I was *made* to notice.

All of us were laid bare to our new element.

Like all immigrant children, ours was to adapt. The desire to become like our peers briskly gathered strength, becoming the driving force in our social development. While my sister and I performed well academically, my brother more readily assimilated socially. He won over his classmates in that easy way boys do—with a prank, a crass joke, or fancy footwork playing football, which he immediately knew to call "soccer."

He fluently adopted the demeanor and lingo of new social groups, and made it seem natural. Confidence neutralized his foreignness, and he sometimes set the irreverent standard of behavior amongst junior high school boys.

I would describe my brother not as the class clown, but as the class *chaos*. The rest of us were working to recognize when we should be noticed and when we should not be. He acted out, always exposed. Looking back, he names the constant feeling of being called up to audition—under inspection, on display, *hypervisible*. His mischief might have been managed with a creative outlet rather than punishment. In detention, he drew—warships, tanks, and airplanes rendered with an astounding level of technical detail. He remained the most vulnerable under our saddle of hypervisibility. Once he was labeled a "problem Black boy," shaking free of that incrimination became his lot in life.

The American South marked the first time I was so exposed to the word "nigger," both as a slur and a reclaimed term. Back then, it made me uncomfortable to hear the word in any context, but my brother incorporated the word into his vocabulary—to assert that it belonged to him, and that he in turn might belong to Black America, which he believed possessed a stronger sense of "Blackness" than our family did at that point. We had been Africans foremost, and culture trumped color. My sister was barely coping in what she called her "beat 'em up" high school. Her tormentors derided her accent, deciding that she was trying to sound posh—that she thought she was better than them.

All three of us were confused as we dealt with the virulent strain of racism preferred by Southern states. Once, my brother called my white friend a "Saltine cracker." I cried and reported him to my father, who didn't understand my reaction and did nothing. We had moved from an English town with a small Black population to a city that was almost a third Black. My new Black American peers didn't know what to do with me. Some held a negative view of Africa and Africans. I was teased and called an "African booty scratcher," that baffling childhood slur. I got over it quickly, but I had such trouble navigating the culture within a culture that is American Blackness within America.

Curious after seeing an ad, I called a chat line for "urban singles." I was connected to a "room" of many voices in overlapping conversations. I raised my voice above the din to introduce myself, and one woman demanded, "Who let this white girl in here?" I immediately hung up the phone, humiliated. I was envious of Black Americans and their ease: the way they knew what to say to each other and how to behave, while I could only observe at a remove.

All over the media, the mannerisms of Black Americans were held up for mockery in the heyday of trashy talk shows, small-minded sitcoms, and political fearmongering. Some Nigerians compare the standard of living in America to the one we left behind, then unfairly conclude that Black Americans should be more grateful, sadly forgetting that we immigrants would not even be here if not for their sacrifices while fighting for civil rights. Some Nigerians dismiss the justified complaints against structural racism in the Western world, seeing only opportunity. And many fall for the ridiculous lie that Black American culture doesn't place the same importance on education that Africans do. How insidious the demonization of Black Americans—that we sometimes believed the worst of them.

Though young, I should have known better, having been saddled myself with negative stereotypes. The North of Nigeria holds a reputation amongst its Southerners as unenlightened. In this way, my native region is the inverse of the

South of the USA. When my family moved there, the American South was terra incognita, except for the slack-jawed foolery I saw in movies. Because of this familiar caricature, a potential new identity as a Southerner appealed; I've an innate desire to defy low expectations. Instead, an identity was chosen for me. In Tennessee, I was told for the first time that I "acted white," and my English accent did not help.

In all this noise, I still clung to immigrants of any background—they understood the minefield of lunch brought from home. Or show-and-tell. They had family photos to explain. They had parents to hide.

After one miserable year of bullying at the public school, my sister transferred into a magnet high school and was happy. At the same time, my mother was hired as a full-time science teacher. She was finally able to buy a good leather purse, a Dooney & Bourke.

Two years after arriving in Nashville, my family moved into a medium-sized house with a two-car garage and had two cars to fill it: our very first home standing as its own structure. Still a rental, it was tucked into a quiet cul-de-sac. As in England, our rented home had a garden—a plot almost our own, our place of planting and hardly reaping. We continued a household tradition of being unwilling conscripts in my father's landscaping projects. Here, he wanted to flatten brush and clear the land behind the house. Though we spent so many weekend hours ripping out roots, we never stayed long enough to find out what came next.

After four years in Nashville, we were beginning to feel like we might make a home. That meant it was time to go. Settling in place was not yet in the cards for us. None of us wanted to leave our schools and friends; none of us were excited about the prospect of a *new* England. Nearing the turn of the millennium, summer of 1999, I was twelve years old and about to enter my last year of junior high school.

We arrived in the town of Mystic, Connecticut, on some nondescript evening, to stay in a long-term residence hotel until we found a house. Again, I could hear my mother saying, "It will be okay. Everything will be all right," but she said it in that tone suggesting the opposite. Her tone proved prescient; after just one week working at the pharmaceutical company Pfizer, my father left his job—the reason for our relocation—under circumstances that have never been disclosed to me. We would be stuck in this sleepy town and in his inertia for three years.

My mother first taught at a public school far away in Boston, as none of the towns and cities leading up the seaboard to that metropolis had openings for a biology teacher. Monday to Friday, she'd wake up at three a.m. to take a three-hour train; at the end of the school day, she'd take the train home again, arriving after ten p.m. Sleep-deprived and ragged, she did this for an entire year. Sometimes, she missed the last train after school events or meetings, and she'd spend the night at a Nigerian acquaintance's apartment.

As when she'd moved to Oxford, I didn't see her much that year, and I missed her. I missed her so much that when she began working at a local science center, I accompanied her on weekends and after school. At the center, she led workshops for elementary school kids and gave tours of its collections— giant reptiles in terrariums, crystals, and cockroaches. In the back office, I played the two computer games they had, *The Oregon Trail* and *Where in the World Is Carmen Sandiego?* I passed my time searching the world for an international thief or trying to avoid dying of dysentery.

I was such a sad little kid in that apartment in Groton,

the cheaper neighboring town we moved to after being priced out of quaint Mystic and dreams of homeownership. Mystic routinely appears on lists of the prettiest small towns in America; Groton does not. Groton is a suburb without the benefit of a city. This summer barely registers as anything but a muggy prelude before three dreary winters. I lost all tolerance for cold, and I turned inside myself. New England's charm never rubbed off on me, though it tried with those fall leaves I'd never seen before, and with its bodies of water. Waters of the navy base; the harbor where crowds heralded tall ships as returning heroes; the pier where many first kisses were had, though not mine.

But coming home from school in late afternoons, it was already dark. Frost early, every morning. Winter and I never became civil again after those years in Connecticut. Years that bullied through boredom—browbeating boredom in a subtopia totally new yet utterly uninteresting. Even the secret pathway through the woods I found while exploring our apartment complex led to nowhere.

I escaped—into chat rooms where I improvised new personas, always pretending to be twenty-three, the oldest age I thought I could imitate—contriving glamorous backstories about careers I researched within our heaving set of thirty-two leather-bound encyclopedias. Usually, I pretended to be white; I learned in Tennessee that the most popular girls were white and pretty, so I associated popularity with prettiness and prettiness with whiteness.

I stayed inside. Inside the apartment, inside chat rooms, the interiors of myself. My few friendships were superficial and shy. Once again, I had to repeatedly explain my accent and manner of speaking. This time around, the exercise only seemed tedious, and these were the years I was quiet for good. Placeholder years—years of such nothing that I want them to take up more space *here*, as if that might make up for the speechless years that seemed all winter, sleep, and silence.

That was me in preteen tumult. Meanwhile, the world at large proposed it was approaching an expiration that boiled down to ones and zeros.

A klaxon cutting through white noise. Nonstop through 1999. The warning sound of Y2K hysteria. Experts speculated that when computer clocks ticked into the midnight of a new millennium, they would automatically roll back to the year 1900, losing all data that didn't exist a century earlier—obviously, *everything*. While frantic programmers worked to fix the bug, the global media catastrophized total social collapse starting the second after 11:59:59 on December 31, when our essential technologies malfunctioned.

For my family, the specter of Y2K eclipsed anything technical or even terrestrial. We feared no failure in electronics. Instead, we fixed fearful eyes upon the End Times.

My family claimed to follow The Word closely, but we really took bits and pieces from our cultural traditions; our practice was heavily syncretic. We bought red currant juice and value packs of wafers to take Holy Communion after prayer meetings at our house. Sometimes, my mother wore a tallit, a fringed shawl some Jewish people wear during prayers. Superstition took up so much space. Once, the five of us were going out, and my mother spotted a praying mantis on the windshield. It wasn't just a bad omen; she feared some intention of the insect itself. We sat in our minivan with the doors locked—as if that would be a sufficient form of protection—while my mother prayed against the praying creature. My father got impatient and threw the car into reverse. The mantis moved. We were safe.

Leaving behind England and its moderate and subdued Anglicanism, in America my parents found houses of worship that followed a more familiar tradition. Here, some enclaves in our immigrant community fomented an idio-syncratic style of evangelism. Within these Protestant sects of nonspecific denomination, the popular philosophy was Pentecostal—one's experience of the Holy Spirit should be direct, intense, and personal. Some endorsed the prosper-ity gospel, a doctrine affiliating righteousness with wealth. People prostrated themselves before pulpits, crying out for dollars and green cards.

Our life in the church revolved around charismatic preach-ers: prayer warriors who led with the fire of their rhetoric and hyperemotion. I grew up around routine exorcism—before a devoted flock, preachers seemed to cast out demons. Congre-gations tried to drive out disease using only their hands and the hallowed names of Jesus. *King of Kings; Bishop of Souls; Fountain of Living Waters; Lion of Judah; Lamb.* Worship-pers outdid each other in their performative displays of gifts of the spirit, like prophetic vision; the ability to interpret language spoken in "tongues"; and dancing in step with the Holy Ghost. I grew up in churches with eight-hour services (the rationale being that if you can give your boss eight hours a day, you can give God eight hours, too). Churches where chairs were broken when people had fantastic fits. Churches where Hellfire was literal, and a pastor might point to *you*, specifically, to tell you that you were heading there, and sooner than you thought.

During the breathless uncertainty of the Y2K drama, we heard from all those people who never get tired of incorrectly predicting the End of the World—*they were certain this time; we must trust them this time*. We heard about the Rapture, when God would lift the faithful to Heaven, how they would abandon their pets, families, car keys. Even the clothes on their backs would be left on Earth, disheveled and random on the spot they fell—outfits that day just littering the ground. Planes piloted by Christians would fall out of the sky. Those left below would endure the apocalypse, Hell on Earth, before going to another Hell awaiting them in the afterlife.

Sermons on the prophecies in the Book of Revelations felt urgent and immediate. A backdrop of constant prayers like fever dreams intensified as the year spent itself, petering out toward a final installment. My family had always passed New Year's Eve in church, praying the whole night through for the coming year. Suddenly, the notion of a "coming year" was obsolete. We bought anointing oil in bulk at a megachurch gift shop, stocking up on essential supplies for a day that was certainly coming—that day after which every space on our kitchen calendar was blank. Nothing came next. *FIN*.

I must not use that word: "cult."

In my house, I was initiated into apocalyptic paranoia. Religion touched everything in our lives as my parents prepared for the great ride ahead. Little things—I wasn't allowed to watch *Sabrina the Teenage Witch*; dress up for the new tradition of trick-or-treating; or read anything subversive, like *Harry Potter*, which I did read in secret, anyway. Movies with the demon doll Chucky were—are still—banned in our house. At private Bible study sessions, we were trained to look for signs: for the mark of the Beast and potential Antichrists. We listened for the sound of trumpets signaling the return of the Son of God.

I believe my parents were agnostic regarding the precise date of the apocalypse; mostly, I think they saw no harm in leaving the door open. Paranoia needs only that little bit to take hold. Once those preachers whipped up my mother, my father hadn't the will to stop her. I had no doubts about *their* fate, only mine. Every time my parents were late picking me up or coming home, I panicked, thinking that the Rapture had come unseasonably early and taken them.

Throughout that silent stage, my mind wouldn't turn itself off. "Please don't send me to Hell; Don't send me to Hell," I bargained, trembling with the violence of my involuntary thoughts. I was taught that the singular unforgiveable sin is cursing the Holy Spirit. Against my will, intrusive thoughts made me cross this line—my own treasonous thoughts began dancing around the ultimate and irrevocable taboo.

My life became *Hell-centric*. In my journals from that time, I can see my scrawl and scribble like demented memos begging pardon and entreating eternal life. Over and over, like punitive lines assigned to a naughty student in detention: *I will not go to Hell; I will be good; I will not go to Hell; I will be good.* All things remotely religious grew burdensome, weighted with a physical dread. It became intolerable to see my father watching the Christian channel TBN or hear my mother cooking and singing that damned song, "Holy, Holy, Holy." I took two-hour showers to avoid family prayers before bedtime. I hid my Bible.

Each Sunday, I was woken up just before seven a.m. by something unseen. Every other day, I slept until an alarm sounded, and if one didn't, then clear into midafternoon. Only on Sundays would I wake unnaturally early, as if my body had internalized the routine of churchgoing days and roused itself in anticipation, knowing something loomed.

Those Sunday mornings, I always tried to fall back to sleep, wanting to wake up safely on the other side of the morning. If we missed church, that would mean a week's reprieve, a week of relief from obsessive thoughts: *There must be devils somewhere; somewhere must be the Devil.* On most Sundays, no such luck. Shuffling in my parents' bedroom.

Quiet, bright gospel music. Footsteps. When my parents came to wake me, I would feign chronic pain; I was too ill to rise. Pathetic but rarely convincing.

The morning for which all the world was holding its breath arrived dressed in demure half-light, nudging my windowsill. *Understated*: it came not at all like a thief in the night. Passing the uneventful morning, every hour thereafter—an hour of overwhelm.

By nighttime on New Year's Eve—the last night I was supposed to be on Earth before being judged and sorted as saint or sinner—I was stupefied. Catatonic in the cold of our inaugural Connecticut winter, in the distance I felt from my family, who all seemed oblivious to my imminent damnation. I couldn't express my fears to them, as I thought that voicing doubts made them stronger. Of what I was taught, I believed in only the bad and trusted no concept of mercy. Maybe if I died in a mass casualty event, I might go unnoticed in the bedlam at the Pearly Gates. My best hope was oblivion. I was numb to their God. I heard nothing in response to my prayers. He, too, had fallen silent that year, His speechlessness matching my own. We were both struck dumb.

The great anticipation for the finale of the known world left our community collectively disappointed after all our morbid curiosity to see such a thing come to pass. Like the rest of that year: *nothing actually happened.* No . . . In the second after the clock clicked over into the year 2000, and everything was as before, *something* happened . . . I lost my little faith.

The one story I was always promised was true was the "Good News" of the Christian gospel. But in this good news, there is one original flaw: there in the name. The Classical Greek word *"euangelion"* ("evangel" in English) referred to good tidings brought by an auspicious messenger—an angel.

The direct translation in Old Saxon was *"gōdspell"* (*"gōd"* meant "good" and "spell" meant "news"). In English, the word *"gōd"*—which originally only meant "good"—was mistaken for a similar word: "God." An error made the *good spell* divine: the literal word of God. Godliness became gospel. Gospel truth replaced all truths.

The gospel was good news, but it was a mistake.

If I was not a Christian—or a girl desperately trying to become one—*what was I?*

I wasn't English anymore—if I had ever been close to any such thing. English being my second language, my British accent was always "off." In high school, I found out that some students thought I faked a British accent the entire time just to be quirky.

After serving a year of our sentence in Connecticut, my family returned to England for the first time since we left five years earlier. We were there for three days in the summer of 2000, a long layover on our way to Nigeria. This trip stunned me—how little everything in England had changed, compared to how much I had. I was thirteen.

Our first morning in Reading, we took the bus straight to the town center. We spent it walking around, marking what remained the same. Smelly Alley reeked of fishmongers' stalls. The department stores we knew were all there, precisely as we knew them. Ruins by the abbey were decomposing haphazardly, as they had been. Now that I was a teenager, the unsupervised graveyard was finally an appropriate place to hang out. We stopped to satisfy our five-year craving for bangers and mash. In America still, we sample and never find pork sausages that taste like British ones; our hunt began in

Tennessee with the hopeful name of the Southern chain "Piggly Wiggly."

Leaving the town center, we walked back to our old neighborhood the same way we always did—never needing directions or losing our bearings, the route imprinted within us. We stopped at Wycliffe Baptist Church and found it empty, as the congregation was picnicking elsewhere. My mother was disappointed, but I was more interested in seeing if Gold Coin Chinese next to the Laundromat was still there (*it was*) and if their lo mein tasted the same (*it did, exactly*). It was midday as we approached Redlands Primary, and we heard the lunch lady Mrs. Rafiq yelling, using the same inflection I remembered, as she called kids in for lunch by the names of their classes: "Lydford dinners and packed lunches!" At a corner shop, the Pakistani proprietor immediately recognized my mother, and they fell into a conversation, picking up right where they'd left off half a decade before.

The exterior of the house I grew up in, the same. I was the first to reach to open the iron gate; it occurred to me that I'd left it unlocked after being the last one to walk away the morning of our departure. We knocked, and the landlady's daughter invited us inside to see its renovation. The interior of our close-to-condemned home was our great surprise—it had repudiated its classic dysfunction and dirt. Gone away, the gauntlet of spider corpses. No slime residue from snails that nightly found a way inside.

I wonder if my conscientious mother barely planned this trip because she didn't think we or the world would be there in the year 2000. She arranged our layover at the last minute, so we hadn't had time to tell anyone we were coming. When we arrived at our friends' houses, we had no idea if they still lived there. Over and over, my siblings and I were amazed to find every person at the same address. We'd knock on the door and be met by an old friend (*taller, wider, leaner*) or a parent (*gray now, more lines creasing eyes*). So clearly I remember their looks of bafflement turning into sudden recognition and smiles; their exclamations of shock and thrill; then calls to the rest of the family to "Come quick, come see who's at the door!"

That weekend, five old friends and I sat on the grass behind a closed council office and talked all day. Despite grand mutual promises, we hadn't once spoken by phone after I left. They wanted to know everything about America. As I answered relentless questions about school, guns, fashion, and music, I perceived the gulf that had opened between us: not the natural rift formed after missing milestones—five years of birthday parties and crushes—but a cultural chasm.

My speech had mutated, the texture of our conversation changed. I showed off a new vocabulary of American slang and felt awkward using Briticisms. For the first time since I was about seven, I could hear the earmarks of a Reading-English accent. My friends thought to praise me; they said I sounded American.

But I wasn't American yet—only *Americanized*.

Every junior high morning in homeroom, the Pledge of Allegiance piped in through the intercom. And every morning, my teacher, Mrs. Marino, watched me to make sure I placed my hand over my heart and mouthed the words. I wasn't sure I should even be saying them, as I was still not a citizen, but it was imperative to her—mother of a navy veteran and wife to another—that every student in her class pledged aloud. Out of a feeling of chagrin, when she fixed her hawklike glare on me, I complied with minimal protest.

My family had been permanent residents for five years, but we wouldn't secure citizenship for another year. We traveled to Hartford for our final immigration interview in the spring of 2001, when I was fourteen. As a minor, I couldn't participate in the swearing-in ceremony confirming us within the ranks of American citizenry and was simply handed a certificate. My sister had to do her own separate interview; she'd turned eighteen. We were lucky it only took six years to process our naturalization, the minimum amount of time a green card holder must wait before applying for citizenship—it can take more than ten.

The day our blue passports arrived in the mail, I refused to sign mine. My mother, exasperated by my reluctance, gave me no choice. I resisted becoming American; leaving my signature on that line felt like losing. *Losing what?* Perhaps my bonds to Nigeria, quickly deteriorating.

I began to hate my mother calling Nigeria, when she would hand me the phone and instruct me to greet one person after another. The call quality was invariably poor, and we had to scream to be heard. This is the soundtrack to my adolescence: my mother hollering in Hausa to a numberless series of relatives, inquiring about health and weddings, and meddling in the dramatic dynamics between first, second, third, and fourth wives in a marriage. I began to worry I was butchering Hausa and struggled to think of what to say and how to be appropriate: conversations followed strict protocols respecting age, gender, and other distinctions. The personal connection frayed as the calls dropped.

My allegiances: *unclear.*

My African identity shifted through stages of grief.

My native language shamed me when my parents spoke in public.

Maybe I tried to renounce my new passport out of guilt.

In honesty, I would have given anything to simulate that eternal emblem of cool, the American teen. I was a fraud.

Connecticut was the worst place we ever lived.

I quieted the internal screaming by exhausting myself mentally, taking the hardest classes in school and redirecting uneasy energies toward becoming an obsessive student. It was soothing to fret over nothing, like the thickness of printing paper used for an essay or the best font for the cover page, which no teacher asked for. After a day of extravagantly empty anxiety, I could sleep soundly in the room I shared with my brother in our two-bedroom apartment; my sister had left for college, so we economized. I never woke up wanting to go to that flat, featureless high school, but I escaped through perfectionism and grade-grubbing.

The full world had become small, my personality misshapen in distasteful reaction. I never came out of my shell. Rather, I replaced one shell with another and another, trying on and discarding selves like discount dresses. I remodeled myself at the beginning of each of the three years we spent in Connecticut—adopting three radically different styles. Most adolescents do something similar, but my peers' experimentation was organic compared to my own methods. I researched the niche or subculture I wanted to infiltrate and strategized how I might ingratiate myself within a clique. Each time they sniffed out my inauthenticity, I plotted the next façade I would present.

I initially tried to be trendy, seeing an opportunity at the dances held twice a year. The first semester in that new school, I stole tube tops from my sister's closet, which hugged me after I began to develop quickly. I bought tight metallic silver jeans so shiny they were reflective. Tight clothes were new for me, but surprisingly, my mother was okay with the fit, thinking I'd lose the extra weight she nudged me about. Those jeans and tube tops didn't make me any more popular on the dance floor, but they sometimes worked with the boys living in navy base housing, where I was intermittently invited to waste delinquent fall days.

I couldn't decide which era of American history I should belong to. My musical taste developed after I fell for those ubiquitous TV commercials in the early 2000s that offered twelve CDs for twelve cents. I signed up with my parents' credit card, getting myself into a lot of trouble after we discovered the catch making that low price possible: enrollment in an expensive monthly subscription service. I was put on parental probation for years, but I never had to return those twelve CDs. One of them was the hyped, heavily promoted compilation of the Beatles' number one hits. Listening to those songs, I became fixated on that bygone era. I started listening to albums popular during the '60s and '70s in the order they were originally released. When came the late '70s, punk music like the Sex Pistols, the Clash, and the Ramones made me destroy my clothes.

I practiced at this: changing what I was, projecting and pretending.

After school, I nested and shopped in a Goodwill frequented by geriatrics—because it was cheap and close to home, and I wasn't allowed to take the bus to the mall. I joined the theater club to gain access to the drama department's sewing machine and accessory closet. The cynical punk kids never found me convincing—me, the poser who was too annoying even to teachers to be their pet. I saved lunch money to outfit myself in a camo jacket held together with rock band buttons and oversized safety pins; in combat boots; in the splurge item of a $20 pleather moto jacket.

Tiring of trying to fit in with the surly punks, I regressed to the heyday of hippies—dressing like the earthy type, not the psychedelic or the radical. My look: real and fake flowers and flowing bohemian skirts. I was a product out of time.

After our visit to Nigeria the summer before high school, I brought back a tunic, which I tucked away in the back of my closet. I picked its pattern because there was nothing like it in all the fabric markets—not a typical, bold West African print, but a modernist composition of pastel cubes: pale mathematics. The seamstress tailored the fit to my body; this garment was mine and made for me. I didn't know it at the time, but it would be the last custom apparel I'd personally select and oversee in my country. Had I known, I would never have given it away to a girl I was trying to impress, someone I hoped would induct me into her society. She didn't cherish the tunic, of course, not recognizing its significance, while I resented the prettier way it hung on her thinner, tall body. I didn't want to see it on myself—nor myself in it. That material *meant* something, and I only wanted it draped over someone else. I wanted to be draped over someone else.

I gave another classmate a bracelet of dear Indian gold acquired during the same trip home. In my culture, gifts of gold passed down along a female line are a priceless, delicate inheritance. When I regifted the bangle, I didn't think it was real gold because of the casual way my great-aunt had slipped it off her arm and handed it to me; she remarked that I looked like her and was pleased. I thanked her and thought it was painted tin. I didn't know Indian gold is *supposed* to look almost orange. I never appreciated how soft it was—how if I wore it with other bracelets, their edges would cut into its yellow meat, marring its filigree.

10

TRIBE AND TONGUE DIFFER

M ary" is my original mystery.

Somewhere, its meaning went missing. Bitter or beloved. Ocean or child.

My first name was the most popular American girls' name from the time anybody started keeping track until just two generations ago. It no longer cracks the top one hundred. Its first form in Classical Hebrew, which was transcribed without vowels, was "Mrym." Miryam was the sister of Moses and the earliest Biblical prophetess, introduced in Exodus singing the "Song of the Sea." She crossed dry land in the miracle of the parting Red Sea; then "deep waters congealed" to drown her enemies. She survived leprosy. In the later centuries of the New Testament, her name was common enough to belong to the mothers of James, John, and Jesus.

A Greek translation modified the name into Mariam. Early Latinate Bibles gave us Maria. The modern Mary first appeared in 1530 in a Middle English Bible, an Anglicization of the French Marie. Other forms render it: Muire in

Irish; Meryem in Kurdish; Miren in Basque; Malia in Hawaiian; Maija in Latvian; Moira in Scottish; Voirrey in Manx. The Quranic Arabic name is Maryam. In Hausa, it is also Maryam—as well as Mairi, Mairo, and Mariamu.

My name's influence is evident. But its ancestry remains unclear. Mary has a mysterious etymon—that essence or truth of a word revealed within its origins. It is not even known if Mary is originally a Hebrew name, whether from the Hebrew root "*mr*," meaning "bitter," or "*mry*," meaning "rebellious." Some etymologists argue that it comes from the early Egyptian language: from a possible expression for a "beloved" daughter, a "wished-for child." Every inquest into a definitive root or precise meaning dead-ends in disagreement.

Mary is a name made sense of in water. Most often, the meaning of Mary is given as "ocean of misery"—likely referencing the historic suffering of the Israelites. "Sea of bitterness" is an accepted alternate.

Ocean of misery. Sea of bitterness. Drop of sorrow.

I have wondered: *Why would anyone call their child this?*

While in my mother's womb, I was called Amina. Like Mary, Amina is the name of a mother of divinity, that of the Prophet Muhammad's.

The inspiration for my gestational name was a queen of Zaria, one of the seven medieval Hausa states. Queen Amina ruled the southernmost state in Hausaland in the late 1500s. When we visited Nigeria, we spent much of it in this former queen's territory—within ruins of the city walls she erected for her people's protection, still called "Amina's walls." She built her empire through conquest; ironically, her name means "peace" in Arabic.

Amina was raised to rule as the eldest daughter in a royal

Muslim family that invested in her political education. Queen in her own right, she is the only female empress of Hausaland in a millennium of oral and recorded history; according to the *Kano Chronicle*, she was the first to bring us eunuchs and kola nuts. Her forty-year reign came at a time when the Hausa had wholly embraced rigid gender roles: when women—who once prominently led as priestesses of traditional religions—began to withdraw from public life.

In our songs celebrating her, she is a lady of war, one who rides horses immodestly, and a woman as masterful as men. Queen Amina expanded the reach of her dominion to unprecedented bounds. As one of the most famous Hausa women of any period, her history is so mythologized that her life and her legend are hopelessly entangled. I hope this is true: that the first order she issued her people was "Sharpen your weapons." Like my mother, Amina was said to have received aggressive proposals of marriage daily, but she refused to marry and share power. Rejecting all offers, she defied convention by taking lovers. Then (according to legend) she killed every last one of them. After occupying a territory, each night she slept with a different man from that place. And each morning, she had him beheaded to keep their secret.

The university where my parents met is in the modern-day state still called Zaria; the women's hall where my mother lived was named for the queen. My mother taught me to revere Amina because I am her direct descendant, though this cannot be true. Most likely, my young mother, falling for my father—to date, the only man she's ever kissed—looked to Amina to make her fearless in the face of first love.

The idea of naming me Amina was disavowed after one of my aunts married a polygamous Muslim man, becoming his third wife. In the Hausa Muslim tradition, the firstborn male should be called Muhammad. My mother wanted to minimize the number of Islamic names in her family and re-affirm her own devotion to Christianity by inscribing faith in the name of her lastborn.

In an alternate history, I keep my original name—"Amina" comes from the same Hebrew root that evolved the word "amen," meaning "truth."

In my culture, a name is a living thing with such power that it spells life or death. In a Hausa tradition, picking a name with a repellent meaning makes malicious spirits believe your infant is unwanted and therefore leave it alone. Mutuwa is born to die; Rakiya escorts the dead. Yadakunya is thrown away in shame. Some parents whisper a secret name to their child that must never be revealed to anyone else—its disclosure carries the risk of a curse.

Much of my convoluted background can be condensed into the fifteen letters plus one hyphen that constitute my name: Mary-Alice Daniel.

A name is a cipher. Letter by letter, it diagrams the influence of religion or regime. My father, Harold, and his peers have "ridiculous" names like Tennyson and Griffith, because a courtly English name was considered a status symbol in their time and place of birth, pre-Independence. Many of his generation also have names in his native Longuda, but other tribes like the Yoruba or Igbo retain a much stronger tradition of naming in their own languages. The Yoruba name Tokunbo celebrates a child born overseas, commonly in England. My family doesn't know a single Nigerian who has the same name as their father or mother; seldom do parent and child share. In Nigeria, your child's name is given to honor and flatter someone more important or famous than yourself.

Imagine the meltdown when I told my parents I planned

to change my name at eighteen to Johanna Maserati, after my favorite Bob Dylan song and his favorite car. They were furious, knowing very well the kind of administrative nightmares incorrect information can bring down upon you. Within the disarray of documentation I've amassed as a serial immigrant, in some records, I am officially Mary-Alice as one hyphenated first name. In others, Mary is my first name and Alice, my middle. In one file, I am archived as Mary-Alice Alice Daniel.

If another Nigerian happened to come across me by name only, they wouldn't know that I'm also Nigerian. Here in the West, I can readily identify other Nigerians by elements of Yoruba names—*tolu, temi, oyin, ayo*—and by Igbo affixes—*inma, ukwu, obi*, plus the prolific letter *z*. I recognize Christians in sunny abstractions like *Peace, Patience, Blessing*, or *Good Luck* (our last president). But I am usually left explaining my name, even to fellow countrymen and tribesmen.

Mary was an unusual choice for a baby born in the "Holy North" of Nigeria. As was the hated Alice, added in honor of my mother's nicest missionary teacher. Girls of the North typically take names from the Islamic tradition, particularly names of the Prophet Muhammad's wives and family—Zainab, Habiba, Amina. Arabic names are adapted into Hausa with slight adjustments—Mariamu instead of Maryam; Zainabu for Zainab. Had I been named after Queen Amina, I would have a perfectly appropriate name. Instead, my mother signaled her "salvation" by forsaking baby names outside Christendom.

But she couldn't completely shake the Islamic impulse. She chose Mary for me because she imagined it would find favor with all descendants of Abraham: Muslims, Christians, and Jews.

A name may be magic. It may spell out protection. The

Hand of Mary—an emblem of an open right palm—is protective in those three Abrahamic faiths, a talisman against envy and the evil eye. The symbol, also known by the Arabic term *hamsa*, is seen throughout the Middle East and beyond to North Africa and the nomads. A lidless almond eye stares knowingly from the centers of palms in jewelry and in amulets placed around the home. In henna, the *hamsa* adorns the bodies of Northern Nigerian women. The "woman's holy hand" represents virgin, wife, prophetess, goddess. Jews call it the *Hand of Miriam*. Its five fingers—the five books of the Torah and the five pillars of Islam. To Christians in regions where the Hand is familiar, it represents the reaching Hand of God, its sole masculine form. The symbol predates all three religions as a fertility fetish representing the Ancient Egyptian deity Isis: the Hand of the Goddess bearing fruit.

I have a measure of agency in the name "Mary."

When I was in Year 1 in Reading, my class held regular sessions with parent volunteers. One day, I was paired with another girl's father. At the top of our math worksheet, there was a blank after the word "Name." I filled it out, and he gently said, "No, write *your* name." I replied that I had, and he repeated, "No, write *your own* name." It took a few exchanges for me to realize I'd written the word "Name" instead of "Nana." We laughed it off—a silly mistake, a momentary miscue because the two words look similar—but I did wonder if he might actually have thought I didn't know how to write my own name. This little moment. The first time I thought my name odd.

When we moved to Nashville, I took advantage of being in a new place where no one knew me. At eight years old, I abandoned Nana, the only name everyone in England had called me. I feared Nana was too conspicuous—that it sounded infantile and that its vowel sounds exposed my foreign accent. Upon moving to the US, I immediately noticed how Black American names were mocked, even though their inventiveness should be admired. I heard that story of the twins called Lemonjello and Oranjello and their sister, La-a (pronounced "Ladasha")—and wanted nothing original for myself.

I started going by a "normal" name. In Tennessee, "Mary-Alice" seemed tailor-made for assimilation. "Mary" still enjoys top-twenty popularity across Southern states, and both my double first name and last name, Daniel, are coded as American Southern. One famous Tennessean shares my last name, emblazoned across bottles of aged whiskey: Jack Daniel of Lynchburg. It's most often in the South that people accept Daniel as accurate the first time without me having to clarify: "no *s*."

Replacing the name you always responded to takes getting used to. A name taken out of shame will feel unnerving. Though I made my American debut as Mary-Alice, all my new classmates and teachers immediately shortened it to Mary, and I was too cowed to correct them. For months, I would fail to respond to Mary, forgetting that she was who I had become.

I have felt estranged from the name Mary because it never seemed to match me. After a rapid generational decline in popularity, those who now share my name are typically older, commonly Catholic, and generally white. If only knowing my name, people are often surprised when I materialize.

I have quarreled with Mary. Immersive water of misery.

But maybe this name's admission of wretchedness is more honest. If names hint at the aura, even the marrow of us, perhaps they should all be less lovely.

I have come to admire my name's incongruity. That I find it ill-fitting is fitting.

My name tells an essentially Nigerian story—the same story of colonization told by the name of Nigeria itself. Mrs. Flora Shaw—the wife of the mastermind behind the British system for ranking our tribes—was also a journalist covering the colonies from London. The name *Nigeria* was first printed in her column in 1897. "Nigeria" is a portmanteau of "Niger" + "Area": clinical language parceling out property. In 1908, the *Oxford English Dictionary* christened the earliest "Nigerian." All of us now—regardless of tribe or faith—affectionately call our country "Naija."

A bizarre drama recalled us home to Naija in 2000. My uncle's fourth wife bit the ear off his third wife. The fight was triggered by a rote accusation of theft against the junior wife; it turned violent when the missing cookware was located, damaged. Over the phone, my mother played the mediator, a role that made her miss our country, its conflicts. Later, settled within the privacy of my uncle's compound—designed to keep his four wives separate and peaceful—we saw the pared ear: ulcerating around its edges, so slow to heal.

This scene unfolded the summer before I started high school in Connecticut, which my family spent in Nigeria for an extended visit after our three-day layover in Reading. In the year 2000, we returned to the same, stable state of crisis as before, as ever. The familiar dangers worsening—petty crime, violent crime, terror, police.

Some things had changed—there was a new "queen" amongst our younger cousins, a new label on tins of canned beef. All summer, we noticed silly things about a place that no one else did because they'd lived there too long. The entitled cow sauntering around a gas station. The retro airport lounges: straight out of the '70s or Soviet era. That impossible sea of crisp white collared shirts on men defying air pollution.

That summer, there was a burial. Actually, there were three. One: *Tuberculosis.* Two: *Old age.* Three: *No guardrail along the overpass on the road from Katsina to Kano.*

In the summer of burials, we traveled like this: three or four days staying with one relative before moving on, taking day trips to see everyone we knew within a twenty-kilometer radius, then returning each night to sleep under unreliable ceiling fans. On the morning of a departure, breakfast was fried eggs and sweet processed bread dipped into tea thick with canned condensed milk. Always tea over coffee—Britain's stamp.

Midday, we'd stop at open-air markets to buy fruit and Fanta for ourselves and meat pies for thin children, and we stood out enough to be accosted by the curious. Foods tasted abnormal to us: water and cake and what my relatives called "Irish potatoes," the miniature, tasteless yield of unpredictable Nigerian agriculture. The summer of funerals was also the summer of weddings, and there was a shortage of wheat flour. Wedding cake was made with potato flour instead.

Once a month, the government ordered people to stay home and clean their houses and land. On "Cleaning Saturdays," we couldn't go anywhere until afternoon; police closed markets and set up roadblocks along main roads—anyone caught without a permit could be arrested. These shutdowns were ruled unconstitutional and retired in 2015, but while they lasted, their approach to environmental sanitation was characteristically Nigerian—bold and chaotic.

Navigating Nigeria—*bureaucracy, infrastructure*—can be a god-awful experience. Solving a simple problem requires superhuman resourcefulness and a minimum of an entire day. Any matter more challenging to sort out takes weeks, months. The infuriating incompetence is a holdover from the colonial period. In the 1950s, as the independence movement crested, the human cogs in the colonial machine made sure nothing worked smoothly as a way of frustrating the British. Inefficiency became a feature, not a bug, in their resistance. The problem is that this inefficiency, once ingrained, was not banished along with the British. Things are still upside down.

The roads were so bad that it took hours to get anywhere: a whole day to travel fifteen miles. Meters and meters and meters and mirages. A road through a country is particular about what it shows you—only one side of things at once. We traveled beside red chalk cliffs and looked for roadblocks. Looked for bandits. We couldn't travel at night and risk encountering armed robbers and kidnappers, so if dusk found us still in transit, an ill feeling would brew inside the convoy as we became anxious for shelter. It was best journeying from villages to cities, leaving places too remote and dark to feel safe and moving toward industry and light.

The road got worse. The road could not even be called a road. It was more an obstacle than a way. In the cities, we stalled in traffic for hours—pedestrians outpaced cars while buses plodded through, glutted with people stuffed in and limbs spilling out like rags, limp and wet. My brother and I started a contest counting Mercedes: hundreds of them, one of the most popular cars on the road. We counted accidents and saw horrific things, motorcycles and bodies smashed and strewn along the hot highway.

We were terrified of medical emergencies as we road-tripped; there were no decent clinics or hospitals. The few accessible had gruesome reputations for unsanitary conditions and malpractice—you were more likely to die from the hospital stay than from whatever brought you there. My brother-in-law's sister went into labor after a high-risk pregnancy, and hospital attendants forcibly removed her from the grounds while in childbirth because they predicted she would die and didn't see why her corpse should be their problem. Once home, she died in her own bed. These were the stories we would tell our American friends when we returned.

And my mother sat in the front, telling the driver stories from her childhood that made me love her more. At boarding school, she joined the choir every term despite being tone-deaf. Like clockwork, she was nominated but never elected head of the hall. Every Friday, when the girls received bones from the cow butchered that day—a treat to tide them over while awaiting its flesh—she never fought over them. She crept into peanut farms to steal as many as she could carry; she climbed mango trees.

I sat in the back with my baby cousin on my lap, wearing a seat belt across us both, shielding her tiny face from blasts of superheated air and all the exhaust. I played Dylan's "Visions of Johanna" on a loop—"*We'll sit here stranded, though we're all doing our best to deny it . . .*"—finding a cocoon in his haggard voice though it was hard-edged. Even as my cousins teased me about his grating rasp, bewildered by my choice of music when they expected me to introduce them to the latest American pop—I hid right inside it.

The old Range Rover Classic was a tough thing that my parents had bought for our trip with the intention of leaving it to relatives afterward. The way it bore us over potholes, byways, and dirt with a lumbering gait. Those roads instilled in me a fondness for rough patches of air during long flights. Airplane turbulence reminds me of that grueling motion over places in poor condition. *Feeling every kilometer within our bodies.*

The landscape passed. It was yellow, orange, and red.

Our daily rituals revolved around water and light—*the lack thereof.*

We arrived in some places on rainy days when the power had already been cut. We could barely see the faces greeting us in the drizzle and dimness, but knew they were like our own and familiar. Everywhere we went, every few hours, the power went out, cut by NEPA (the National Electric Power Authority) in unpredictable rolling blackouts. We had power less than half the time; we used that time to charge appliances, cook, and see. During the day, power cuts halted household activities, and at night, they pitched us into the density of sudden black. I adapted by developing a sense of where things were spatially—practicing how to get from one room to the next in starless darkness, never forgetting where I'd left my flashlight or where the sharpest table edges waited to wound.

One night, our only light came as unexpected fire—the fallout from improperly stored batteries. We lit kerosene lamps; their burning scent mingled with the chemical odor of our industrial insecticide. We sometimes had a generator, but fuel was costly, so they were not consistently used. It was sweltering without air-conditioning: when the power went out for too long, throughout the night one heard a stream of curses invoking the names of the Lord and NEPA.

The Sokoto house had no running water, so every morning, water had to be gathered from the small well shared with neighbors to either side of us. Several buckets were kept on the cool tile floor of the bathroom: half a bucketful poured in quickly to flush a toilet. One bucketful was heated over the stove—about two gallons per person—to take bucket baths twice a day: one cupful to wet yourself enough for a soapy lather and each precious cup thereafter mentally accounted to ensure enough to clean your body, wash your hair, then rinse.

The basic rhythms of Nigerian life were offbeat—difficult to get used to, day by day. One generation ago, the enterprise of an entire household for the whole day centered on water and food. Modern convenience is now evident at the table; Nigeria is one of the largest global markets for instant noodles, a new national staple. Most of my relatives, however, never changed their protocol: buying fresh ingredients and cooking thrice daily, sometimes on the stove, sometimes over open fire. Special meals feted my family's return, and we were drafted into their labor-intensive preparations. Crushing seeds into flour was the women's work I was assigned. That I tired so soon—evidence of never having developed the muscles needed to beat the oversized wooden stick and steady the vessel—always inspired laughter. I'd be given easier tasks: grinding vegetable skins to paste or splitting coconuts.

I was embarrassed about being noticeably Westernized in Nigeria. Then, back to being embarrassed about being identifiably African in America. When American friends came over to my house, I prayed my father wouldn't be wearing one of his dashikis made of the cruder fabric used in his home village, which my friends called "decorated sheets." I hoped against all hope that my mother wouldn't clean her teeth with a chewing stick, a popular West African product made from wood of the "toothbrush tree." She'd picked up the habit young and always brought back a stockpile. She used the softened splinters to scour her back teeth, the bark to polish them, contorting her face into a grimace.

I no longer belonged anywhere, and it was never more present a truth than when returning to the USA after visiting Nigeria. Always, just when I was beginning to acclimate after spending a long time in Africa, the act of returning to the West brought culture shock in reverse, as I stepped again into that malformed mold of "immigrant." When speaking Hausa in Hausaland, I spoke with an accent that instantly outed me as "other" to locals. Wherever I went in the West, the same issue followed me. There is no one I ever speak to who immediately recognizes me as theirs. I envy those who feel this affinity. Knowing your people as soon as they open their mouths must feel abundant.

Back Home once, my siblings and I rehearsed and performed the Nigerian national anthem, "Arise, O Compatriots," for an audience of cousins. We sang a prayer, a benediction, an appeal to corrupt leaders in "one nation bound in freedom, peace, and unity." These lyrics appear in the second attempt at our anthem, which combined phrases from submissions to a nationwide contest open to all citizens. The first anthem was written by a white Englishwoman and adopted on Nigeria's Independence Day in 1960, when it was predictably met with protest. Lillian Jean Williams's lyrics rang false: "Our own dear native land! Though tribe and tongue may differ, in brotherhood we stand, Nigerians all."

My cousins were unimpressed. I knew all the words to both anthems, and they did not, and I thought that proved something about my connection to our mutual country, but the bizarre performance only laid bare desperation and cultural degeneration. How my brother couldn't play football barefoot anymore, having no calluses, yet the local boys wouldn't let him play with shoes. How I went to the market stall and insulted the owner by handing him money with my left hand, the taboo hand.

Lacking light in more than one way, I moved unsteadily through darkening fields of misunderstanding and miscommunication.

Of course, I saw how my "truly Nigerian" family and I moved along unlike orbits: how we would never again sync. But I didn't want it named. Did they have to be spoken— the small shames isolating a girl estranged from her ancestral home and the people she was ferried away from? If I couldn't feel at home within my own family, itself within a culture built upon welcoming the lost stranger, providing water and refuge in the desert: Was there not something wrong with me in particular? Some impossible, incongruent element of my character?

We went on the road like a family of bandits, trying to grasp language, people, history—*trying to steal our culture back.*

Our visits were a big deal. To everyone who knew us or had heard of us, there was no such thing as not coming to greet us, the lost ones from "Amirka." Whichever place we stayed, people descended upon us in droves. Some came so far: one caravan drove for days from a city called Jos, which I was told stands for "Jesus Our Savior," though it does not. Visitors took over every room in a house and streamed outside into improvised seating—asking just to see me, asking how tall we had grown, their voices overlapping: *The girl is well but thin; Come stand in formation for photos; You have forgotten how to eat prettily with hands.*

My mother was patient as she explained how everyone was connected to us and had the great talent of remembering the exact nature of our ties to every person, even if she hadn't seen or spoken to them in decades. "Here is the youngest sister of my Head Girl . . . This woman and I played pranks in the dormitory . . . She was the only one you would let comb your hair . . . He brought you a blue dinosaur when you were born . . ." I love her more for the ways she tried to bind us in fellowship: to counterwork our unraveling.

Some of my unschooled relatives didn't speak English well, so our communication suffered. Nigerian Pidgin, a creole language spoken by more than half of the people in the country, serves as a common dialect mixing English and various tribal languages. Pidgin is casual, used to navigate markets and mass transport. Able to understand Pidgin, I was too self-conscious to use it; I felt it only sounded right with a certain accent, one I didn't want to fake. In Pidgin, to ask how someone is, you say, "How you dey?" or "How market?" Telling someone not to bother you, you warn, "Make you no vex me." If they persist, you might say, "I go scatter you! You dey craze!"

Nigerians take pride in the cutting way we insult one another. Roasting is an original Nigerian art form. *See your head like a calabash! Your legs dry like yams!* Some insults can't translate their impish clevernesses and won't sound like much to outsiders, but I assure you can devastate: *You bombastic element! Radio without battery!* My brother's childhood nickname was "Fanta Face, Coca-Cola body" because of the lighter tone of his face. When I overslept, my mother would say I have flat buttocks because I slept through the meeting where the angels handed them out. I never took these gibes personally and recognized the difference between lighthearted putdowns and curses uttered in anger, also heard often.

But I never laughed as hard as my family did. And I felt like a pest, interrupting the flow of conversation to ask what someone meant. I was having more and more trouble constructing complex, fluent ideas in Hausa. One curious reality of language retention became apparent—that the part of the brain responsible for understanding a language is different than the part responsible for recalling it. One understands much more than one can say.

Hausa has its own simplified pidgin, called "Barikanci." Its name refers to the British Army barracks, where soldiers from various parts of Northern Nigeria had to find a way to communicate. The language of the barracks is full of English and associated with non-native speakers. I related to its nature; I always kept one ear open for this pidgin, known as "Bastard Hausa."

Sometimes, I pretended to understand less of our language than I did, so I could hear what personal quarrels my cousins had with my voice, my accessories, the way I clung to my mother like a life raft. Sometimes, I didn't want to fit in. I so resisted that subtle bow I had to make when handing something to an older person, or the curtsey expected when being introduced to a senior. I was happy using respectful titles (regardless of relation, every older woman was "Auntie"; every elderly woman was "Mama") and maintained that deference in the West, but submissive physical gestures felt like vulgarities in my body.

Upon rising, Hausa children engage in a sequence of questions greeting their elders: *How did you sleep? Are you well? Are you tired?* This exchange is supposed to be an earnest inquiry into their health and well-being. I stumbled through; I *did* care, but I wasn't used to the social scripting. I couldn't show concern with a formula. The extended ritual of morning greetings made me reluctant for that first encounter of the day with my family; I favored the informal address my parents allowed, just a simple "G'morning." In Nigeria,

I risked shaming my parents for having failed to raise proper children. It didn't help that there was always someone quick to catch every minor mistake I made.

Etiquette was enforced. Courtesy was compulsory. Tradition took over. There was a social hierarchy based on gender and age, which I moved up each return visit as I got older. At first, I was the last to eat and the first sent to fetch things, the one told the most to be quiet. In later years, I lorded over a gaggle of younger cousins who looked up to me as I corralled the legions of children swarming every household.

I had many girl cousins close to my age—we experienced adolescence worlds apart. They were my age until they were suddenly expected to start their own families. They were my age and had to choose between going without one necessity and another and another; my age and wed too soon.

In my maternal family's sphere in the sharia states, most marriages were arranged until the middle of the twentieth century, when more parents gave their children choices. Under the Islamic laws, a man is limited to four wives and expected to provide well for all; in Northern Nigeria, a few famously take many more. Arranged marriages remain common in rural areas. They ensnare the daughters of my mother's brothers and sisters who readopted Islam for love, safety, or social acceptance. Four cousins were married this way—two in polygamous marriages—all by the age of seventeen.

I felt guilty that I lived an easier life, one where I was able to be a child: no grunt work or weddings worried me. All my female cousins woke up early to fetch water, then spent the rest of their day cooking, cleaning, and taking care of younger ones. I helped ineptly. When they finished the work, we would talk outside about America—under open sky while toxic sprays fumigated our rooms before bedtime. We never talked about boys.

Through the years, my siblings and I played a competitive game with our cousins to see who could list all the cousins the fastest, by birth order or alphabetically. Bonus points if you could list your cousins' cousins, who are really your own cousins, too. My mother was the eldest of nine or ten fruitful siblings, and there came a point where I could not remember all their offspring: over forty. In this game, my score dropped over the years—*every point less, a person lost.*

My family put something in the hands of every person we greeted. Our itinerary was punctuated with exchanges where we emptied hard-shelled suitcases of their offerings. Good candy, toys, and clothes—bursting stores of mass-produced treasure along with a few luxuries for favorites. We filled our Samsonite again with cheaper gifts; illegal meat; curios. One set of distant relatives made me rich with plastic beads and with booklets flaking gold leaf in a script I could not read.

11

ALLOW SPIRITS TO
ENTER AND LEAVE

There was once a _____ who was my grandmother.
I struggle to resolve how to refer to my paternal grandmother and her beliefs—beliefs that invited accusations of witchcraft. Her nervous habits during prayers, like shuffling her feet back and forth, were interpreted by certain members of our family as attempts to undo those prayers. They say she sacrificed her children—my father's three brothers who died young—to preserve her youth and extend her own life. As proof, they cite the fact that she still lives. Nothing but her death would satisfy them.

The word "pagan" immediately comes to mind; my mind immediately rejects it. This Latin term's original connotation was unrelated to religion and referred to a villager, a bumpkin. *Pagan* later came to identify the adversaries of the earliest Christians, who fashioned themselves "soldiers of Christ." A pagan became the enemy of this new army—"One who worships false gods; an idolater; a heathen." *Wild, savage, wicked.*

I see my grandmother in her village, unprepared for the onfall of compulsory religion. I see her becoming the enemy. In modern, neutral usage, a pagan is one who adheres to non-Abrahamic religions, especially earlier polytheistic, nature-worshipping religions. Her name, Samailah, is the feminine Hausa version of Samuel, one of the last ruling judges in the Old Testament, who anointed the Kings of Israel. She, too, was a kingmaker. She is proud of her name and calls herself not pagan but Protestant. She is both, neither.

The Longuda, my paternal tribe of one hundred thousand, are obscure. *Obscure*: I mean both *remote* and *difficult to discern*. Small in size and status, they are notable as Nigeria's only matriarchy and known for frustrating missionaries with their pattern of pseudo-salvation. My great-grandfather was the first person in the Longuda tribe to be baptized after Danish evangelists arrived in 1911. His daughter, my grandmother, followed suit in adolescence. But she continued to make charms—out of wood from ebony trees where good spirits lived; out of bones, the small hands of animals that doubled as bushmeat. Instead of attaching charms to her body or bedclothes, she buried them.

Before the mass conversion of the Longuda, each member of a family kept a personal idol by their cooking hut. Idols are hollow vessels made of clay, like thin flower vases. At the top, where the mouth flares out, a second and third hole on either side allow spirits to enter and leave. The vessel is a holy space for welcomed spirits; evil spirits are cast out, sometimes only by its breaking. When a loved one dies, their soul might get trapped inside. Rituals must be performed to release them—for if they do return, they return cursed. By my grandmother's generation, most Longuda Christians had gotten rid of their idols—or they hid them. Instead of a clay congregation with a whole host of family gods, one shut away idols in shame. A neighbor might claim to have seen one in some dark corner.

Accusations of idol worship often preceded accusations of witchcraft. A Longuda witch—a *swanya*—has innate, inherited supernatural abilities and the will to harm. The *swanya* is blamed for disaster, for death itself—in folklore, her mere existence explains why people have to die at all. Missionaries teaching the Longuda hoped belief in witchcraft would dissipate as people converted. That didn't happen, not even after a long century of Christianization; in 1995, 80 percent of Longuda who identified as Christian reported a strong traditional belief in witches.

And witches are women. Longuda matriarchy was oriented around the feminine. The ideal of descending from a strong line of women lived alongside the idea that evil passes down *through* women. Since you belong wholly to your mother, if *she* belongs to the Devil, that is your inheritance. Your heredity might be of Hell.

Fortunately for my grandmother, the rumors swirling about her proved powerless. Because of her status and reputation in the village, they were endorsed mostly by in-laws and those with trivial vendettas. This is a mythos most in my family will not speak of, except in warning—to mention witchery is to summon it. Their silence is one of many spiritual paradoxes I grew up with. *That witches don't exist. That they once did. That they still do. They hold no power over us since Christ vanquished them. They hold so much power we must never speak of them.*

Years ago, when I first began experiencing sleep paralysis, it was always this grandmother I saw while I couldn't move. Her presence lurked by the far door even as I felt her weight oppressing me in the bed. I never know how to interpret her presence. Is she my protector or am I her prey? I have been taught that God is greater than the wicked. I ward her off. I consider that she brings blessings—

Of my 4.5 grandparents, she alone lives.

Yes, I want to live, too.

The last time I traveled to Nigeria, in 2011, I was twenty-four.

A few years before, a Danish newspaper depicted the Prophet Muhammad in twelve offensive cartoons. The resulting firestorm swept over and outside the European continent via demonstrations in countries with large Muslim populations. The cartoons were the spark that lit the match in regions already simmering in religious misease; the provocation destroyed tense truces and incited renewed animus. In the eternally agitated North of Nigeria, riots over the caricatures claimed one hundred lives.

My final visit had clouds over it—and some bright spots.

The trip was conceived after my sister got engaged to a man then living in Nigeria, who we've known since we were kids. My sister grew closer to him during our family trips in childhood, and they nurtured a long-distance relationship. My mother, sister, and I were anxious about the grim outlook for our safety, and we questioned if we could return. We decided that performing my sister's betrothal rites Back Home was worth the risk.

We three women traveled to our extended family home in Sokoto for my sister's Na Gani Ina So ceremony. *Na gani ina so* literally translates to "I have seen; I have loved." The groom's family visits his future bride's home bearing gifts, such as kola nuts and palm wine, that symbolize prosperity and attract fortune. If the proceedings are carried out in accordance with sharia, wine is forsaken for fruits and other objects of abundance. Presenting gifts, the groom declares his intentions before the two families.

Traditionally, this formality takes place before the courting stage, an opportunity for the suitor to express his official desire for a particular woman. It occurs after both families vet each other and consent to the match. My sister's fiancé is also a Hausa-Fulani Christian, the firstborn of a neighboring family that converted under the tiny circle of influence my grandfather exerted as the only local pastor. The two of them had already been dating for years; every effort was made to call attention away from this "vulgar" fact. In love matters, my family is illiberal.

On the morning of my sister's Na Gani Ina So ceremony, I woke up as soon as the roosters in the courtyard started crowing. *But maybe this I misremember*—roosters don't start crowing at a certain hour; most of them disturb through the night. My aunts and the rest of the household rose early to clean and prepare for the feast in the evening afterward. As with every event dependent on traversing Nigerian roads, no one could predict the hour that guests would arrive.

Aside from the unorthodox timing at a late stage in their relationship, we followed tribal customs closely. My cousins did my sister's traditional makeup—naturally, with a celebration that means the groom "loves what he sees," the focus is on feminine beauty. They applied henna, called *lalle* in Hausaland, where the ink of ground leaves has ornamented us for a thousand years. Ubiquitous in the Muslim world, *lalle* is an art my cousins have worked to master—learning to steady their hands for neat lines and wanting to outdo one another in intricacy. They practiced lettering *ajami*, the Arabic script used to write Hausa. They offered indulgent flowers; mandalas; fractals; teardrops. My sister chose curlicues and vines. My cousins modified the ink so its color would show up on the dark skin of her arms and hands, adding secret ingredients they refuse to reveal. I know that kerosene is one additive. They swear it is safe.

Next came the ritual with a flower I know only by the name *jan fure*: "red flower." We crush its petals as we rub them across our mouths, leaving a red stain for days on lips and teeth. With a closed mouth, *jan fure* looks like lipstick; when our crimson teeth show, we look like we've been drinking blood. My cousins finished her ceremonial cosmetics with kohl—*kwalli*—to shadow and line her eyes. The liner is made from crushed minerals, mainly the abundant galena found in deposits around Northern Nigeria. It is enshrined in Hausa culture to protect against the dry desert clime, against the evil eye. Ironically, some Nigerian *kwalli* carries toxic risk due to unsafe levels of arsenic and heavy metals. In our family photos, baby boys as well as girls wear it. They say it is not good to hold a baby with naked eyes.

My sister wore a hand-beaded yellow lace top with a matching skirt and head tie, an outfit that took months to make and was worn for this occasion and never again, like a wedding dress. She had to stand out. Unlike at other Nigerian functions, my relatives didn't match our own outfits with hers—nor with each other's—to avoid upstaging her. The rest of us dressed uncharacteristically, in understated style: in the Nigerian rarity of monochrome.

Her fiancé's family finally arrived. A pair of representatives from each family convened in the front room of my grandparents' house. Traditionally, the representatives are men, but my auntie Habiba appointed herself with no objections. The bride's parents are never permitted to represent her, because the honor is reserved for relatives who have been closely involved with the young woman's rearing. While the rest of us waited outside, a scripted conversation played out in Hausa. My relatives said to the groom's side, "We sowed some seeds." His representatives responded, "What kind of seeds?" The answer: "Some blessed seeds." His relatives concluded, "We want those seeds to be our own."

We came together to pray. Prayers were the mandatory bookend to all our affairs, even to unmistakably pagan traditions—sometimes, the wrought prayers felt reactionary. Later that night, my sister inspected the gifts from her fiancé's family. A tote bag stuffed with clothes she'd never wear; costume jewelry; two pairs of underwear; an ill-fitting bra. We were later told that the task of procuring her trousseau was handed off from one relative to another until the duty ultimately fell upon someone who barely knew her and was too timid to ask for any information or money to buy them. My sister happily redistributed them.

Where is the god of my life, the bringer of songs in the night?
Colonial West Africa was known as the "White Man's Grave" because of the tropical diseases that ravaged Europeans upon first exposure. The earliest missionaries to Nigeria embarked upon so-called evangelical suicide missions due to their high mortality rate. They sought both death and everlasting life. They were driven by faith, the thing that diminished within me.

That final trip, I managed expectations to profess a faith I no longer felt but could not safely reveal I lacked. I remember a church service. As the hymns started, I was distracted by some piles of tires outside being melted down into mirror frames. My step-grandmother noticed I wasn't paying attention. She would always watch me while we were in church, an overseer confirming I was making all the motions and being deeply moved. *"Ki yi waka,"* she commanded. She was telling me to sing, but I wasn't familiar with any of the Hausa songs. *"Je ne connais pas ces chansons,"* I said in the French she knew better than English. Then my mother turned to me as well, asking, "Why aren't you singing?"

I imagined a scene: The full congregation pressing around me—tawdry, red, tall—urging, "Sing, sing" in dozens of undecipherable languages. My step-grandmother leaned over to ask: "Are you ashamed of God?" I pretended not to hear her. She began singing louder, as if to overpower my blasphemy with her raised voice. That was the only harsh interaction I ever had with this otherwise sweet, mild woman. Something remarkable stands between me and my family of faith and cannot be reconciled. (More than a leap I can never take.)

Nigeria must be the world's most prayed-over nation. My country is divided into wartime parallels—a grand field of spiritual warfare. Within it, all those marathon, multiday revivals and vigils. Ninety percent of Nigerian Christians go to church at least once a week; this rate is one of the highest globally, double that of American Christians. I remember those services held by late-night lighting: bare bulbs in cool white, insecticide candles, butane, flashlights. Touring the South, you'll see a King of Israel Barber Shop; a Light of the World Boutique; a Salon of the Begotten Son. In Hausaland, to express agreement in prayer, Christians and Muslims alike say, "Amin." Across a scattered diaspora, our country is the top priority on prayer cards: *Father, put an end to economic recession. Let our prayers destroy every power of Hell at work here. Pray without ceasing for all thirty-six states of Nigeria. My country, oh!*

And Nigeria must be one of the most superstitious countries in the world. That women shouldn't pluck hairs in the dark; that women shouldn't sweep in the dark. Always about women, always about our activities in the nighttime. My mother passed these notions down to me out of some instinctual, protective fear: never quite believing them, never not. She warns that fake crying, like children do—*Saran kuka*—calls the worst luck, as I risk turning my pretend tears into real ones.

If someone admires the softness of your skin too intently, consider that she may want to eat you. You must rebuke her, saying, "If you're a witch, eat yourself." Avoid sleeping with your face uncovered and exposed to wandering, wicked spirits who might like your looks. Eating in the dark may be taken by the dead as an invitation to join you at your meal. In Western culture, food that has a familiar face feels forbidden: cats and dogs. In Nigeria, superstition determines what is evil to eat. In extreme cases, the food taboos of a tribe lead to malnutrition. The unthinkable fare in my native area: lizards, horses, donkeys, frogs.

The country became an international laughingstock in 2009 after police arrested a goat for witchcraft. BBC News reported that a goat was being held in custody at a police station after vigilantes made a citizens' arrest, believing the cloven-hoofed suspect was a robber with the power to shape-shift. In 2018, the current Nigerian president made a national address in order to discredit a conspiracy theory accusing him of being a clone. Of course, his public appearance only raised more questions for the paranoid speculators who picked apart his countenance and mannerisms.

In such a nation, hallucinatory voices are not automatically dismissed as insanity. Rather, possession might be good or bad, depending upon the spirit. In much of West Africa, auditory hallucinations are received as welcome messages from God or gods. Surveying schizophrenics about the voices in their heads, researchers found that some cultures do not always interpret "hearing voices" as mental illness. West Africans often report positive, personal conversations with the audible spirit world.

My maternal grandmother, a preacher's first wife, had passed a few years before this trip. After her death, my parents paid their tithes—10 percent of gross income—toward a new chapel being built in her honor. On this our final trip, we visited her village to see what our donations funded: a malformed skeleton of concrete block, and there was no roof. All work was stalled due to mismanagement. It looked decayed before it was half-built. We were patrons of embezzlement—of entropy.

My mother went into the room where her own mother lived and died. Upon my grandmother's death, all my aunts and uncles went into that room to pray and found a hidden cache of bills. The value of my grandmother's secret naira was $200; she had no reason to leave a will, so my family split it evenly. Each share so small, this was symbolic. My aunt told my mother all that happened; I heard them outside in the courtyard. My mother said, "What stops me from becoming so depressed is that I believe I will see her again." My aunt said something like, "Yes, we will see her again." My mother repeated the same thing five times during the conversation—*I believe I will see her again*. It hurt every time I heard it because, you see, I feel she is wrong.

The last time I was in Nigeria, I'd started writing about my family's miscellaneous and often mystifying religious record. One night, an aunt described how during one crisis, men with machetes went from house to house and door to door in search of Christians, attacking whoever they found within. The men spent their bloodlust a few doors down from where she and her children hid. This was her personalized miracle. It remade her.

I began to wonder who I would be had I never left Nigeria: meaning the mood and humor of my feelings for God.

Here I need a word that continually approaches—but never touches—"cult."

The version of Christianity my parents passed down to me took on a life of its own. If you are ill and do not heal, your faith is not strong enough. There is power in the tongue, they said, so I learned to avoid cursing myself by saying anything negative—to avoid speaking the truth if it was any less than idealized. *It shall be well with us. It shall be well.*

Our prayers were spectacles: *Prayers Soliciting the Sword of the Lord; Prayers Commanding High Places; Prayers to Root Out; Prayers Quenching Enemy Fire; Dealing with Horsemen; Destroying Marine and Leviathan Spirits; Deliverance from Animalistic Spirits; Prayers Releasing Shame unto an Enemy; Speaking to Mountains.*

I grew up in competition with my mother's God. She and I had a minor falling-out after I asked if she would sacrifice me if God commanded her to—like Abraham was prepared to do with Isaac in the ultimate test of faith. When she said she wouldn't kill me for anyone, I didn't know if I believed her: What else could a mother tell her child?

I never ran out of babyish questions about belief. If I asked them at Sunday school, I'd usually be dismissed. At home, I received unsatisfactory answers. How can Jesus be the Shepherd, the Lion, *and* the Lamb? Who did Adam and Eve's children reproduce with, if there were no other humans on Earth: With their mother or with each other? In the Book of Job, after God and the Devil murdered all of Job's children, why is the fact that Job had more children portrayed as fair restitution? Can children be replaced? In Hell, after trillions of years, wouldn't all memory of your sins be forgotten—would you remember what you were being punished for? In Hell, do they have difficulty creating a form of physical pain souls can perceive? Can a soul burn? Do they have to keep remaking souls when the undying fires burn through them? Is it sinner souls they are punishing—or brand-new baby souls?

Much of what I was taught wasn't rooted in Biblical texts but based instead on what a few preachers concocted. My faith community claimed strict adherence to fundamental Christianity while entertaining notions at odds with The Word, like belief in hexed and sacred places—a "moral geography" of rivers, rooms, and storefronts. Even now, when I confront my mother directly, I can't pin down or square her true mind. When I once called our cat my "baby," my mother made what I hope was a joke—that calling him that might curse me to bear a deformed child.

She has a prayer closet. It's just the abandoned walk-in wardrobe of an empty nester's house. In it, she keeps her prayer shawls, books, some candles. She prays kneeling on a pretty mat like Muslims do, facing no particular direction. During bad times, I can hear her wailing until three a.m. It seems a place of pain.

I was twenty when I finished reading the Bible, having started at the beginning at seven—the Age of Salvation. I discovered a passage at the very end, which I started regularly pointing out to my mother. Revelations 22:18–19 prohibits adding or taking away anything from the Good Book. These two verses from the final chapter of the final book of the Bible are threats: "For I testify unto every man that heareth the words of the prophecy of this book: If any man shall add unto these things, God shall add unto him the plagues that are written in this book. And if any man shall take away from the words of the book of this prophecy, God shall take away his part out of the book of life, and out of the holy city . . ."

I hoped this warning would discourage her more adventurous doctrines. It made no difference; I came home from college to find our cat's forehead greasy with anointing oil. My mother insists "Boo is a Christian cat" because of his tendency to show up and stick around whenever people are praying. She supposes he means to acknowledge his Creator in his lazy way. According to her, "Even animals must be anointed."

I try to understand why she believes as she does. She grew up in a world defined by absolutism and sharp divides along gender, class, and religious lines. Within that culture, she spent years in draconian boarding schools. Inside such a bubble—almost in captivity—young minds are molded by ideology to an extent beyond what is healthy. And now, her family faces genocide. Instead of being angry at God for not existing like I am, safe and spoiled, they seek Him in frenzy. All that senseless death is given meaning, some transcending design. It is hard for me to even *look* at news about our native region, the printed images always nightmarish. My blood curdles; I notice a body that could be my aunt. Could be me, if my mother hadn't taken me away.

My mother is stronger than I am. In spite of such suppression, Nigerian women are known to be bold, not permitting sexism to silence or render them passive. She taught me not to care about people's opinions. She says, "Care only what God thinks of you." Recently, I watched a home video of my seventh birthday party in England. While I played with friends, you can hear my mother off to one side saying, "I have to go to Whiteknights after I clean this mess." Whiteknights is the main campus of the University of Reading, where she cleaned lavatories while writing her dissertation. She used to take me on bike rides through the woods to the university, where I'd play or sleep under her desk while she worked at her Apple Macintosh. I was oblivious to everything she did for me.

Until I left home for college, we were so close. Generational differences and our polar mentalities pull us apart. I can't now say I know her well. Not long ago, she showed me a photo of herself at eighteen, a token of unrequited love kept in mint condition by one of her many admirers. Fifty years ago, his handwritten caption listed her hobbies: *Music, Photography, Visiting, Poetry.* I never knew she liked poetry. I went to her for a comprehensible answer, but she said, "I used to, but you are better, so I did not mention me." If she weren't my mother, we would find no reason to speak. Yet she is the love of my life and the main force within it, always pushing me toward or away from something. *Toward medical school; away from moving out of state; toward her Nigerian friends' sons; away from poetry.* Ultimately, she pushed me away from God.

I don't like her God. Despite growing up as a global stray, I was sheltered inside the confines of my conservative home, where His terrifying nature was the only one I knew. As I progressed through the Bible in adolescence, I came upon the undying problem of working out what was allegorical, what was literal, and how much fiction may be in "fact."

Driftless and without a home for most of my young life, I identified with the story of the Jews overcoming bondage in Egypt before wandering in the desert for forty years. Exodus presents like a historical narrative; archaeologists on countless excavations have tried to corroborate the timeline of the book in which my namesake, Miryam, first appears.

Sifting through all that sand, instead they found evidence precluding the possibility of most events in Exodus. When I learned that this story cannot be true as it happened in the Bible, the whole thing started to seem like it had nothing to do with me.

For twenty years of bedtime sessions, I hated having to pray aloud in front of my family. The five of us assembled in the living room most nights a week, most of my life. My father always prayed first, my mother second. After them, we children went in an arbitrary order dictated by my father—I think to make sure we stayed awake. We kneeled over couches and chairs, which actually makes for a comfortable position to nap. Female worshippers must cover their heads; I used my scarf to block out light for deeper sleep. My bored siblings and I used signals, blinking and making funny faces, hoping our parents wouldn't open their eyes and catch us in one of the more egregious childhood offenses. Sometimes, I volunteered to go first and get it over with, so I could sink into pillows and uninterrupted daydreams about unwholesome things.

My mother took the longest time to pray, spending thirty-plus minutes thanking God for minutiae ("every pore on our faces"); asking Him to protect us in random, unlikely scenarios ("arrows"); listing all His names and titles in various languages and all *our* full names, too; quoting long verses; finally, speaking in tongues, avidly at first, then winding down . . . Over her holy babble, my father appointed the next speaker. When his turn came, my brother would ask for stuff—material things like video games; sometimes favors, sometimes inappropriate ones like revenge. My sister complained.

In prayer, my father was formal, almost corporate. But not one of us suspected that he questioned his faith—or for how long. He hid this huge secret, maybe for decades.

When my father was ten, his younger brother fell onto a knife. Their father carried his injured son on his motorcycle to the missionary hospital; the strain of shouldering him made his hernial repair come apart. Their mother ran the five miles to the hospital, ripping open surgical stitches over an abscess in her breast. My father ran there and then back to his village to muster people to donate blood. Doctors found a match with a cousin—his blood didn't coagulate when mixed with my uncle's blood. This elderly relative insisted the doctor take the necessary two pints of blood from him immediately, then fainted and was also admitted. A total of four members of my father's family were hospitalized that night. His seven-year-old brother survived. Running from the hospital to the village not knowing if his brother would live—that was the first time my father felt afraid of the familiar darkness.

After this ordeal, his house became a house of prayer. All in the household lived in gratitude for His miracle of healing. God spared my uncle only for him to contract HIV in Nigeria after going to a dentist who used unsterilized equipment (he had a toothache). He died at the age of thirty-nine, the year after we arrived in America. We tried sending medications through the post, but our packages didn't always arrive, and anyway, the disease had been caught late and initially misdiagnosed. No hope to have. For his brother to be saved then lost to a preventable disease the same way his other two brothers had succumbed in childhood—both dying within five years of their original family "miracle"—this broke my father.

After Christmas dinner a decade ago, we were all five sitting in the living room, and my father had something to say. He announced that he was an atheist and cited a litany of abuses perpetrated by the church. Maybe there had been clues pointing to his creeping apostasy. He got frustrated by my mother's superstitions, having a more analytical mind. He approached God as if in a seminar; long ago, he'd walk us through the lectures he prepared on different theological topics—*How to Have Faith; How to Have Doubt; The Correct Pronunciation of "Hallelujah."* He loves things worldly and freewheeling—Malbec and James Brown.

I hadn't noticed my father's metamorphosis, because once I was out of his house, I didn't notice anything about him. When I visit, he burrows in his office full of out-of-print anatomy and sci-fi books. The two of us have never discussed our mutual skepticism, because without the dynamic of him leading prayer meetings, he retreats in aloneness, as if he's lost his position in our household. Maybe he has lost purpose on a grand scale. He sulks like a man cheated; settling this score is between him and the God that is gone. My father, speaking four languages almost fluently, increasingly couldn't speak to me. When I go home for holidays, we communicate through Scrabble games. When I am away, we don't call. Around him, I experience *jamais vu*—sometimes I see him for the first time.

His dramatic announcement that Christmas night marked the end of our tradition of family prayer. I was relieved to be done with it. Following a brisk mental checklist, for decades I reliably kept my prayers under three minutes:

Thank God for health, safety, and family; Ask Him to keep us safe; Say good night.

Nigerians sing in our national anthem to a neutral "God of Creation"—either the Islamic or the Christian iteration of the

divine—*but only One.* One powerful enough to cry out to—
"*Oh God of Creation!*"

I think I understand why the Black Diaspora is drawn to
an omnipotent creator God: why West Africans and Black
Westerners alike embrace the religion imposed on us. Our
traditional gods are numerous but modest—small spirits at a
family shrine watching over just one hearth. They deal with a
harvest or with a farmer's flock. They are not gods who could
unmake the Middle Passage or intervene in a continent's colonization. They are gods miniature in the face of cataclysm. In
vast, collective desolation—in reaction to ruin—it is comfort-
ing to hold on to One; a Father; everlasting and omniscient;
of whose all-seeing eye you are the apple.

I have tried to be tactful in my utter rejection. Of all of it.

As an adult, my tactic of distancing myself from religion
while in my parents' house had been to fabricate some pressing obligation that excused me from church or prayer. My father's confession made me feel like a coward, but I told myself
I had good reason for not admitting my own faithlessness: if
my mother would genuinely believe I might go to Hell, I was
sparing her pain. I have since consigned that worry to her
alone. These past few years, I am open about my irreligion,
having revealed it little by little. I even ask her why she worships a god who would condemn me, but I don't think she
feels any choice.

She testifies that years ago, she went forward during a
church service for a laying of hands after a concerning mam-
mogram. She felt white-hot fire in her left breast and knew
God was healing her. She told me—only one time—that when
she was a girl, she saw Jesus walking amongst distant mango
trees. I do believe her. She doesn't lie that way.

She insists that I still believe. She maintains the convic-
tion that if she says I will come back to Christ enough times,

then I will. She repeats her Biblical directive: "As for me and my house, we will serve the Lord." My email inbox is full of her forwarded videos with titles like "I saw the Eyes of JESUS in PERSON!" She wants to pray for me on the phone, in the flesh, and I let her. She points out small miracles in my life, evidence of His signs and wonders.

Our good Christian home is now a mother and father living in awkward opposition. A trial separation a few years ago didn't take; forty-five years of marriage proved too stubborn a habit. My mother sees my father as a temporarily misplaced sheep, as the same devout man she wedded. After my father briefly moved out of their house during their separation, she found a document he'd left in his printer titled: "Oh God, I Have a Problem." Two pages expressed grievances with a God who failed him. His ominous objective in boldface: *"Write as a letter to God and say Goodbye."*

I have not quite said goodbye. I talk at God when I remember I must die. I still hold superstitious beliefs against my will. There's a not-insignificant chance I am going to Hell. I cannot sleep looking into a dark hallway. I will never start a love affair on a Saturday; never challenge a snake to sing.

On our last night in Nigeria during the trip for my sister's prewedding ceremony, which was the last time I went back, we stayed in a hotel on our long way to the airport. In my room, a Nollywood soap opera flickered on the only working channel. I kept the television blaring because the hotel grounds were too quiet, positioned at a distance from the city in a nervous perimeter patrolled by armed guards. In a surreal plot, the actress realizes she's been cursed by a rival for a man's affections. As the image on-screen began to warp to suggest the supernatural, I could feel her terror as she feigned it. I faced the real prospect of being haunted or hunted. I was prey.

Before first light, I fled my country—superstition chased me out, and there was gladness at my back.

But a single obsessive thought follows me in waking life:

What if everything I think has happened in my life since leaving Nigeria has all been a dream? Maybe a malaria-induced fever dream?

The last day of our last visit Back Home began—like always—with fast-breaking and prayer. That dawn, a goat had been slaughtered just outside my bedroom window. I imagine waking up to find myself back in that bed, some bright morning along the border.

12

THE NAME ONE GIVES ONESELF

Some Fulani clans wander after all around them settle. The last holdouts refusing to set up permanent camps, the most intractable transients. They eschew anything that might hamper free movement or infix them in one place. Of their few possessions, the one most dear to drifting Fulani is a bed built from the heavy woods of the mahogany family. This bed is always taken with them from place to place.

Their attachment to the bed tells us: that we must carry sanctuary with us; that the morphology of "home" is makeshift. To tarry too long on one plot of land is to let the land unnaturally claim and control us—*tame us*.

My immediate family and I have shared a dozen residences across three continents. I remember those addresses so generic they might exist anywhere: Church Street and Riverfront Drive. I remember each spice jar in one old cabinet as its layout materializes in fine memory.

Wherever we went, we faced *undoing*—in many valences.

What is left is a singular culture, mixed-up and multidimensional. Wherever my family displays red-white-blue, we *must* show Naija green-white-green. My father tells us the most powerful weapon of colonizers is their talent for making people ashamed of their own history and traditions. In our culture of five, we have a private language featuring an unstandardized vocabulary we argue about using in Scrabble. We have our own cuisine. Always Heinz Salad Cream in our fridge, and it only goes on stews too spicy. Before anything, we sauté these things in palm butter: onions, green onions, garlic, ginger, Scotch bonnet peppers. Our inside joke, singing hymns contralto. We all have one signature posture when posing for family photographs. We do not talk to outsiders about the things I write in this book.

For the decades we prayed together as a family, each of us began our prayer the same way, admitting God's presence: Wherever two or three are gathered in Your name, You are there in their midst. In my prayers when I was small, I would recite our current address as soon as I memorized it, as if God Himself could lose track of us.

They say there is a feeling of minor pride when someone stops you on the street to ask for directions. The asking means that you look as if you belong there. *You're* the one at home; everyone around you is lost. Once, a stranger asked me which road went into town. Which town, I can't recall. There were four roads. I couldn't guess.

I joke that Maryland combines the worst parts of the South and the north—humidity devoid of charm. In retrospect, it was the best move we ever made. Three years in Connecticut had dragged plodding feet through cold and crisis. Nothing to do, less to see, no room to move in or grow. *The place-*

holder years. Until again it was time to repeat our signature and uproot ourselves. A steady sequence of disruption, our serial of disaster.

My family first arrived to the pseudo-South when I was fifteen.

Summer 2002: My father secures a research position at Howard, a historically Black university, where he researches *diabesity*, the intersection of obesity and diabetes—a fatal combination that will kill both my grandfathers. Dick Cheney serves as acting president for the few hours W. is incapacitated during a routine colonoscopy. Forty years after murdering four Black girls with a homemade bomb at the Sixteenth Street Baptist Church, Bobby Cherry is convicted by a jury of his peers. Halle Berry receives the Academy Award for Best Actress, becoming the first Black woman to win. I never miss an episode of the first *American Idol* season, the one token of continuity from June to September.

I am entering the eleventh grade. My sister comes home from college to crash on the couch. We move to Silver Spring and a three-bedroom apartment in a moderately high-rise building—ten stories, so much taller than any terrain in our Connecticut. We live on the tower's ninth floor. A huge window in our unit faces west, so we see sunset. I go into our kitchen to look at the technique of particolored light over walls. Our small city is six miles from DC, one stop on the Red Line train.

Maryland means home to the fourth-highest concentration of Nigerian immigrants in the States. One reason we flock around DC is our cultural supposition that a capital city must be the most functional. My family has long been "alien" in the official language of immigration and even beyond bureaucracy—even within our community of incomers. Famously nomadic all over the African continent, the Fulani rarely relocate to the West. Beyond the desert, Fulaniland doesn't give up its own.

When we lived in Nashville, we joined the Igbo Union, an organization for the second-most-populous tribe within the US. At their events, we lacked a common language and culture. We were lost during conversations in Igbo, we misfits who danced instead when we couldn't speak. It was sometimes enough to be around other Nigerians who did their best to welcome us. My parents and siblings now belong to Zumunta, an association of Northern Nigerian immigrants. They finally found their place there in the long shadow of the capital. For the rest of my family, Maryland felt less like a repeat of every prior move—more like a reset.

But for me, even in my own private room for the first time in my life, a real bed was too permanent an investment. My final two years of high school, I slept on a plush, rolled-out chair cushion: orange tie-dye. I decorated my room with throwaway, thrifted knickknacks my mother begged me to discard; with peacock feathers from that sad pet store in Connecticut I'd walked to after school most days for no reason. My parents moved into the first house they'd ever owned the semester I left for Yale, and it was during the homesick winter that I would see it for the first time.

Against regulations, I stayed on Old Campus a week into winter break after every other student had left. I couldn't leave my dorm building because my key card wouldn't allow reentry, and I might be spotted by the maintenance crew and tossed out. I locked myself inside the few rooms I could access and kept quiet when I heard workers in the hallway. Sotto voce, I murmured what I learned that semester, my party trick of reciting the first eighteen lines of Chaucer's *The Canterbury Tales* with precise Middle English enunciation. I scavenged food from common areas and for seven days survived on bad snacks while I watched DVDs looted from adjoining suites and tried not to think.

My maternal grandparents were waiting for me at my parents' house, having flown in from Nigeria—their only trip outside that country in their lifetimes aside from Niger. Their presence meant putting on the performance of "God-fearing daughter" required of me. The greetings, those prayers. It felt bleak.

I missed my family, but escapism was one of many new vices I picked up in college. I was paranoid they could sense my sin. Is there such a thing? When I finally went home out of hunger, I was shown to my new bedroom and its furniture appointed by my parents. A coherent set of heavy fixtures meant to last, standing in contrast to the junk I knew. My mother had tossed my things while I was away playacting as a serious student. No one could figure out why I'd chosen to return to that cold—to the Connecticut I always cursed.

My siblings stayed put. The four members of my family now cluster near to one another: in a core, in communion—excluding me. Maryland marked the final place I was ever taken against my will: to every place since that followed, I went on my own.

I alone have gone out; I have gone out alone.

Ten years into the millennium. Ten years on borrowed time the younger version of myself didn't think would come to pass. *Maybe the Hand of Mary spared me.* I don't think I believe in God; I don't know about goddesses. I am grown; on my own; alone.

I am more accurately "American-African" than its inverse—"African-American"—the term Black American descendants of the enslaved claimed a generation ago and a label

I have never used for myself. I am now more American than I ever was English. Maybe more American than African, having stopped frequently going Back Home.

Some observable faults remain in my evolution toward becoming fully American. I still have British-trained habits concerning some minutiae in grammar; I don't feel whole without the Oxford comma. I put quotation marks *outside* commas and periods ("Learn this convention!" my favorite professor complained on my papers). I've dropped most superfluous *us*—color (not "colour"). I have internalized American spelling and pronunciation—mischievous (not "mischievious"); aluminum (not "aluminium")—but my accent remains unstable. My decades-long, self-conscious battle about how I sound has pushed me to prefer my voice on the written page. I make a bare living from it.

The day I graduated college, I moved to the one city I always imagined I would belong to, New York. I was so close to NYC when we lived in Connecticut, but I only ever saw the most direct route to, then the inside of, the Nigerian Embassy whenever we were summoned to solve some immigration problem. Instead, I memorized guidebooks.

My New York—half spent in a railroad apartment in Crown Heights, where the figure of the contrary Jamaican landlady recurred as a central conflict in my life. Half in Harlem: I moved in with my sister, and we argued over balcony use. My parents surprised us by driving up from Maryland hauling a decrepit leather couch, and I mistook accommodating this large object as a sign I would be there for a while. In the city so magnified in my young mind that it represented the entirety of the USA, I made it a year.

I fled to California after I decided it's impossible to understand America without spending time *Out West.* The farthest west I'd ever been was Kentucky Lake, Tennessee. My best friend convinced me it would be a waste of my time and little money to visit first.

Just come. So. I just went.

The first time I moved to LA was on New Year's Day, and that first morning, waking up by a glaring sun through the window, my body recoiled reflexively—not understanding why it should be so bright. I was repulsed by early, unrelenting sunshine like an intrusion. Having been drawn out here twice, I refer to a *first time* and a *second time* I've lived in Los Angeles—like I'm stuck in a loop: echoing and outside time, as if doomed to déjà vu.

Los Angeles has a nickname, "Lotusland," after the island of lotus-eaters in *The Odyssey* where narcotic flowers made islanders moony, made them forget whatever they knew, whoever they were. Time operates differently here. Telling a tale temporally, even a simple one, is more difficult when talking about LA than about any other place. The sunniness—how it becomes the *sameness*—begins to affect one's memory. I cannot piece together a timeline.

I remember weather in New York. I remember heartbreak that aligned with sharp drops in temperature. Of course, I remember the climate when we sat on his stoop and he fixed the broken zipper on the back of my dress. I will never be reconciled to New York winter, but I can say when something happened just as well as I can say what happened. When I attempt to remember *when*, my mind first feels around for a sense of the season—what the weather is like; the debris on the ground; what the trees bear.

In LA, the weather is almost the same day after day, and there are no real seasons. When recalling an instance within the decade I've called it my home, the mental image of

November looks and feels exactly like June. Heat waves and increasingly frequent infernos puncture this pattern somewhat. When record highs made the hottest October in history, that must have been 2015; I slept in the bathtub, then checked into a motel because I had no AC.

In the beginning, I lived in the way of my tribe of a different desert. *Semi-settled*—a way that would tie me to this place as impermanently as possible. On the move, a Fulani nomad dismantles her entire home, woven with reeds and wooden pillars, and takes it with her. My first apartment was so sparely furnished that when I moved out a year later, I had nothing more to take than what I'd come with—two suitcases, the free allotment on my Southwest flight. I had no car and lived centrally in Koreatown, a walkable neighborhood close to bus lines and the subway I didn't know LA had. I'd signed the shortest lease I could find, a six-month contract, then renewed it month to month. I slept on a mattress with no frame.

I needed to know I could get out fast. Before I came here sight unseen, I had never entertained the idea of living in Los Angeles. The heartbreaker was the one who brought this speculative thing into being—he muttered some passing thought of moving here. (I wasn't invited.) He said, "LA has a certain ethos." He said that, exactly. He destroyed a city for me; he drove me to a new one. When we reconnected after five years of silence, he said he couldn't imagine what he was thinking.

Falling for LA came as a surprise: I'd shared some of the general public's antipathy toward it. In a movie theater back on the East Coast, I saw the trailer for a disaster movie featuring scenes of LA being destroyed: the Hollywood sign exploding, palm trees on fire. People in the audience hooted and clapped, cheering their approval with a passion more appropriate for an enemy nation in wartime. I knew I desperately loved California when earthquakes rocked me to sleep, and when I begged a friend with a truck to help me bring home a bed frame. I loved that one friend moved into low-income haunted housing and took me ghost hunting; I loved how another found a way to live with coyotes.

When I tell people that Los Angeles is the greatest city in the world, their reaction is laughter. Most times, when people think about a place, they imagine the version presented by Hollywood. The standard complaints about LA are that it's "fake" and that its celebrity culture spews toxic ills through Western society. However, outsiders perceive Hollywood's own rendition of Hollywood. My LA is far removed from that glitz and glam—just as Hollywood's projection of itself is removed from the lurid reality of its streets.

Like the lotus-eaters, I cannot think to leave. The definition of "lotusland": "a place inducing contentment especially through offering an idyllic living situation." Some see LA as the opposite of paradise: not dream but nightmare. Some would say I *am* in fact gone to Hell—the Hell on Earth of this city always on fire.

Meaning the world *did* end.

In this city's short 240-year history, the dead became a feature of infrastructure with unusual immediacy. Human bodies classified as indigent, unclaimed, or unidentified repose communally in mass graves attached to missions and churches. LA develops around monster sloths and extinct elephants—Ice Age fossils regularly disturbed by paleontologists and public works. Major construction projects, including the

Metro system, work through the substratum of skeletons beneath our streets.

Los Angeles is a menagerie made of corpses.

Are *they* the angels we invoke when we pronounce the name of our city—whether softly, as it sounds in Spanish, or with the accent of Anglos? An ongoing debate amongst historians questions the initial name of the city of Los Angeles when it was first settled as a Spanish pueblo in 1781. The historical record is marred by errors on early maps, particularly the frequent misidentification of the Los Angeles River. Conflicting sources—books, church rolls, commemorative plaques, almanacs—present different possibilities:

El Pueblo de Nuestra Señora de los Ángeles.

El Pueblo de Nuestra Señora de los Ángeles de la Porciúncula.

El Pueblo de la Reina de los Ángeles Sobre el Rio de Porciúncula.

El Pueblo de Nuestra Señora la Reyna de los Ángeles del Rio Porciúncula.

Pueblo del Rio de Nuestra Señora la Reyna de los Ángeles de Porciúncula.

The most widely accepted original toponym—*El Pueblo de Nuestra Señora la Reina de los Ángeles*—refers to Mary, Queen of Heaven, after whom I also was named. This name means: "The Town of Our Lady the Queen of the Angels." Angels are certain. A queen is certain.

In Downtown LA, near the on-ramp to the 101, the major street currently named Los Angeles Street once included a block called Calle de Los Negros—meaning "Street of the Blacks." This section was referred to as "Nigger Alley" and "Negro Alley" ("politely"). It appears with all three titles on street maps from the nineteenth century. In the 1840s, Negro Alley was home to "men of very dark complexion," according to a local newspaper report, likely describing Afro-Mestizo laborers. On the Street of the Blacks, one prominent establishment was a bordello called La Prietita ("little dark-skinned lady"). Historian James Guinn, writing in real time, portrayed a space-efficient corruption: "In length it did not exceed 500 feet, but in wickedness it was unlimited."

Negro Alley's evil was tied to its name: the name of the dark-skinned people who fueled the Gold Rush economy by legal and less-than-legal means. In Guinn's words, Calle de Los Negros was "as black in character as in name." It was officially renamed in 1877 in a campaign to sanitize and redeem that section of the city—to rehabilitate its reputation as the base of the criminal element. Any trace of Negro Alley disappeared from maps by the middle of the twentieth century. Today, it is populated by the overflow from shelters, men surviving in tents.

In a repeating pattern, the Black histories of California become obscured: the Black pioneers in Western boomtowns go missing. In the 1781 census of the first forty-four settlers of the new Pueblo of Los Angeles, only two belonged to a racial category we might now consider white (Spaniards from Spain). Twenty-six—over half—had Black ancestry, some listed as "Negro," some as "Mulata/Mulato" (of mixed Spanish and African descent). In much storytelling of the city, these demographics are whitewashed. At the LA Bicentennial, a plaque on Olvera Street publicly recognized the ancestry of the forty-four founders for the first time.

Hernán Cortés came to California accompanied by the first free African to arrive in America. Alongside thousands of the enslaved, free *negros ladinos* (Hispanicized West Africans who settled in Spain and Portugal) left Iberia in early expeditions to the West Coast—many as soldiers, some in skilled capacities as crew. From its beginnings, California has steeped in Black influence; it is hidden there inside the name of our state. Like the name of Los Angeles, it refers to a queen. Again like that name, it involves a mistake on a map. To understand the name of the Golden State, enter the island of California, the island of Blacks.

Such an island first took form within the pages of a sixteenth-century Spanish novel, *Las Sergas de Esplandián* (*The Exploits of Esplandián*). In his epic chivalric romance, author Garci Rodríguez de Montalvo fantasizes an island kingdom—"*Una isla llamada California . . . de mujeres negras.*" An island called "*California*" of Black women. He directs us there: "Know, then, that on the right hand of the Indies there is an island called California, very close to the side of the Terrestrial Paradise, and it was peopled by Black women, without any man amongst them, for they lived in the fashion of Amazons."

Montalvo places a dark-skinned empress at the helm of his legendarium. Queen Calafia reigns over a mythic matriarchy, a race of Amazonians "living manless" in a realm he designates "the island of Blacks." Its imaginary geography made a deep impression on a generation of explorers. Wave after wave hunted for it—all the while hunting the people indigenous to the land. In 1535, when Spanish conquistadors enamored with her legend moored their ships along our coast, they believed they had reached the sublime shores of Calafia's island. Settlers of a state of delusion: they named it after her. *California.*

The etymology of our heroine's name and namesake territory is derived from the Arabic *khalifa*, referring to a ruler (caliph) of an Islamic kingdom (a caliphate)—such as the former Sokoto Caliphate in my tribal home. In 1510, a newly unified Spain instated autocratic Catholicism after reconquering the caliphates held by Muslim caliphs, who had occupied parts of southern Spain for eight centuries. The Treaty of Granada, signed in 1491, signaled the cessation of engagement with Moorish armies, who retreated by strait or sea to North Africa.

After the Reconquista, the Inquisition: Christianity was unchallengeable in Spain. A trifle like a trinket with the *hamsa*, the Hand of Mary, became heresy. Impelled by the Doctrine of Discovery, conquistadors desolated the New World in service of an empire under Isabella the Orthodox. This is the religious and imperial context in which the character of Queen Calafia—the female *califa*—was conceived. She is at once a symbol of centuries-old conflicts and new worlds: a "pagan" and a "heathen" confronting interlopers at the mouths of her caves.

Queen Calafia is sovereign over an island where male infants are eliminated at birth. Where women domesticate griffins and fatten them on the flesh of male trespassers. For fun, their pet griffins fly the bodies of men up to a great height and drop them. Calafia's subjects are of "hardy bodies, of ardent courage and great force." With its "steep cliffs and rocky shores," their habitat's natural defenses complement a militaristic society of women. Black warlike women, born to battle even nature.

The island of California is El Dorado. Montalvo's descriptions of its gold were so tantalizing that Hernán Cortés himself lusted after it obsessively, willing it into existence.

For two hundred years after they first arrived, Spanish settlers believed California was an island, misunderstanding the terrestrial and marine divide. They erroneously believed a large expanse of water lay to the east: that there was no land route connecting this tract to the main body of the continent. Faith in the legend interfered with mapping California long after there was evidence that the Baja California Peninsula was in fact continentally enjoined. California appeared on maps as an island well into the eighteenth century. The five-hundred-year-old myth's sorcery is in its promise—not only of gold, but of infinite quantities.

When I was fifteen, after a bad fight with my mother, I packed a bag and my inscrutable guitar, stole her credit card, and left home meaning to buy a bus ticket to Hollywood. A cross-country journey of four days. Once there, I planned to join a commune, having never divorced the California in my imagination from the flower-child era of the '60s. Lucky she noticed and followed me on the Metro to Union Station; I would not have made it back. In that mind-boggling moment of teenage stupidity, I glimpsed something of the mania that compelled men west.

I tell you, I saw more than the prospect of panning fortune out of dirt.

California still exists in collective imagination as an island. The state is envisioned and experienced as distinct from the rest of the nation, separated by impenetrable boundaries.

In a reverse engineering of this island, we find Calafia in its code. Too few people know the creation myth of California: those who do know recognize her as the "Spirit of California." See her in San Francisco at the Stock Exchange Tower, in Diego Rivera's first American mural. A lone female figure amongst men and their machines. A giantess whose hundred-year-old hands brace the earth and its instruments. A team of painters upraised her elsewhere in the Golden City—bare-breasted and brown, cradling a ragged lump of gold and guarded by two of her tribe, all armored and bejeweled. In a grand hotel hall, they set her against a gold-leaf backlight and set upon her head an exaggerated crown. Immortalized in art, inhabiting public space, she possesses her eponymous island.

Calafia's name is an *asteroidonym*:
341 California, an asteroid unusually bright.

A *cosmonym*: the California Nebula,
which resembles the shape of the state.

A *hydronym*: the Gulf of California.

An *oronym*: California Hill in Nebraska, the first major peak confronting travelers along the Oregon Trail.

A *speleonym*: California Caverns, a limestone system under the mountain backbone through Gold Country.

She gives her name to flowers: *Eschscholzia californica*, the California poppy—also called California Sunlight, the golden poppy, the cup of gold.

Her name to Californite,
a mineral making jade-like jewelry.

To Californium,
an extremely radioactive element synthesized in 1950.

To at least twelve cities and municipalities,
neighborhoods, unincorporated communities,
and boroughs across America.

One ghost town in West Virginia.

An *isulonym* is the proper name given to an island: California counts, marked by the unreality of the myth that birthed it. This place has never rid itself of an early association with a fool's paradise—the locus of a lost city, like Eden, Arcadia, or Atlantis. All reverie and illusion. Our shapeshifting state. When I sleep through an earthquake, I begin to dream . . .

Perhaps we'll break off into a true island any day now . . .

Coast.

Obsolete: "the frontier; the line, limit, or border of a country." Its verb form once meant "to travel around the borders of a place."

Even earlier, it referred to a "rib as a part of the body."

A coastline is an immeasurable thing. Depending how close you zoom in, twists and turns can extend any boundary to infinity.

I was born near a vanishing body of water: Lake Chad has at most a century to live. If you zoom out after pinpointing my birthplace on satellite maps, you see its pin piercing the lowest border of yellow—the edge of arid land, the last bit of sand. Future maps may show regreening in the desert where we plant the Great Green Wall: a barricade of saplings to protect soil and savanna. The desertification of SoCal and the Sahara present similar environmental calamity—still, I am drawn to deserts. I left one caliphate only to end up in another.

America, I didn't choose, but California—an island distinct—I did choose. It feels increasingly natural to reply, "California," when someone wants to know where I'm from. This response seems to make people happy, perhaps recalling sunshine and movie magic. In my sunny chosen setting, I began writing about the uncanny valleys surrounding La La Land. How this city interlaces specter and light—the underbelly, the airbrushing. *Anti-glamour.* I write of Hollywood and Hausa: one accent an unlikely echo of the other. Poems make my cosmology of past and present countries.

The mistaken magic that manifests the island of California

has much in common with Nigeria. Each a fantasy creation. A fabrication. Each one coveted and swallowed up by the curse of resources: their lands enticing, their inhabitants a nuisance. *Gold Coast; Slave Coast; Pepper Coast; Grain Coast*—English names given to West African territories seen only as commodities. In West Africa, early European invaders were inflamed by the same greed for gold that drove their contemporaries to the New World. The Age of African Exploration galvanized their wild ambition to mine Timbuktu, called the Lost City of Gold after the gilded hidden things said to be buried under its sand.

California and "Niger + Area," both of butchered borders. Both were mislabeled on maps drawn by intruders. In the early 1700s, English mapmakers labeled a parcel of land just below the Sahara that stretched from the Nile to Atlantic water: "Negroland." Nigeria was part of their Negroland. This nomenclature appears in constant use on British maps until the middle of the nineteenth century. My ancestral home and my adopted home were identified as *lands of the Blacks*. The Land of Blacks and the Island of Blacks were both branded "uninhabitable" by those expecting promised lands to come easy.

Curious nations of a nature better perceived in dreamscapes: each made of myth. Like twin exhibits of romantic racism, projecting someone's make-believe of Negros. In the Calafia myth, the island of California represented Africa in the author's imagination. Maybe the golden coastline of California is the Gold Coast of Africa, extended. Maybe the Sahara expands until it swallows the world whole.

Monster or Black Madonna.
   Savage, slave, subhuman, superhuman.
   These are the archetypes Black people embody in precolonial texts. In distorted narratives, we are presented as beastly

or beatific. In the European imagination, we were strange populations to be written about as though we befit the Uncanny Valley—human, but not quite. Always more than or less than human. *Machine, animal, goddess.*

The plot of the Calafian story reproduces Nigeria's colonial past and mirrors the catastrophe of my native land. As in the myth, colonization changed our society at its most intimate levels, and conversion transformed us spiritually. Old traditions and beliefs were outlawed, lost, libeled. Colonizers held up our practices as exaggerated cruelties. In mythical California, infanticide and human pet food indicate the barbarity of its "natives." Nigerians were called cannibals, said also to make meals of men.

Calafia's arc leads me down a familiar path—repression; rebellion; submission. Early in her timeline, she waged war against invading Christians and Muslims, resisting both to adhere to ancient practices. She astonished her foes, who came to regret underestimating her. But at last, the compulsion of crusaders overwhelmed her, and she capitulated to the "ordered order" of Christianity. Montalvo abolishes her matriarchy, scorning the idea of her tribe "doing nothing but what their grandmothers did." When women follow the path of their foremothers, they must live and die as "very brutes."

Her marriage to a Catholic prince ended a way of life going "so far back that there is no memory of the beginnings of it." At once, Calafia perceived fatal flaws in her previous regime: ". . . it is clear that the law which [Christians] follow must be the truth, while that which we follow is lying and falsehood." In Montalvo's telling, scales have fallen from her eyes, and she is delivered from ignorance. His paternalism reflects one definition of pagan: an "unruly, badly educated child." We are to understand that Christian wedlock "civilizes" Calafia. We see this trope over and over in colonial narratives—*that we are tamed.*

Author Montalvo's descriptions of Calafia's body veer toward the grotesque, an aesthetic paradox wherein one is simultaneously fascinated and repulsed by an object of curiosity. His language presents her physicality as extreme, his superlatives placing her outside the norm: "very large in person, the most beautiful of all of them." With aggressive traits—ferocity, hypersexuality—she is almost feral. Somehow, she never seems mortal. And in my musing, Calafia slips the bondage of her own origin story.

She remains wild. She becomes mine.

To claim the demonym "Californian" is to fantasize a kinship where I belong to Queen Calafia's tribe. I am claimed by her fabled sisterhood called the "California Blacks." When I began my inquiries into my ancestry, I never imagined I would add a fifth possible answer to the question of my tribe.

I speculate that this possibility has lived with me all along.

Growing up in England, I was called *kali* by some of the South Asian girls in my class. *Kali* is a slur in Hindi and Urdu—it means "black" or "dark" with a derogatory connotation. One girl recoiled if I accidentally touched her, as though fleeting contact between my skin and hers would infect her, rub off on her—perhaps burn her.

In Hindu mythology, Kali—"The Black One"—is a female deity, the wife of Shiva. Her titles: Divine Mother of the Universe; the Black Goddess; Goddess of Time, Creation, Destruction, Violence, and Power. She wears human arms entwined to make her robe; she wears a crown of the living heads of humans. She is depicted with skin so dark it brims midnight blue. She is the Black Wrathful Lady. The Dark Black Night. She Who Is Death.

Had I known then what I know now about divine and

darkling feminine beings, I might have proudly adopted the title *kali*. I may have embraced this epithet were it not for the way it was spat at me. There is no linguistic connection between my childhood label, *kali*, and the shortened state name, "Cali," except for their similarity in sound—I make this connection myself. And the slur I was called makes Kali my namesake, placing another ancestor in my personal pantheon. Yet another black-skinned warrior goddess.

I pretend I am a princess.

I grew up around a father who lacked names for things. The language of his tribe, the Longuda, evolved a distinctive feature: the tradition of word taboos. These are words one must never speak aloud, frequently terms used for deities or kings. Longuda names and titles often reference personal attributes—a brave chief might be called a lion, a steady man, a mountain. Because word taboos require replacing common words like "lion" or "mountain," the language of the small Longuda tribe has elaborated into a slew of dialects. Each of the twenty-five-ish tiny villages that make up the totality of Longuda territory has its own. A Longuda man traveling just twenty miles might find the vocabulary of a neighboring tribesman unintelligible. He would have to ask him to speak very slowly.

The Longuda come up with different ways of expressing those words they may not say. If they cannot speak of lions, they invent a new term for this animal. My father makes up silly names for things for no reason: "Wandansencras!" he exclaims to describe anything spectacular. My mother thinks it means "one dancing craze," but he will not disclose its etymology. It could be nonsense.

The words people choose to name themselves often mean,

in the plainest terms: "human." The Longuda word for their tribe simply marks their own people as mankind. *They* need no distinction; only outsiders require articulation. As a child, I was sensitive to expressions that indicate belonging or exclusion from a group; I needed to know how they might be weaponized against me. My body instinctively tensed around words I knew were used to identify outsiders. *Oyinbo* is any white person. *Baturiya* names European women. *Akata*, meaning a wildcat, refers to those separated too long from African cultures, usually Americans. During visits to Nigeria, my cousins teased me by calling me *'yar Ingila*, and later, *'yar Amirka*. I was *daughter of England* before becoming *daughter of America*.

My names change as I do. Moving around this world. Might be some form of magic. I am Nana in native naming, in a tradition against the taboo of speaking the name I share with my grandmother. Mary is who I am for Anglos and America. *Bitter or beloved ocean or child.*

I will return Back Home to Nigeria one day soon: I say this praying no petty spirit just now passing in the wind turns my confidence into a curse. *Inshallah*, I should add. *God willing.* God of All Creation, God of Colony and Caliphate.

The name one gives oneself is called an *autonym*. Greeting the unreconcilable coastline of that infinite desert, I might insist cousins call me:

'yar Kaliforniya.

ANTILOGUE

(noun)—a contradiction in related terms or ideas; an inconsistency

The way we keep finding facets to fact.

I didn't start this project as a fact-finding mission in any strict sense, knowing that such an approach would fail. At first, I simply tried to find the right names for things. Peoples, places. Within names, I encounter totems, oracles, odd movement in meaning. My way of truth-seeking refines my way of world-building. I sort fact from phantasm—and wonder what to make with the sketches of a reimagined homeland.

I am a poet of place.

Because I come from nomads, I have a tenuous, less tactile relationship with place. Both physical and mythical landscapes compel me—to distill the mythos and ethos of a place; to venture through vast architectures of personal and cultural identity. My writing is charged by the friction created by conflicting ideas at work in my history. They rub against each other—God of Abraham against animism; superstition against science; sacrilege against the sacred; ghosts against industry; the mystical against the mundane. My tribal mythology was estranged by an Evangelical dogma that made no room for invocation or enchantment—that made the magic in our stories inherently evil. Their revelations became bad omens: *unlucky.*

But these our stories are wonderwork—some struggle and survive.

Within my family, mine is the first generation turning from that cold colonial eye: seeing us for ourselves. I realized that our relationship with our own culture need not feel instinctive or innate. We may pursue it, pick at it, pull it apart. People removed should not feel inadequate or undeserving when reattaching severed ties. We are neither true outsiders nor true insiders—but a litmus test is never the point. "True" is pointless. For our part, we immigrants are *integral*, even when we are not *integrated*. We are the embodiment and evidence of our unrooting: the tensile connective tissue in all diaspora.

My last trip to Nigeria at twenty-four was also the last time I saw my maternal grandfather alive. After overcoming leprosy in his youth, healing in the sanitarium where he became a Christian, he never entered another hospital and ever refused all medical intervention. Baba died where I had left him, in his favorite cool spot in the courtyard. On that trip a decade ago, my grandfather told me a story. Since his death, my mother repeats it as fact.

In my grandfather's village—when he was in that stage of life when young men seek high reputation and reward—there skulked an armed bandit who no one could catch. The Sultan of Sokoto announced that whoever arrested him would receive a purse of gold coin. My grandfather surveilled the layout of the village and surmised the likely approach of a crafty robber. Night after night, he set out to wait. He hid in the brush and high grass along the fringe of a walking path for weeks without success, but he was not deterred.

Far into one night, he heard someone stealing into the village. Knowing that no one honorable came and went at such a late hour, he leapt from his hiding place, startling the thief, and gripping him by the neck. Disarming him (the thief carried a knife), he held his face up to moonlight and recognized him from the artful descriptions given by victims. After the ambush, he tied up his captive, having brought rope, and frog-marched him to the one house in the village that had a car. Borrowing the auto, he drove the wailing burglar thirty miles and presented him to sultanate officials. My grandfather won his purse.

He becomes our hero in this tale we grandchildren hear often. Most times, we hold our questions. We keep it glamorous: this one untarnished image to hold in memory as our gospel truth. Though dubious, this legend always feels like *luck*.

I begin escaping some generational curse.

I was blessed to be born in the least-lucky place, because where I come from, we turn leprosy into luck. My self-mythologization is desultory—working past a past of no true home. I now navigate illusory locations. The island of California, a Nigeria that makes sense. I did chart my own Africa. I keep turning over the truths I was told, that I now tell.

ACKNOWLEDGMENTS

Good friends are the greatest blessing in a writing life, and I have had the best. Will Nguyen, without your sense of humor and cynical goodness, life would be very bleak and very bad. You always help me recognize when I'm not making any sense, and you encourage my growth in every way. Juan Castillo, you shape how I perceive beauty in art and in all places while constantly cracking me up. Melissa Campos, thank you for your preternatural patience. Safiya Sinclair, my love, you're my role model. I thank you so much for your brilliance in each incandescent part of you; for your uplifting confidence in me; for being who I want to be as a woman and a writer. Nicole Richards Diop, thank you for the singular way you choose to be in the world and the exquisiteness you add to it. Reyna Camps, thank you for the many, many joys over half my lifetime; thank you also for the pessimism. Cody Farthing, you're everything at once—thank you for your strength, which you use to pull me out of my obsessive spirals when you can. Shari Sharpe, I cannot ever thank you enough. The most generous person I know, you offer life-giving support and spend boundless time and energy agonizing with me over endless minutiae. You make all things clear and mirrorlike.

I am extremely grateful for the professors who have supported me since I was seventeen. Anne Fadiman taught me that writing must be paired with compassion. Laura Kasischke is so wildly weird in everything she does and brought kind light to my experience of academia. Bill Deresiewicz helps me feel less lost and hopeless while figuring out my path as a young writer.

I extend my deepest gratitude to my academic advisors. David St. John, thank you for helping me stay the course with your guiding wisdom. Bill Handley and David Bridel, thank you both for your kind notes and edits of my project drafts.

I sincerely thank the people who listen to me ramble: Hiba bint Zeinab, for commiserating over a past of religious violence, and Brian Souder, for being a sounding board. Thank you, Tim DeMay, for being my harshest critic.

I have been so lucky in this process to know Dan Halpern, who saw this book before I did. Jin Auh has been my life raft during the long years of this difficult undertaking. Thank you, Jin, for advising me to trust my instincts and for urging me to the seemingly simple but radically unfamiliar task of writing what I *want* to write. You empowered me to delete this six-word phrase from my vocabulary: "I don't want to be difficult." Gabriella Doob and Norma Barksdale, thank you for drawing out ideas and truths I was afraid to put on paper.

I hope to do justice to my immediate family's unstable and strange experience of this world. Daddy, thank you for countless days spent telling and untangling our family histories. Uwani, you taught me how to read and raised me; I owe you a lifelong debt of gratitude. Ishaya, you made childhood an adventure, and I am so proud of the man you have become. Mommy, you made me dream about writing your life, whose sacrifices I only now begin to understand. You are selfless. You shoulder all of us. I love you so much.

NOTES

Prologue

1 blindness, sleep, pride, worry, and death: David Adams Leeming, *Creation Myths of the World: An Encyclopedia* (Santa Barbara: ABC-CLIO, 2010), 111.

2 Restlessness, rootlessness: references Kate Mayberry, "Third Culture Kids: Citizens of Everywhere and Nowhere," BBC News, November 18, 2016, https://www.bbc.com/worklife/article/2016 1117-third-culture-kids-citizens-of-everywhere-and-nowhere.

5 presented as a monolith: ideas were influenced by Chinua Achebe, "An Image of Africa: Racism in Conrad's *Heart of Darkness*," *Massachusetts Review* 57, no. 1 (2016): 14–27, https://doi.org/10.1353 /mar.2016.0003.

5 routinely flattened in representations: ideas influenced by Chimamanda Ngozi Adichie, "The Danger of a Single Story," uploaded July 2009 by TED Global, video, https://www.ted.com/talks /chimamanda_ngozi_adichie_the_danger_of_a_single_story.

1: Fortune Far Away

8 FBI warns Americans: "Nigerian Letter or '419' Fraud," Scams and Safety, Federal Bureau of Investigation, accessed September 10, 2021, https://www.fbi.gov/scams-and-safety/common-scams-and -crimes/nigerian-letter-or-419-fraud.

12 "the story of how Europeans": Margaret Thatcher, "Speech to the College of Europe," Keynote Address, European Economic Community Conference, Bruges, Belgium, September 20, 1988.

12 "tale of talent": Thatcher, "Speech."

12 "Disposing of some myths": Thatcher, "Speech."

12 "Britain does not dream": Thatcher, "Speech."

24 According to a recent census: "Reading Population and Demographics," Reading Borough Council, 2020, https://reading.berkshire observatory.co.uk/population.

2: Irregular Universe

39 "Wax" refers to a print: information about wax-print designs is drawn from Julie Halls and Allison Martino, "Cloth, Copyright, and Cultural Exchange: Textile Designs for Export to Africa at the National Archives of the UK," *Journal of Design History* 31, no. 3 (2018): 236–54, https://doi.org/10.1093/jdh/epy007.

39 A radio once meant "modernity": Melanie Abrams, "8 Vibrant African Wax Prints and Their Unique Stories," *British Vogue*, April 18, 2018, https://www.vogue.co.uk/gallery/eight-stories-behind -traditional-african-wax-prints.

42 "full of Nigerian babies": Jordanna Bailkin, "The Postcolonial Family? West African Children, Private Fostering, and the British State," *Journal of Modern History* 81, no. 1 (2009): 87, https://doi .org/10.1086/593156.

45 "children who accompany their parents": Ruth Useem and Ann Cottrell, "Adult Third Culture Kids," in *Strangers at Home: Essays on the Effects of Living Overseas and Coming Home to a Strange Land*, ed. Carolyn Smith (Bayside, NY: Aletheia Publications, 1996), 22.

45 immersed in the cultures: discussion informed by David Pollock and Ruth Van Reken, *Third Culture Kids: Growing Up Among Worlds*, 3rd ed. (repr., Boston: Nicholas Brealey Publishing, 2017).

45 floundering cultural identity: ideas discussed in Andrea M. Moore and Gina G. Barker, "Confused or Multicultural: Third Culture Individuals' Cultural Identity," *International Journal of Intercultural Relations* 36, no. 4 (July 2012): 553–62, https://doi.org/10.1016 /j.ijintrel.2011.11.002.

3: Land Like a Firearm

47 "hold Africa like a gun": the translated quotation "Africa has the shape of a revolver, whereof the trigger is placed in Zaire" is

attributed to Frantz Fanon by then-president of Zaire Mobutu Sese Seko in a 1973 speech to the UN. "Mobutu à l'ONU 1973," video, uploaded November 7, 2012, https://www.youtube.com/watch?v=tKcMLmtSp3k.

48   Where-to-Be-Born Index: information is sourced from Laza Kekic, "The Lottery of Life," *The Economist*, November 12, 2012, https://www.economist.com/news/2012/11/21/the-lottery-of-life.

48   critical killing ground: "Citing 'Horrifying Acts of Cruelty' in Nigeria, UN Rights Chief Urges Justice for Victims," *United Nations News*, June 5, 2015, https://news.un.org/en/story/2015/06/500792-citing-horrifying-acts-cruelty-nigeria-un-rights-chief-urges-justice-victims.

48   was established in 1907: information about Maiduguri colonial history sourced from Amy McKenna, *Encyclopedia Britannica*, "Maiduguri Location, Facts, and Population," last updated July 9, 2019, https://www.britannica.com/place/Maiduguri. Also from *Encyclopedia Britannica Online*, "Borno," last updated November 8, 2021, https://www.britannica.com/place/Borno.

48   destruction ten years ago: "Boko Haram Militants Arrested at the University of Maiduguri Teaching Hospital with Bomb Parts," June 10, 2011, *Sahara Reporters*, http://saharareporters.com/2011/06/10/boko-haram-militants-arrested-university-maiduguri-teaching-hospital-bomb-parts.

49   Global Terrorism Index: information is sourced from "Global Terrorism Index: Measuring and Understanding the Impact of Terrorism," Institute for Economics and Peace, 2015, https://reliefweb.int/report/world/global-terrorism-index-2015-measuring-and-understanding-impact-terrorism.

49   pledges allegiance to Isis: Libby George, "Boko Haram Fighters Pledge to Islamic State in Video, Worrying Observers," Reuters, June 28, 2021, https://www.reuters.com/world/africa/boko-haram-fighters-pledge-islamic-state-video-worrying-observers-2021-06-27/.

50   their dawning in 2002: information about Boko Haram is sourced from "Boko Haram," National Consortium for the Study of Terrorism and Responses to Terrorism, University of Maryland, March 2015, https://www.start.umd.edu/baad/narratives/boko-haram.

50   "purify the land": Akinola Olojo, "Islamic Clerics Can Shift Boko Haram's Ideological Narrative," Institute for Security Studies,

August 27, 2018, https://issafrica.org/iss-today/islamic-clerics-can -shift-boko-harams-ideological-narrative.

50   at least one million people: "Nigeria: Plans to Close IDP Camps in Maiduguri Could Endanger Lives," Amnesty International, December 15, 2021, https://www.amnesty.org/en/latest/news/2021 /12/nigeria-plans-to-close-idp-camps-in-maiduguri-could-endanger -lives/.

51   Maiduguri names the place: information about Maiduguri's etymology from Babagana Abubakar, "Origin and Meaning of Maiduguri," ResearchGate, July 5, 2017, https://www.researchgate.net /publication/318215165_Origin_and_Meaning_of_Maiduguri.

51   animals in every stage: information about Maiduguri commodities sourced from McKenna, "Maiduguri Location, Facts, and Population."

51   fragile and "failed states": "2021 Annual Report," Fragile States Index, Fund for Peace, May 20, 2021, https://fragilestatesindex .org/2021/05/20/fragile-states-index-2021-annual-report/.

52   Unilever corporation until 1987: "History of the United Africa Company Ltd," Unilever Archives, accessed January 9, 2021, http://www.unilever-archives.com/Record.aspx?src=CalmView .Catalog&id=GB1752.UAC&pos=1.

52   annexed the delta: information about palm oil industry from Ayomide Tayo, "How Nigeria Transformed from a Business into a Country," Pulse Nigeria, July 26, 2019, https://www.pulse.ng /news/local/unilever-royal-niger-company-and-how-nigeria-trans formed-from-a-business-into-a/15tym8p.

52   colonizers deceived tribal chiefs: information regarding colonial contract deceit from Tayo, "How Nigeria Transformed."

53   "When the missionaries arrived": quoted in John Frederick Walker, A Certain Curve of Horn: The Hundred-Year Quest for the Giant Sable Antelope of Angola (New York: Grove Press, 2004), 144.

54   telegram to the Colonial Office: John Carland, The Colonial Office and Nigeria, 1898–1914 (Stanford: Hoover Institution Press, 1985), 108.

56   "sea coast, shore": Online Etymology Dictionary, "Sahel," accessed November 16, 2021, https://www.etymonline.com/word /Sahel#etymonline_v_37561.

56   "grassy plains": "Sahl," Wiktionary, accessed December 5, 2021, https://en.wiktionary.org/wiki/%D8%B3%D9%87%D9%84.

56   habitation of one hundred million: Henry Ridgwell, "Africa Could

See World's First 100-Million-Person City by Century's End," *Voice of America News*, March 29, 2018, https://www.voanews .com/a/african-city-of-100-million-by-centurys-end/4321998 .html.

57 population will surpass China's: "Nigeria's Population to Overtake China, US by 2100—Study," News Agency of Nigeria, *The Guardian*, July 15, 2020, https://guardian.ng/news/nigeria-to-overtake -china-u-s-by-2100-study/.

57 outrage over a beauty pageant: Lydia Polgreen, "Nigeria Counts 100 Deaths over Danish Caricatures," *New York Times*, February 24, 2006, https://www.nytimes.com/2006/02/24/international /africa/24nigeria.html.

57 bad end of international indexes: statistics about maternal mortality rate and HIV/AIDS rates from "Nigeria," *The World Factbook*, CIA, last updated March 8, 2022, https://www.cia.gov/the-world -factbook/countries/nigeria/#people-and-society.

57 Gallup global survey: Magali Rheault and Bob Tortora, "Nigerians Express Optimism About the Future," Gallup News, August 22, 2007, https://news.gallup.com/poll/28483/nigerians-express -optimism-about-future.aspx2.

58 nearly 400 tribes: Onigu Otite, *Ethnic Pluralism and Ethnicity in Nigeria: With Comparative Materials* (Ibadan, Nigeria: Shaneson, 1990).

58 speaking 502 languages: Roger Blench, *An Atlas of Nigerian Languages*, 3rd ed. (Cambridge: Kay Williamson Educational Foundation, 2012).

58 configurations they form today: information about Nigerian tribal chronology from Toyin Falola, Ann Genova, and Matthew Heaton, *Historical Dictionary of Nigeria*, 2nd ed. (Lanham, MD: Rowman & Littlefield, 2018).

60 strategy of mass prison breaks: Alex Thurston, "Are Recent Prison Breaks in Nigeria Part of a Southward Expansion by Boko Haram?," Global Observatory, December 16, 2014, https:// theglobalobservatory.org/2014/12/are-recent-prison-breaks-in -nigeria-part-of-a-southward-expansion-by-boko-haram/.

60 350,000 deaths in 20 years: Aliyu Tanko, "Nigeria's Security Crises —Five Different Threats," BBC News, July 19, 2021, https://www .bbc.com/news/world-africa-57860993.

60 *"Be extra vigilant"*: "Security Alert," *Nigeria Travel Advisory Update*, U.S. Embassy and Consulate in Nigeria, last modified

September 3, 2021, https://ng.usembassy.gov/security-alert-nigeria
-travel-advisory-update.

60   "technically defeated": Tanko, "Nigeria's Security Crises."

60   "hunters with voodoo powers": Abdulkareem Haruna, "Borno
Govt in Fresh Recruitment of Traditional Hunters to Help Fight
Boko Haram," *Premium Times*, October 8, 2019, https://www.pre
miumtimesng.com/news/headlines/356661-borno-govt-in-fresh
-recruitment-of-traditional-hunters-to-help-fight-boko-haram
.html.

4: The People Who Steal Thatch

67   spoken by one hundred thousand tribesmen: Anthony Ayodele
Olaoye and Oluseye Olusegun Adegboye, "A Sociolinguistic Pro-
file of Longuda: A Minority Indigenous Nigerian Language," *Nile
Journal of English Studies* 4 (2017): 73–84.

77   affliction known as Brain Fag: Oyedeji Ayonrinde, "'Brain Fag':
A Syndrome Associated with 'Overstudy' and Mental Exhaustion
in 19th Century Britain," *International Review of Psychiatry* 32,
no. 5–6 (2020): 520–35.

5: From Her I Inherit

83   *Essentially, we need not worry*: information about the Fulani creation myth considered with David Newnham, "Why Worry?," *The
Guardian*, April 7, 2000, https://www.theguardian.com/theguard
ian/2000/apr/08/weekend7.weekend1.

83   who they name individually: information about cattle naming from
E. Thys and D. Noye, "Identification des Bovins par Description
de la Robe et des Cornes en Fulfulde, Dialecte des Éleveurs Peul
du Diamare," *Revue d'élevage et de Médecine Vétérinaire des Pays
Tropicaux* 36, no. 3 (1983): 301–305.

83   The first Fulani man: discussion of Fulani mythic origins considered with F. W. de St. Croix, *The Fulani of Northern Nigeria: Some
General Notes,* Reprint (London: Gregg International Publishers,
1972). Also with Ulrich Braukamper, "The Cow Emerges from the
Water: Myths Relating to the Origin of Cattle in the Chad Basin,"
in *Man and Water in the Lake Chad Basin*, ed. Daniel Barreteau
(Paris: Orstom Editions, 1997), 191–205.

83   to become a vagrant: M. D. W. Jeffreys, "Speculative Origins of the
Fulani Language," *Africa: Journal of the International African Institute* 17, no. 1 (1947): 50, https://doi.org/10.2307/1156939.

84 "more than human lives": Celia Lebur, "The Fulani: One of the Last Nomadic People," *AFP Interactive*, 2021, https://interactive .afp.com/features/The-Fulani_613/.

84 "They are like birds": Victor Azarya et al., *Pastoralists Under Pressure? Fulbe Societies Confronting Change in West Africa* (Leiden, Netherlands: Brill Publishers, 2022), xi.

85 you see Red Fulani: Jean Boutrais, "The Fulani and Cattle Breeds: Crossbreeding and Heritage Strategies," *Africa: Journal of the International African Institute* 77, no. 1 (2007): 18–36, http://www .jstor.org/stable/40026696.

86 ten thousand years ago: Lorraine Boissoneault, "What Really Turned the Sahara Desert from a Green Oasis into a Wasteland?," *Smithsonian*, March 24, 2017, https://www.smithsonianmag.com /science-nature/what-really-turned-sahara-desert-green-oasis-waste land-180962668/.

86 grown 10 percent: "New Study Finds World's Largest Desert, the Sahara, Has Grown by 10 Percent Since 1920," National Science Foundation, March 29, 2018, https://www.nsf.gov/news/news _summ.jsp?cntn_id=244804.

86 most populous pastoral group: demographic statistics about Fulani nomads from "Who Are the Fulani?," WorldWatch Monitor, accessed August 11, 2020, https://www.worldwatchmonitor.org/who -are-the-fulani/.

86 exact tribal population: statistics about Fulani population from Boukary Sangare, "Fulani People and Jihadism in Sahel and West African Countries," *Fondation pour la Recherche Stratégique*, February 8, 2019, https://www.frstrategie.org/en/programs /observatoire-du-monde-arabo-musulman-et-du-sahel/fulani -people-and-jihadism-sahel-and-west-african-countries-2019.

87 come into regular conflict: information about Fulani conflicts from Andrew McGregor, "The Fulani Crisis: Communal Violence and Radicalization in the Sahel," *CTC Sentinel* 10, no. 2 (2017): 34–39, https://ctc.usma.edu/the-fulani-crisis-communal-violence-and -radicalization-in-the-sahel/.

87 Fulani herdsmen number four: Rose Troup Buchanan, "Global Terrorism Index: Nigerian Fulani Militants Named as Fourth Deadliest Terror Group in World," *Independent*, November 18, 2015, https:// www.independent.co.uk/news/world/africa/global-terrorism -index-nigerian-fulani-militants-named-as-fourth-deadliest-terror -group-in-world-a6739851.html.

87   "laws as readily . . .": Lebur, "Fulani."

87   Islamized much of West Africa: Virginia Comolli, *Boko Haram: Nigeria's Islamist Insurgency* (London: Hurst, 2015).

87   three shades of meaning: *Merriam-Webster*, "jihad," accessed September 9, 2020, https://www.merriam-webster.com/dictionary/jihad.

87   apply to the Fulani Jihads: information about the military campaign of Usman dan Fodio from Toyin Falola and Matthew M. Heaton, *A History of Nigeria* (Cambridge: Cambridge University Press, 2008), 62–73. Also from Hamza Muhammad Maishanu and Isa Muhammad Maishanu, "The Jihad and the Formation of the Sokoto Caliphate," *Islamic Studies* 38, no. 1 (1999): 119–31, http://www.jstor.org/stable/20837029.

88   Fulani-led militias: information on Fulani army and military movement referenced in Margari Hill, "The Spread of Islam in West Africa: Containment, Mixing, and Reform from the Eighth to the Twentieth Century," Stanford University, January 2009, https://spice.fsi.stanford.edu/docs/the_spread_of_islam_in_west_africa_containment_mixing_and_reform_from_the_eighth_to_the_twentieth_century.

88   "Movement of Restoration": information about Usman dan Fodio's revolutionary jihad from Daniel Agbiboa, "Nigerian State Responses to Insurgency," in *African Frontiers: Insurgency, Governance and Peacebuilding in Postcolonial States*, 2nd, ed. John Idriss Lahai and Tanya Lyons (New York: Routledge, 2016), 83.

88   Fulani who follow another religion: Lindy Lowry, "7 Things to Know About Deadly Fulani Persecution in Northern Nigeria," Open Doors, April 3, 2018, https://www.opendoorsusa.org/christian-persecution/stories/7-deadly-fulani-persecution-northern-nigeria/.

89   "no matter how deep . . .": Rudolf Leger and Abubakar B. Mohammad, "The Concept of Pulaaku Mirrored in Fulfulde Proverbs of the Gombe Dialect," *Berichte des Sonderforschungsbereichs* 268, no. 14 (2022): 303, https://d-nb.info/1106135571/34.

93   A minority of 0.5 percent: Cletus Famous Nwankwo, "Religion and Voter Choice Homogeneity in the Nigerian Presidential Elections of the Fourth Republic," *Statistics, Politics and Policy* 10, no. 1 (2018): 8, https://doi.org/10.1515/spp-2018-0010.

94   initiation ritual called *sharo*: information from Pat I. Ndukwe, *Fulani* (New York: Rosen Publishing Group, 1995), 27–30. Also from Allan Carpenter, *Nigeria (Enchantment of Africa)* (Chicago: Children's Press, 1978), 64.

94   "literacy and numeracy": "Nigeria - Education," UNICEF, accessed March 16, 2022, https://www.unicef.org/nigeria/education.

6: Spirits of Wilderness

99   broad ethnic confederation: information about Hausa influence as an ethnic group from Ibrahim Sabiu, Fakhrul Sanol, and Mohammed Abdullahi, "Hausa People of Northern Nigeria and Their Development," *APJ* 1, no. 1 (2018): 179–89, https://journal.unisza.edu.my/apj/index.php/apj/article/view/21.

99   This group is substantial: Hausa demographics from Mark Cartwright, *World History Encyclopedia*, "Hausaland," last modified May 9, 2019, https://www.worldhistory.org/Hausaland/.

99   At their mercantile peak: information about medieval Hausa economics from Ronald Oliver and Anthony Atmore, *Medieval Africa 1250–1800* (Cambridge: Cambridge University Press, 2001), 79–84.

99   Hausa neighborhoods called *zongos*: Joseph A. Sarfoh, "The West African Zongo and the American Ghetto: Some Comparative Aspects of the Roles of Religious Institutions," *Journal of Black Studies* 17, no. 1 (1986): 71–84, http://www.jstor.org/stable/2784041.

100   legendary founder of the Hausa people: I learned the Bayajidda legend growing up, and there are many versions. I present a version written consulting information from Abba Gana Wakil Mahamadou, "Bayajidda Hausa Historical Legend: Myth or Reality," CSAN Niger, January 20, 2020, https://www.csan-niger.com/bayajidda-hausa-historical-legend-myth-or-reality.php. Also from Dierk Lange, "The Bayajidda Legend and Hausa History," in *African Zion: Studies in Black Judaism*, ed. Edith Bruder and Tudor Parfitt (Newcastle: Cambridge Scholars Publishing, 2012), 138–74. Also from W. K. R. Hallam, "The Bayajida Legend in Hausa Folklore," *Journal of African History* 7, no. 1 (1966): 47–60, https://doi.org/10.1017/S002185370000606X. Also from Abdoulaye Amadou et al., "Bayajida: The Legend of Hausa Land," DW and the Gerda Henkel Foundation, January 26, 2018, https://www.dw.com/en/bayajida-the-legend-of-hausa-land/a-42291985.

100   patriarchal rule in Hausaland: Carmen McCain, "Islam and Modernity," in *The Wiley-Blackwell Companion to African Religions*, ed. Elias Kifon Bongma (Oxford: Blackwell Publishing, 2012), 355–64.

101 integrity as a collective fluctuated: ideas about Hausa state systems considered in J. E. G. Sutton, "Towards a Less Orthodox History of Hausaland," *Journal of African History* 20, no. 2 (1979): 179–201, https://doi.org/10.1017/S0021853700017011.

101 twenty-fifth most spoken: Jennifer Gunner, "30 Most Common Languages Spoken in the World," *Your Dictionary*, accessed December 6, 2021, https://reference.yourdictionary.com/other-lang uages/30-most-common-languages-spoken-in-the-world.html.

101 fifty million speakers: Hausa language information from H. Ekkehard Wolff, *Encyclopedia Britannica*, "Hausa Language," last modified April 4, 2013, https://www.britannica.com/topic/Hausa -language.

101 most spoken indigenous African language: A. Kirk-Greene, "Neologisms in Hausa: A Sociological Approach," *Africa: Journal of the International African Institute* 33, no. 1 (2012): 25–44, https:// doi.org/10.2307/1157795.

102 I speak Hausa: my discussion of Hausa linguistics was written in consultation with "The Hausa Language," Department of African Studies, Humboldt University Berlin, accessed April 3, 2021, www.iaaw.hu-berlin.de/en/africa/linguistik-und-sprachen /african-languages/hausa.

102 Arabic challenged Hausa: influence of Arabic literary traditions discussed in S. U. Balogun, "Arabic Intellectualism in West Africa: The Role of the Sokoto Caliphate," *Institute of Muslim Minority Affairs* 6, no. 2 (1985): 394–411, https://doi.org/10.1080 /13602008508715950.

103 working migrants moves east: information about Hajj route from J. S. Birks, "The Mecca Pilgrimage by West African Pastoral Nomads," *Journal of Modern African Studies* 15, no. 1 (1977): 47–58, http://www.jstor.org/stable/159790.

104 "beautiful country, but the climate . . .": "States of Central Africa," 1902 Encyclopedia (9th and 10th editions), *Encyclopedia Britannica*, accessed March 10, 2021, https://www.1902encyclopedia.com /A/AFR/africa-33.html.

104 seat of Islamic scholarship: information about Kano's religious architecture from Aliyu Barau, "The Kano Emir's Palace," in *Kano: Entertainment, Society and Development*, ed. A. I. Tanko and S. B. Momale (London: Adonis and Abbey Publishers, 2014).

105 southernmost commercial hub: information about Kano history corroborated in Aliyu Salisu Barau, *The Great Attractions of*

Kano (Kano, Nigeria: Research and Documentation Directorate, 2007).

106 blue-dyed textiles: Daniel Flynn, "Ancient Indigo Dye Pits Barely Survive in Nigeria," Reuters, April 27, 2007, https://www.reuters .com/article/us-nigeria-dyers-idUSL2668533920070426.

107 traces the Arab influences: information about Arabic influence in Hausaland from Sabiu et al., "Hausa People," 179–89.

107 enigma of the Arewa knot: information about this symbol from Nura Yunusa, *Arewa Knot (Dagin Arewa): The Origin* (Arewa Intellectuals Forum, 2016), https://www.academia.edu/30465097 /AREWA_KNOT_DAGIN_AREWA_THE_ORIGIN?email _work_card=view-paper. Also from Jeremiah Aluwong, "The Arewa Knot," *Connect Nigeria*, June 19, 2021, https://articles .connectnigeria.com/the-arewa-knot.

107 first written into history: Sutton, "Towards a Less Orthodox History."

107 The *Kano Chronicle* was completed: information about historicity from M. Adamu, "The Hausa and Their Neighbors in the Central Sudan," in *Africa from the Twelfth to the Sixteenth Century*, ed. D. T. Niane (Paris: UNESCO Publishing, 2000), 271–74.

108 The *Kano Chronicle* recounts: H. R. Palmer, "The Kano Chronicle. Translated, with an Introduction," *Journal of the Royal Anthropological Institute of Great Britain and Ireland* 38 (1908): 58–98, https://archive.org/details/v38a39journalofro38royauoft.

108 "There is no cure but resignation": Palmer, "Kano Chronicle," 64.

108 when it was first introduced: "Hausa," Art & Life in Africa, University of Iowa Stanley Museum of Art, accessed September 2, 2021, https://africa.uima.uiowa.edu/peoples/show/Hausa.

108 millennium of Islam: information about Hausa Islamic history from "Arabic Intellectualism in West Africa: The Role of the Sokoto Caliphate," *Institute of Muslim Minority Affairs* 6, no. 2 (1985): 394–411, https://doi.org/10.1080/13602008508715950.

108 set of sharia Islamic laws: information about sharia law from "Sharia Implementation in Northern Nigeria over 15 Years: Policy Brief No. 2," Nigeria Research Network (Nigeria Stability and Reconciliation Program, 2016), https://www.qeh.ox.ac.uk/content /nigeria-research-network-publications#sharia.

109 "main body of civil and criminal law": Jonathan Rosenthal, "Opportunity Knocks," *The Economist Special Report*, June 20, 2015, 13.

109 "alcohol, gambling, prostitution . . .": "Sharia Implementation in Northern Nigeria After 15 Years," Oxford Department of International Development, accessed October 20, 2021, https://www.qeh .ox.ac.uk/content/sharia-implementation-northern-nigeria-after -15-years.

109 religious police enforce laws: information about religious policing from *The Enforcement of Shari'a and the Role of the Hisbah* (Human Rights Watch, 2004), https://www.hrw.org/reports/2004 /nigeria0904/8.htm.

109 "stylish haircuts": Mayowa Samuel, "Bauchi Law Forbids Alcohol, Stylish Haircut, Trouser Sagging: Hisbah Commander," *Peoples Gazette*, May 31, 2021, https://gazettengr.com/bauchi-law-forbids -alcohol-stylish-haircut-trouser-sagging-hisbah-commander/.

110 store mannequins skirt idolatry: Nduka Orjinmo, "Nigeria's Kano State Moves to Ban Mannequin Heads on Islamic Grounds," BBC News, August 16, 2021, https://www.bbc.com/news/world -africa-58175709.

110 "Judge for yourselves": 1 Corinthians 11:13 (New International Version), https://www.biblica.com/bible/niv/1-corinthians/11.

111 Maguzanci upholds a pantheon: information about Maguzanci pantheon sourced from family stories I heard growing up and corroborated by Umar Habila Dadem Danfulani, "Factors Contributing to the Survival of the Bori Cult in Northern Nigeria," *Numen* 46, no. 4 (1999): 420–26, http://www.jstor.org/stable/3270434.

111 spirits of the wilderness and the bush: Danfulani, "Factors," 421.

111 "an island within the ocean of Islam": Danfulani, Factors, 412.

111 hyenas and he-goats: Danfulani, "Factors," 418.

111 A hierarchy of priestesses: Danfulani, "Factors," 427–29.

111 both cause and cure: information about spirits and sickness from Judika Illes, *Encyclopedia of Spirits: The Ultimate Guide to the Magic of Saints, Angels, Fairies, Demons, and Ghosts* (Sydney: HarperCollins Australia, 2010), 579–80, Kindle.

112 *My bones are fat . . .*": interpretation of Proverbs 15:30 from John Eckhardt, *Prayers That Rout Demons* (Lake Mary, FL: Charisma House, 2008), 93.

112 "any spirit causing diabetes": Eckhardt, *Prayers*, 90.

7: The Dark Continent

115 Usually, they point east: my family's speculations are reflected in A. G. Adebayo, "Of Man and Cattle: A Reconsideration of the Tra-

ditions of Origin of Pastoral Fulani of Nigeria," *History in Africa* 18 (1991): 3–5, https://doi.org/10.2307/3172050.

116 represented as black-skinned: information about Ham from David M. Goldberg, *The Curse of Ham: Race and Slavery in Early Judaism, Christianity, and Islam* (Princeton, NJ: Princeton University Press, 2013).

117 use the term "Hamitic": information about Hamitic theory from Edith R. Sanders, "The Hamitic Hypothesis; Its Origin and Functions in Time Perspective," *Journal of African History* 10, no. 4 (1969): 521–32, http://www.jstor.org/stable/179896.

117 shapes of their crania: information about craniometry from Sanders, "Hamitic Hypothesis," 521–32.

117 Fulani "Hamitic" roots: information about the Fulani as Hamites from Frank A. Salamone, "Colonialism and the Emergence of Fulani Identity," *Journal of Asian and African Studies* 20, no. 3–4 (1985): 193–202, https://doi.org/10.1163/156852185X00315.

117 The actual history of the Fulani: information from Mustafa B. Ibrahim, "The Fulani - A Nomadic Tribe in Northern Nigeria," *African Affairs* 65, no. 259 (1966): 170–76, https://doi.org/10.1093/oxfordjournals.afraf.a095498.

117 etymology of the Fulani language: mythic origins of Fula from Jeffreys, "Speculative Origins," 47–54. Also from Adebayo, "Man and Cattle," 4.

117 most likely an admixture: information on Fulani admixture from M. Vicente et al., "Population History and Genetic Adaptation of the Fulani Nomads: Inferences from Genome-Wide Data and the Lactase Persistence Trait," *BMC Genomics* 20, no. 195 (2019), https://doi.org/10.1186/s12864-019-6296-7.

118 "dominant inhabitants": "States of Central Africa," 1902 Encyclopedia.

118 "much more advanced in civilization . . .": "States of Central Africa," 1902 Encyclopedia.

118 "like many North Africans": Carpenter, *Enchantment of Africa*, 26.

118 still resent the Fulani: Simon Abah, "Why Are the Fulani People So Unpopular in Nigeria?," *The Guardian*, July 13, 2019, https://guardian.ng/opinion/why-are-the-fulani-people-so-unpopular-in-nigeria.

119 as many people as Fula: "Fulfulde (Fula)," University of Cambridge Language Centre Resources, accessed August 7, 2021, https://www.langcen.cam.ac.uk/resources/langf/fulfulde.html.

119 "warrior-scholars": Tambari Sidi Yusuf et al., "Sokoto Jihadist Writings as a Blue Print Towards Socio-religious Transformation in Northern Nigeria," *Al-Hikmah Journal of Education* 8, no. 1 (2021), https://www.alhikmah.edu.ng/ajhir/index.php/aje_path/article/view/170.

120 their own "Hausaization": Azarya et al., *Pastoralists Under Pressure?*, 1–29.

120 the fallen caliph fled: Toyin Falola, *Colonialism and Violence in Nigeria* (Bloomington: Indiana University Press, 2009), 370, Kindle.

120 "Next to the Fulani . . .": A. J. N. Tremearne, "Notes on the Origin of the Hausas," *Journal of the Royal Society of Arts* 58, no. 3007 (1910): 767, http://www.jstor.org/stable/41339232.

120 "caliphatarians": Nnamdi Kanu, "Hausas Are Civil, Well Behaved; Fulanis Are Nigeria's Problem," *Vanguard Nigeria*, January 27, 2021, https://www.vanguardngr.com/2021/01/hausas-are-civil-well-behaved-fulanis-are-nigerias-problem--nnamdi-kanu.

121 more contexts as one: Hamzat Abaga, "Hausa and Fulani: Difference Between the Two Ethnic Groups of West Africa," *Transcontinental Times*, November 23, 2021, https://www.transcontinental times.com/2021/11/23/hausa-and-fulani.

122 a contemporary "caliphate": Jacob Zenn, "The Islamic State's Provinces on the Peripheries: Juxtaposing the Pledges from Boko Haram in Nigeria and Abu Sayyaf and Maute Group in the Philippines," *Perspectives on Terrorism* 13, no. 1 (2019): 87, https://www.jstor.org/stable/26590511.

124 from the Arabic "haram": "Winds of the World," Meteorology Office, accessed January 9, 2022, https://www.metoffice.gov.uk/weather/learn-about/weather/types-of-weather/wind/wind-names.

124 an accursed thing: *Wiktionary*, "Harmattan," accessed November 25, 2021, https://en.wiktionary.org/wiki/harmattan.

124 ʿUqbah ibn Nāfiʿ: information from Martin Gray, "Sacred Sites," World Pilgrimage Guide, accessed March 13, 2021, https://sacred sites.com/africa/tunisia/kairouan.html.

125 mythos of our region: referenced in Danfulani, "Factors," 421–22.

125 75 percent of its female population: Stephen Kenechi, "Nigeria Ranked Top Consumer of Skin-Whitening Creams in Africa," The Cable, January 25, 2022, https://lifestyle.thecable.ng/nigeria-ranked-top-consumer-of-skin-whitening-creams-in-africa/.

126 "quicker witted than the dark . . .": Sanders, "Hamitic Hypothesis," 521.

126 "extremely linear in bodily build . . .": Carleton Coon, *The Races of Europe* (New York: Macmillan, 1939), 452.

126 "most pronounced types of the Negro race": quoted in M. D. W. Jeffreys, "Niger: Origins of the Word," *Cahiers d'études Africaines* 4, no. 15 (1964): 443, http://www.persee.fr/doc/cea_00080055_1964 _num_4_15_3019.

8: Daughter of the Wind

129 "ethnicity and occupation": information about spirit family units from Illes, *Encyclopedia of Spirits*, 579.

129 mirror the qualities of mortal members: explored in Danfulani, "Factors," 422–26.

129 House of Fulani is nomadic: sourced from family stories and corroborated in Illes, *Encyclopedia of Spirits*, 1877.

129 Symptoms of the Fulani curse: adapted from Illes, *Encyclopedia of Spirits*, 1878.

130 The idea of *iskanci*: definition of *"iskanci"* adapted from Rudolph P. Gaudio, *Allah Made Us: Sexual Outlaws in an Islamic African City* (Hoboken, NJ: John Wiley & Sons, 2009), 208.

134 awareness of your own heartbeat: John Koenig, "Rubatosis," Dictionary of Obscure Sorrows, accessed April 10, 2022, https:// www.dictionaryofobscuresorrows.com/post/28154792144 /rubatosis.

135 2018 VICE documentary: "The U.S. Green Card Lottery Is Basically Unwinnable (HBO)," VICE News, published May 16, 2018, video, https://www.youtube.com/watch?v=TPc50dQ20S8.

136 dies by firearm: Dave Mosher and Skye Gould, "The Odds That a Gun Will Kill the Average American May Surprise You," *Business Insider*, October 29, 2018, https://www.businessinsider.com /us-gun-death-murder-risk-statistics-2018-3.

136 "I will support and defend . . .": "Naturalization Oath of Allegiance," U.S. Citizenship and Immigration Services, last modified July 5, 2020, https://www.uscis.gov/citizenship/learn-about-citizen ship/the-naturalization-interview-and-test/naturalization-oath -of-allegiance-to-the-united-states-of-america.

137 2.5 stars in a single Yelp review: "Riverbend Apartments," Yelp, accessed December 19, 2021, https://www.yelp.com/biz/riverbend -apartments-nashville.

146 An unexpected theory: Christine Ro, "How Americans Preserved British English," BBC, February 8, 2018, https://www.bbc

.com/culture/article/20180207-how-americans-preserved-british
-english.

146   of all possible worlds: Reference to the phrase "the best of all possible worlds," coined by Gottfried Leibniz in 1710 in *Essays of Theodicy on the Goodness of God, the Freedom of Man and the Origin of Evil.*

9: Allegiances Unclear

159   thief in the night: the Lord's return to the Earth is compared to a thief in the night in 1 Thessalonians 5:2 (New International Version), https://www.biblica.com/bible/niv/1-thessalonians/5.

159   there in the name: Millar Burrows, "The Origin of the Term 'Gospel,'" *Journal of Biblical Literature* 44, no. 1/2 (1925): 21–33, https://doi.org/10.2307/3260047.

10: Tribe and Tongue Differ

167   no longer cracks the top one hundred: "Mary Meaning & History," Behind the Name, last modified January 21, 2022, https://www.behindthename.com/name/mary.

167   Its first form: early timeline of the name "Mary" described in Aili Channer, "In Search of the Meaning of Mary," *Baby Name DNA*, July 16, 2020, https://nameberry.com/blog/in-search-of-the-meaning-of-mary.

167   the earliest Biblical prophetess: information about the Biblical origins of "Mary" from Anthony Maas, "The Name of Mary," *The Catholic Encyclopedia* (New York: Robert Appleton, 1912), https://www.newadvent.org/cathen/15464a.htm.

167   "deep waters congealed": Exodus 15:8 (New International Version), https://www.biblica.com/bible/niv/exodus/15.

167   Greek translation modified the name: information about "Mary" in various languages from "Mary Meaning & History."

167   modern Mary first appeared in 1530: Kent P. Jackson, "Chapters, Verses, Punctuation, Spelling, and Italics in the King James Version," in *By Study and by Faith: Selections from the Religious Educator,* ed. Richard Neitzel Holzapfel and Kent P. Jackson (Provo, UT: Brigham Young University Religious Studies Center, 2009), https://rsc.byu.edu/study-faith/chapters-verses-punctuation-spelling-italics-king-james-version.

167   Other forms render it: information about "Mary" in various languages from "Mary Meaning & History."

168 Some etymologists argue: information on Hebrew and Egyptian etymology from "Mary Meaning," Biblical Name Vault, Abarim Publications, 2010, https://www.abarim-publications.com/Meaning/Mary.html.

168 "wished-for child": "Etymology & Historical Origin of the Baby Name Marie," Oh Baby Names, accessed November 10, 2021, https://ohbabynames.com/all-baby-names/marie.

168 queen of Zaria: Amina biographical details corroborated in Oludamola Adebowale, "The Marvel of Queen Amina of Zaria: 'Sarauniyar Yariman Arewa,'" *The Guardian*, May 31, 2020, https://guardian.ng/life/the-marvel-of-queen-amina-of-zaria-sarauniyar-yariman-arewa. Also in Abubakar Oladimeji, "Queen Amina of Zaria: The Woman Who Led Men to War," *Naija Biography*, May 28, 2020, https://naijabiography.com/queen-amina-of-zaria.

169 eunuchs and kola nuts: Palmer, "The Kano Chronicle," 75.

169 her life and her legend: information about Amina legends from oral history and corroborated in "History of a Queen Who Killed the Men She Slept with So They Don't Live to Tell the Tale," *Opera News*, 2021, https://ng.opera.news/ng/en/military/38436cd2877c3 54424b51ea6afb0ce53.

170 therefore leave it alone: Adelaide Arthur, "Africa's Naming Traditions: Nine Ways to Name Your Child," BBC News, December 30, 2016, https://www.bbc.com/news/world-africa-37912748.

170 a secret name: corroborated in A. J. N. Tremearne, *Hausa Superstitions and Customs: An Introduction to the Folk-Lore and the Folk*, 2nd ed. (London: John Bale, Sons & Danielsson, 1913), 178.

172 the Arabic term *hamsa*: Nafisa Ali Sayed, "The Hand of Hamsa: Interpretation Across the Globe," *Research on Humanities and Social Sciences* 6, no. 20 (2016): 23–26.

172 "woman's holy hand": Sayed, "Hand of Hamsa," 25.

173 top-twenty popularity across Southern states: "Popular Baby Names by State," United States Social Security Administration, accessed February 17, 2022, https://www.ssa.gov/cgi-bin/namesbystate.cgi.

174 the name of Nigeria itself: etymology of "Nigeria" from Jeffreys, "Niger: Origins of the Word," 443.

179 a new national staple: Tanni Deb and Eleni Giokos, "How Indomie Instant Noodles Became a Nigerian Staple," CNN, January 25, 2019, https://edition.cnn.com/2019/01/25/africa/indomie-giant-in -nigeria-intl/index.html.

180 "one nation bound . . .": "Arise Oh Compatriots, Nigeria's Call Obey," National Anthems, accessed February 14, 2022, https://nationalanthems.info/ng.htm.

180 predictably met with protest: information about history of national anthem from Ezekiel Mphahlele, "Nigeria on the Eve of Independence," *Africa Today* 7, no. 6 (1960): 4–6, http://www.jstor.org/stable/4184128.

180 "Our own dear native land! . . .": "Nigeria We Hail Thee," National Anthems, accessed February 14, 2022, https://nationalanthems.info/ng-78.htm.

182 Nigerian Pidgin, a creole language: information from Ogechi Florence Agbo and Ingo Plag, "The Relationship of Nigerian English and Nigerian Pidgin in Nigeria: Evidence from Copula Constructions in ICE-Nigeria," *Journal of Language Contact* 13, no. 2 (2020): 351–88, https://doi.org/10.1163/19552629-bja10023.

11: Allow Spirits to Enter and Leave

187 Latin term's original connotation: etymology of "pagan" from *Merriam-Webster*, "pagan," accessed May 30, 2021, https://www.merriam-webster.com/dictionary/pagan.

187 "One who worships false gods . . .": *Fine Dictionary*, "pagan," accessed May 27, 2021, http://www.finedictionary.com/pagan.html.

188 adheres to non-Abrahamic religions: modern, neutral definition of "pagan" adapted from *Your Dictionary*, "Pagan Meaning," accessed May 27, 2021, https://www.yourdictionary.com/pagan.

188 evangelists arrived in 1911: information from Todd M. Vanden Berg, "Culture, Christianity, and Witchcraft in an African Context," in *The Changing Face of Christianity: Africa, the West, and the World*, ed. Lamin Sanneh and Joel A. Carpenter (New York: Oxford University Press, 2022), 50.

189 the will to harm: information about Longuda witches from Vanden Berg, "Culture, Christianity, and Witchcraft," 45–62.

189 80 percent of Longuda: information from Vanden Berg, "Culture, Christianity, and Witchcraft," 53.

190 caricatures claimed one hundred lives: Polgreen, "Nigeria Counts 100 Deaths."

192 Nigerian *kwalli* carries toxic risk: I. Y. Zakari et al., "Radiological and Toxic Risk Assessment of Nigerian Kohl as Cosmetic Compared with Imported Kohl Cosmetics," *Research Journal*

of Applied Sciences, Engineering and Technology 7, no. 14 (2014): 2970–75, http://dx.doi.org/10.19026/rjaset.7.628.

193 *songs in the night:* Refers to Job 35:10 (New Living Translation), https://biblehub.com/job/35–10.htm. Original verse: "Where is God my Creator, the one who gives songs in the night?"

193 evangelical suicide missions: ECWA Editorial Board, "ECWA History," *ECWA USA Magazine*, December 16, 2017, https://www.ecwausa.com/2017/12/16/ecwa-history.

194 Ninety percent of Nigerian Christians: Joey Marshall, "The World's Most Committed Christians Live in Africa, Latin America—and the U.S.," Pew Research Center, August 22, 2018, https://www.pewresearch.org/fact-tank/2018/08/22/the-worlds-most-committed-christians-live-in-africa-latin-america-and-the-u-s/.

194 top priority on prayer cards: prayers adapted from "5 Prayer Points to Pray for Nigeria," *Every Day Prayer Guide*, May 20, 2021, https://everydayprayerguide.com/2021/05/20/5-prayer-points-to-pray-for-nigeria/.

195 the power to shape-shift: Andrew Walker, "Nigeria Police Hold 'Robber' Goat," BBC News, January 23, 2009, http://news.bbc.co.uk/2/hi/africa/7846822.stm.

195 Surveying schizophrenics about the voices: Tanya M. Luhrmann et al., "Hearing Voices in Different Cultures: A Social Kindling Hypothesis," *Topics in Cognitive Science* 7, no. 4 (2015): 646–63, https://doi.org/10.1111/tops.12158.

197 Our prayers were spectacles: descriptions of prayers adapted from Eckhardt, *Prayers*.

198 "moral geography": Molefi Asante and Emeka Nwadiora, *An Introduction to African Religion* (Lanham, MD: University Press of America, 2007), 27.

201 most events in Exodus: Teresa Watanabe, "Doubting the Story of Exodus," *Los Angeles Times*, April 13, 2001, https://www.latimes.com/archives/la-xpm-2001-apr-13-mn-50481-story.html.

205 "As for me and my house . . .": Joshua 24:15 (Berean Study Bible), https://biblehub.com/joshua/24-15.htm.

12: The Name One Gives Oneself

208 Wherever two or three: Refers to Matthew 18:20 (New King James Version), https://biblehub.com/matthew/18-20.htm.

209 fourth-highest concentration: Pamela Constable, "African

Immigrant Population Doubling Each Decade; D.C. Area Among Group's Top Destinations," *Washington Post*, October 1, 2014, https://www.washingtonpost.com/local/african-immigrant -population-doubling-each-decade-washington-area-among-hi ghest/2014/10/01/efbada70-498f-11e4-891d-713f052086a0_story html.

215 "a place inducing contentment...": from *Merriam-Webster*, "lo-tusland," accessed June 6, 2021, https://www.merriam-webster .com/dictionary/lotusland.

215 indigent, unclaimed, or unidentified: "Los Angeles County Burial of Unclaimed Dead," St. Camillus Center for Spiritual Care, ac-cessed February 16, 2022, https://stcamilluscenter.org/news/los -angeles-county-burial-of-unclaimed-dead-december-3-9-30-am.

215 disturbed by paleontologists: information from "The Los Angeles Subway System Has Been Hiding This for over 11,000 Years," *Sci-ence 101*, last modified February 14, 2022, https://www.science101 .com/los-angeles-subway-system-hiding-this-over-11000-years.

216 An ongoing debate: Bob Pool, "City of Angels' First Name Still Bedevils Historians," *Los Angeles Times*, March 26, 2005, https:// www.latimes.com/archives/la-xpm-2005-mar-26-me-name26 -story.html.

216 historical record is marred: list of Los Angeles names from "Where Did the Name *Los Angeles* Come From?," *Los Angeles Almanac*, accessed March 4, 2021, http://laalmanac.com/history/hi03a.php.

216 a block called Calle de Los Negros: information from William Es-trada, *The Los Angeles Plaza: Sacred and Contested Space* (Austin: University of Texas Press, 2010), 59–78.

217 "men of very dark complexion": Estrada, *The Los Angeles Plaza*, 279.

217 one prominent establishment: information about commercial activ-ity from Dave Rogers, "Calle de Los Negros, the Wickedest Street in the American West," *Frontier American Illustrated News*, Jan-uary 2, 2021, https://www.frontieramericanillustratednews.com /post/calle-de-los-negros-the-wickedest-street-in-the-american -west.

217 "In length it did not exceed 500 feet...": James Guinn, *A History of California and an Extended History of Los Angeles and Envi-rons* (Los Angeles: Historic Record Company, 1915), 268.

217 "as black in character as in name": Guinn, *A History of Califor-nia*, 351.

217 1781 census of the first: "Original Settlers (*Pobladores*) of *El Pueblo de la Reina de Los Angeles, 1781,*" *Los Angeles Almanac,* accessed February 24, 2021, https://www.laalmanac.com/history/hi03c.php.

217 a racial category: referenced in Tom Fassbender, "Los Pobladores: The 44 Founders of Los Angeles," Los Angeles Explorers Guild, September 4, 2021, https://losangelesexplorersguild .com/2021/09/04/los-pobladores-the-44-founders-of-los-angeles.

217 At the LA Bicentennial: Victoria Bernal, "These Two Women Spent Decades Highlighting the African Heritage of L.A.," KCET Public Media Group of Southern California, November 16, 2021, https://www.kcet.org/shows/lost-la/charlotta-bass-and-miriam -matthews.

217 first free African: Peter Preskar, "The Fascinating Life of the First Free Black Person in America," History of Yesterday, June 18, 2021, https://historyofyesterday.com/juan-garrido-11e2243d 198e.

218 free *negros ladinos*: "African Explorers of Spanish America," Park Ethnography Program, National Park Service, accessed April 10, 2021, https://www.nps.gov/ethnography/aah/aaheritage/Spanish AmB.htm.

218 steeped in Black influence: John William Templeton, ed., *Our Roots Run Deep: The Black Experience in California 1500–1900,* vol. 1 (San Francisco: Aspire Books, 1991).

218 "*Una isla llamada California . . .*": Garci Rodríguez de Montalvo, *Las Sergas de Esplandián* (Barcelona: Castalia Ediciones, 2003), CVIII.

218 "Know, then, that . . .": quoted in Edward Everett Hale, "The Queen of California," *His Level Best: And Other Stories* (Boston: Roberts Brothers, 1885), 245–46.

218 "living manless": Gregory P. Schmidt, "California - The Golden State," Office of the Secretary of the Senate, 2010, https://secretary .senate.ca.gov/sites/senate.ca.gov/files/the%20golden%20book%20 2010_0.pdf.

219 from the Arabic *khalifa*: *Online Etymology Dictionary,* "caliph," accessed April 10, 2021, https://www.etymonline.com/word /caliph.

219 Hand of Mary, became heresy: Ryan D. Giles, *Inscribed Power: Amulets and Magic in Early Spanish Literature* (Toronto: University of Toronto Press, 2017), 3–25.

219 the female *califa:* Ruth Putnam, *California: The Name,* ed. Herbert

Ingram Priestley (Berkeley: University of California, 1917), 358, https://archive.org/details/cu31924008278347.

219 "hardy bodies, of ardent courage . . .": quoted in Hale, *His Level Best*, 246.

219 "steep cliffs and rocky shores": quoted in Hale, *His Level Best*, 246.

219 Hernán Cortés himself lusted: William T. Little, "Spain's Fantastic Vision and the Mythic Creation of California," *California Geographer* 27 (1987): 33, https://scholarworks.calstate.edu/down loads/4j03d332m.

220 into the eighteenth century: "California as an Island in Maps," The Glen McLaughlin Collection: Stanford Libraries, accessed February 10, 2021, https://exhibits.stanford.edu/california-as-an-island.

220 Diego Rivera's first American mural: "The Allegory of California," *Atlas Obscura*, accessed November 14, 2021, https://www.at lasobscura.com/places/the-allegory-of-california.

221 A team of painters: Maynard Dixon and Frank Van Sloun painted Calafia in 1926. Information from "Intercontinental Mark Hopkins Hotel History," Historic Hotels of America, accessed August 1, 2021, https://www.historichotels.org/us/hotels-resorts /intercontinental-mark-hopkins-hotel/history.php.

221 341 California, an asteroid: "341 California (A892 SE)," Small-Body Database Lookup, California Institute of Technology, accessed November 11, 2021, https://ssd.jpl.nasa.gov/tools/sbdb_look up.html#/?sstr=341.

221 the California Nebula: Lee Dyson, "Pictures of the California Nebula," *BBC Sky at Night*, June 14, 2021, https://www.skyat nightmagazine.com/astrophotography/nebulae/california-nebula.

221 California Hill in Nebraska: "California Hill," Oregon National Historic Trail, National Park Service, accessed September 29, 2021, https://www.nps.gov/oreg/planyourvisit/california-hill.htm.

221 the California poppy: "California Poppy," California Native Plant Society, accessed March 5, 2021, https://calscape.org/Eschscholzia -californica-(California-Poppy).

221 Californite, a mineral: "Californite," National Gem Lab, accessed January 16, 2022, https://nationalgemlab.in/californite.

221 extremely radioactive element: "Californium," Royal Society of Chemistry, accessed December 3, 2021, https://www.rsc.org/per iodic-table/element/98/californium.

222 "the frontier; the line . . .": etymology of "coast" adapted from *Academic Dictionaries and Encyclopedias*, "coast," accessed Decem-

ber 31, 2021, https://etymology.en-academic.com/9746/coast. Also adapted from *Merriam-Webster*, "coast," accessed December 31, 2021, https://www.merriam-webster.com/dictionary/coast.

223 Nile to Atlantic water: "New and Accurate Map of Negroland and the Adjacent Countries Also Upper Guinea," Maps of Africa: Stanford University Libraries, accessed January 7, 2021, https://exhibits.stanford.edu/maps-of-africa/catalog/tg858rf9015.

224 "ordered order": quoted in Hale, *His Level Best*, 274.

224 "doing nothing but what their grandmothers did": quoted in Hale, *His Level Best*, 274.

224 "very brutes": quoted in Hale, *His Level Best*, 248.

224 "so far back that there . . .": quoted in Hale, *His Level Best*, 274.

224 ". . . it is clear that the law which . . .": quoted in Hale, *His Level Best*, 274.

224 "unruly, badly educated child": *Your Dictionary*, "Pagan Meaning."

225 "very large in person . . .": quoted in Hale, *His Level Best*, 247.

225 *Kali* is a slur: information from "Kali Meaning in English," UrduPoint, accessed April 30, 2021, https://www.urdupoint.com/dictionary/roman-urdu-to-english/kali-roman-urdu-meaning-in-english/10649.html. Also from *Shabdkosh English Hindi Dictionary*, "Kali," accessed February 14, 2022, https://www.shabdkosh.com/search-dictionary?lc=hi&sl=en&tl=hi&e=kali.

225 In Hindu mythology, Kali: information about Kali from Mark Cartwright, *World History Encyclopedia*, "Kali," last modified June 21, 2013, https://www.worldhistory.org/Kali. Also from David R. Kinsley, *The Sword and the Flute: Kali and Krsna, Dark Visions of the Terrible and the Sublime in Hindu Mythology* (Berkeley: University of California Press, 2000). Also from Wendy Doniger, *Encyclopedia Britannica Online*, "Kali," last updated December 26, 2019, https://www.britannica.com/topic/Kali.